ADVANCE PRAISE FOR

after spirituality

"*After Spirituality* is an ambitious attempt to chart a new path in the study of mysticism. The collaborative vision of Philip Wexler and Jonathan Garb to examine the mystical phenomenon from both a textually informed phenomenology and a theoretically sophisticated sociology has shaped the contours of the volume as a whole. The multidisciplinary orientation, and particularly the effort to combine social scientific and humanistic methodologies, is a refreshing and generative contribution that will surely have an impact on further research into mysticism and esotericism. Each of the essays included in the volume reflects that vision, albeit from the unique perspective of the given author. The breadth of this collection is attested in its pursuit of a sophisticated comparative approach that is not reductive either historically or conceptually. Common aspects are allowed to emerge in their singular expression. I am confident the book will be of interest to scholars of mysticism as well as the historians, sociologists, and anthropologists of religion."

—*Elliot R. Wolfson, New York University*

"Scholars of comparative mystical literature have increasingly realized that the rules of the game are quickly shifting, if not completely changing, in front of their eyes in our globalizing cosmopolitan world. But seldom have a group of scholars taken these sociological changes so seriously and thought about them so deeply and in such fruitful dialogue. The result is a collection of essays "after spirituality" that challenge those binaries (text/context, past/present, particularism/universalism, immanence/transcendence, spirit/society) that have to this day hampered truly radical theorizing—a rich and nuanced book announcing a promising new series."

—*Jeffrey J. Kripal, Author of* Esalen: America and the Religion of No Religion

after spirituality

Studies in Mystical Traditions

Philip Wexler and Jonathan Garb
Series Editors

Vol. 1

Advisory board:
Professor Jeffrey J. Kripal
Professor William B. Parsons, Rice University

The After Spirituality series is part of the Peter Lang Education list.
Every volume is peer reviewed and meets
the highest quality standards for content and production.

PETER LANG
New York • Washington, D.C./Baltimore • Bern
Frankfurt • Berlin • Brussels • Vienna • Oxford

after spirituality
Studies in Mystical Traditions

EDITED BY **Philip Wexler & Jonathan Garb**

PETER LANG
New York • Washington, D.C./Baltimore • Bern
Frankfurt • Berlin • Brussels • Vienna • Oxford

Library of Congress Cataloging-in-Publication Data

After spirituality: studies in mystical traditions /
edited by Philip Wexler, Jonathan Garb.
p. cm. — (After spirituality; vol. 1)
Includes bibliographical references and index.
1. Mysticism. I. Wexler, Philip. II. Garb, Jonathan.
BL625.A335   204'.22—dc23   2012032459
ISBN 978-1-4331-1739-8 (hardcover)
ISBN 978-1-4331-1738-1 (paperback)
ISBN 978-1-4539-0933-1 (e-book)
ISSN 2167-8448

Bibliographic information published by **Die Deutsche Nationalbibliothek**.
Die Deutsche Nationalbibliothek lists this publication in the "Deutsche
Nationalbibliografie"; detailed bibliographic data is available
on the Internet at http://dnb.d-nb.de/.

The editors wish to thank the Jules and Gwen Knapp Charitable Foundation for their generous support towards the publication of this volume and the entire series.

© 2012 Peter Lang Publishing, Inc., New York
29 Broadway, 18th floor, New York, NY 10006
www.peterlang.com

All rights reserved.
Reprint or reproduction, even partially, in all forms such as microfilm,
xerography, microfiche, microcard, and offset strictly prohibited.

*Philip Wexler dedicates the book to
Ilene, Helen and Ava for the journey to Jerusalem*

*Jonathan Garb dedicates the book to
Ronna, Evyatar David and Ariel for joining the adventure.*

Contents

After Spirituality: Introducing the Volume and the Series..................1
   Jonathan Garb and Philip Wexler

Part One: Jewish Mysticism

Contemporary Kabbalah and Classical Kabbalah: Breaks and Continuities.......19
   Jonathan Garb

Between Tsaddiq and Messiah: A Comparative Analysis of Chabad
and Breslav Hasidic Groups...47
   Yoram Bilu and Zvi Mark

"The Besht Passed His Hand over His Face": On the Besht's Influence
on His Followers: Some Remarks 79
   Moshe Idel

Society and Mysticism...107
   Philip Wexler

Part Two: Traditions East and West

Initiation and Communities of Secrecy in Papua New Guinea, Tantric Buddhism,
and Contemporary Serial Drama.......................................129
   Louise Child

Sacrament and Medicine: A Comparison of Roman Catholic and
Native American Church Confession 147
   Thomas J. Csordas

Beyond Transcendence? A Buddhist Perspective on the Axial Age 155
   David R. Loy

Freud's Last Theory of Mysticism: The Return of the (Phylogenetic) Repressed..173
   William B. Parsons

Contributors..187

Index 191

One

After Spirituality
Introducing the Volume and the Series

Jonathan Garb and Philip Wexler

Dialogue of Discourses

This volume, and the series which it inaugurates, are the outgrowths of collaboration between us, the editors, which began long before now, in a dialogue across discursive and academic disciplinary worlds. Fittingly, for religious studies, it began with a joint reading of texts, an instructional reading that was at once mutual and different in its orientation. We came to similar questions, but from divergent origins, and the collaboration and convergence which we have experienced and begin to represent here are not entirely idiosyncratic—embodied only in our dialogue, but reflect broader, analytical and field interests.

On the one side, the relatively young academic field of Jewish mystical studies has included within its unequivocally dominant commitment to hermeneutical, philological, textual study an apparently contradictory internal voice, calling to go beyond the text, beyond the "ideology of textology," as Moshe Idel (in his *Kabbalah: New Perspectives*) first deemed it.[1] Before Idel, Gershom Scholem, the undisputed founder of this field, already criticized scholarship on mysticism for "scanting" on an understanding of mysticism in society, and attempted to reverse the overwhelming textual focus which he had himself initiated.[2] Scholem wanted to contextualize Jewish mysticism, to put it back into society, and he drew upon the social analysts of religion best known for his times and tradition, Ernst Troeltsch and Max Weber.[3]

On the other side, Sociology, and social science, more generally, has had its own openings, beginning with Frankfurt School Critical Theory, and later challenges to the legitimacy and false universalism of an ethnocentric, institutional, academic social science.[4] Sociology, however, has been hardly shaken by such theoretical forays, and it succeeded in recognizing multiplicity, multiculturalism and diversity by expanding the inclusion of its objects of study: not its subjects. This has served the interests of religious scholarship well, since the once entirely peripheral sub-discipline of sociology of religion, has now become more salient and academically established.[5] Of course, empirical, historical events have something to do with this, since the "religious turn" is very much a question of social practice and not "merely" of social theory and research. The so-called spiritual revolution[6] is grist for the sociological mill, as a salient object of study, as part of the emergence of the "new social movements."[7]

Garb's dialogue with Wexler emerged from his interest (expressed already in his Foucauldian *Manifestations of Power in Jewish Mysticism from Rabbinic Literature to Safedian Kabbalah*) in analyzing kabbalistic texts in light of social and political theory. All this, reflecting his ongoing attempt to study Jewish texts within both historical-contextual and phenomenological-comparative frameworks.[8] Wexler, however, did not come to the dialogue with Garb, and through him, to religious studies and mysticism, as a sociologist of religion. Rather, it is the exhaustion and analytical incapacity of social science to fully grasp and explain contemporary social phenomena, along with a pluralization, and analytical polyvocality, resulting from the critique of established, hegemonic sociology, that drives this exploration of mysticism—not simply as an object of study but as a discursive resource, a no-longer reductive subaltern in the analytical work of understanding. Rather, as a co-equal conceptual power, a discourse historically suited to make sense of a present in which the classical sacred/profane divide is no longer persuasive, any more than the classical social theories that once announced its centrality. On this side, the dialogue comes from a newfound social science respect for mystical texts, which are not merely artifacts, but vibrant and systematic rational voices which represent conceptual order in this, lived, visible world, as well as in the beyond

A Community of Scholars

It was this mutual opening of fields and desire for dialogue that led us to convene a research group at the Institute for Advanced Studies in Jerusalem, which we entitled "The Sociology of Contemporary Jewish Mysticism in Comparative Perspective." It had its start from Jewish mysticism and Sociology, but it quickly broadened out, as we included anthropologists, like Yoram Bilu,

Louise Child and Thomas Csordas, psychologists like Tanya Luhrman and psychoanalytical theorists of religion like William Parsons. While this group that worked together—some for an entire academic year and others for shorter visiting periods—kept an anchor in Jewish mysticism, with the participation of Moshe Idel, Zvi Mark and Elliot Wolfson, we partook of work in Christianity (Parsons, Luhrman), Buddhism, with David Loy and New Age spirituality, as in the work of Boaz Huss, Rachel Werczberger and Robert Forman.

This volume reflects that highly enjoyable and active year, which included a full program of seminars, as well as a larger conference at the end of the year. It presents work from an incipient new universe of discourse, keeping the integrity of disciplinary languages, as well as their explanatory power, but also moving outward, toward: systematic interaction and comparisons across mystical traditions; relations between historical and contemporary phenomena; explorations of the text/context relation and the new paths in the study of mysticism which emerge from that; and, also in the critical discussion of the core terms themselves, including "mysticism" and "spirituality."

In this first volume of the series which begins with selected contributions from the community of scholars which we were privileged by the Institute of Advanced Studies to initiate and nurture, we see examples of these tendencies. We began from where we came from, Jewish mysticism and Sociology, but we expanded, even at the beginning, to see these interests as catalysts for a new integration on a wider horizon, including a broad range of social sciences and the worlds of mystical scholarship and practice well beyond the academic walls of the textual work natural to its setting in Jerusalem. Thus, we included visits by a Mussar teacher and a Haredi hypnotist and field trips to kabbalistic festivals and events in our program.

The study of contemporary and recent forms of mysticism enabled us to transcend the well-known paradigm clash between universalist and contextualist approaches (the first having been represented within our group by Robert Forman): in the increasingly globalized mystical culture of the twentieth and the early twenty-first centuries, the comparison between Buddhist and Christian mysticism, to cite but one instance, is a matter of actual historical contact rather than a phenomenological conjecture.[9] Thus, a more moderate contextualist like Louise Child and even a more radical contextualist such as Boaz Huss within our group were able to comfortably collaborate within an explicitly comparative framework.[10] This being said, our project was carefully designed so as to avoid the fallacy of studying the present and recent past in isolation from many centuries of tradition. Through a blend of expertise in the classical and the contemporary, we sought to anchor current globalized phenomena in the history and cultural background of the discrete mystical traditions that we studied. As a result, the interplay of "continuous," traditional streams and "discontinuous" and more obviously contemporary developments played a central role in our discussion, as explicitly presented in Garb's article. Obviously, the study of continuous trends requires a stronger base in classical, textual scholarship, whilst the study of discontinuous groups that are more in tune with the global mystical culture calls more for comparative skills and social science analysis.

The blend of resources exemplified in the group was also designed towards overcoming the growing divide between two forms of study of Jewish mysticism, that are perceived as falling into the geographical and cultural space between Israel and Western centers (mostly in the United States): on the one hand we can be gratified with strong textual scholarship, enjoying both relatively rich libraries and a cadre of students whose native tongue is Hebrew. In recent years, this form of scholarship has increasingly availed itself of the ever-expanding human and bibliographical resources of the Yeshiva world (mostly Haredi). Despite all of its achievements, this world, mostly publishing in Hebrew, is usually not greatly in conversation with recent advances in comparative mysticism, literary theory, philosophical and theological reflection, or even cultural and intellectual history of Europe and the Middle East. In this climate, it is not surprising that there is little integration of social science methods, such as sociology, cultural studies, anthropology and psychology (social and individual). It is, however, rather surprising that usually Kabbalah scholars of this type do not even consult exemplars of textual scholarship, such as David Greetham, who has indeed greatly influenced a paragon of manuscript scholarship, Daniel Abrams.[11] Despite some minor administrative changes, the general practice of locating the study of Jewish mysticism within rather insular departments and institutes devoted to Jewish studies has strongly maintained this tendency. [12]

On the other hand academic activity outside Israel is usually integrated or in close proximity with Religious Studies or other Humanities departments and institutions, though generally not in close conversation with the social sciences. As a result, one can discern a far greater presence of theoretical and comparative literature. In other words, institutional deployment affects scholarly practice. However, for the very same reasons, this discourse is at times not greatly in contact with the necessary textual basis, especially in terms of anchoring Jewish mysticism in the wide frame of Jewish culture and religion. Thus, it is rather rare, in such studies, to find comparison between kabbalistic texts and their historical and conceptual parallels within the vast corpuses of Halakhah (Law), Mussar (so-called ethics), Piyyut (religious poetry), etc. Indeed, the ratio between texts, especially manuscripts or lesser-known printed books, and theory at times differs sharply from that found in the first kind of studies.

However, especially in the years since our group was conceived, one can observe various hopeful signs of a diminution of this sad gap (which is not exactly unknown in other branches of Jewish studies). Obviously, one cannot do justice here to all of these developments, and the following paragraphs mostly focuses on the immediate context of our group. Elliot Wolfson's ongoing synthesis of comparative study, philosophical and theological reflection, and gender theory and poetics with far-ranging textual study has been expressed lately in two far-ranging works. One of these, *Open Secret: Postmessianic Messianism and the Mystical Revision of Menahem Mendel Schneerson*, was concluded during the semester in which he participated in our group. Another, *A Dream Interpreted within a Dream*, has appeared since. Moshe Idel's longstanding call for integration of comparative religious studies and other branches of humanistic studies in order to offset the 'conceptual aridity' of much of earlier Kabbalah scholarship has most recently been echoed in his *Old Worlds, New Mirrors: On Jewish Mysticism and Twentieth-Century Thought*. Here Idel follows the traces and presences of Kabbalah in the work of theorists such as George Steiner and Jacques Derrida. Needless to say, the presence of both Wolfson—as a fellow—and Idel—as a year-long visitor—greatly enriched the scholarly discussion in the group (as is evident in the influence of the former on Child's article). Garb's *Shamanic Trance in Modern Kabbalah* (largely written at the IAS) continues his earlier work on empowerment within the frame of social contextualization and comparative study of Jewish mysticism, but in new ways; following the pillar of modern comparative religious studies, Mircea Eliade (in his *Shamanism: Archaic Techniques of Ecstasy*),[13] while updating and expanding this perspective through contemporary social psychological and hypnotic theory. Our series of guest seminars for group members opened with a fascinating presentation by David Sorotzkin, whose recent Hebrew volume,[14] though not dedicated to Kabbalah, has placed Hasidic and other mystical texts (most notably those of R. Loewe, or Maharal, of Prague) in the proper context of European modernity. It is striking that one may again find some parallels to this integrative mode in very recent scholarship on Sufism, as in the sophisticated study *Sufi Bodies* by Shazad Bashir, as well as in a manuscript on Christian mysticism partly written at the IAS—William Parsons' *Freud and Augustine in Dialogue: Psychoanalysis, Mysticism and the Culture of Modern Spirituality*.[15] So that while mystical studies may remain largely textual, if not "textological," the opening toward extra-textual discourses, not simply as critical "lenses," but as discursive interrogators of mystical traditions has now occurred strikingly.

From the direction of the social sciences, Bilu and Mark's article here marks a pioneering, full integration of textual study of Jewish mysticism and the social sciences in one study, joining Bilu's ethnographic and comparative work on contemporary Habad (that was also addressed from the textual angle in Wolfson's presentation in our seminar) with Mark's textual and ethnographic work on contemporary Braslav (as expressed in his *Revelation and Rectification in the Revealed and Hidden Writings of R. Nahman of Breslav*, part of which was conceived at the IAS).[16] This fine example of comparative analysis describes not only the differences between these two messianic groups, but also their commonalities, in crossing and blurring common-sense boundaries, even highlighting how the most effective paradigm of leadership might be the one in which the leader is absent, as a sentient being, though not as a formative presence. Idel's article likewise addresses the meeting of Hasidism and the social sciences, through an innovative study of the fascinating image of the founder of the movement, the Besht, as depicted in central hagiographical accounts. Idel's detailed textual analysis shows that the charisma of this founder of a social movement that evolved into a much larger one that is still very much with us drew on his employment of hypnotic techniques. Echoing Bilu and Mark's article, Idel concludes his reflections with the last rebbe of Habad. Garb's article here juxtaposes contemporaneous and historical influences on the shape of modern Kabbalah. Against the trend of finding the power of modern Kabbalah in the later "non-continuous" twentieth century figures (as in the above-mentioned Habad and Braslav), Garb shows how contemporary Kabbalah carries the classical tradition through apparently conventional, nomian, ultra-orthodox forms of Jewish mysticism. Philip Wexler also begins with a classical tradition, albeit of Sociology, and describes several canonical sociologies of mysticism, but especially the direction of Max Weber's turn-of-the-last century approach. Here, however, the vibrancy of the classical tradition is put into question, and Wexler argues for a break with sociology, in favor of the explanatory power now demonstrated by the discourses of the "new mystical scholarship," some of which are represented in this book and in the volumes to follow.

Louise Child illustrates the integration of social science with Tantric Buddhism, in a Durkheimian rethinking of secrecy and initiation rituals, and then shows how the analysis works, far from Papua New Guinea, in a contemporary British serial drama. This social intervention in ritual explication does not mean that we would deny the continuing value of psychological, and indeed, psychoanalytical interpretations. Thomas Csordas employs anthropological theory and fieldwork in comparing practices of confession in the Roman Catholic and Native American churches. Exemplifying sensitivity to the emic perspective, Csordas offers "medicine" as an indigenous Native American parallel to the Catholic term "sacrament," while addressing the ritual role of the ingestion of substances following confession in both traditions. The resultant "dialogue" between the terms underlines divine immanence and transfiguration of everyday reality in the former tradition, in a manner that invites future comparison to Hasidic views as well as practices, especially those surrounding the Sabbath meals. William Parsons takes the discussion from the more 'outside' of ritual practice to the inner world of mystical experience, to Freud's evolving theory of mysticism. From his earliest observations, to the middle period of Freud's famous "oceanic feeling" approach to mystical experience, Parsons reflects on the less-often cited interest of the late Freud in historical survivals in the unconscious, in our "archaic heritage." Loy takes the tone of the discussion further from either social science or psychology, when he takes a normative, critical Buddhist position against the social damage of hierarchy and inequality and the environmental damage caused by dualism, which he urges can be overcome by the non-duality and evolutionary views which enable a therapeutic orientation to our current, planetary condition, views inspired and informed by a Buddhist perspective.

It would be extremely naïve to posit that our group's activity, even if situated in a crown jewel of Israeli academia, had a decisive impact on these developments. Rather, one should properly see our efforts as part of an emerging wave in global scholarship that is dialectically strengthened precisely by the extremity of the prevailing polarization. Furthermore, just as that split reflects insular and parochial tendencies in the contemporary Jewish world, the new desire for integration cannot be divorced from the globalizing and integrating tendencies of the contemporary spiritual world. It would be highly surprising if a new generation of students exposed both to Jewish and Far Eastern spirituality (though sadly far less to Christian or—incredibly—barely even to Sufi worlds) would not respond to a wider agenda.[17]

Thinking beyond the volume and towards our series, we aspire to maintain the strong focus on Jewish mysticism while branching out to further traditions, reaffirming their important place in the study of contemporary society, while critically examining the comparative approach itself. We offer now a very brief overview of some recent and current developments in the traditions surveyed in this volume: Kabbalah, Western Christian mysticism and Buddhism (especially Tantra). Though it was somewhat addressed in our concluding conference, Sufism does not take place in the present volume, though we do aspire to include an entire volume devoted to this central tradition within the series. Here we will but say that the vast geographical and cultural diversity of recent and contemporary Sufism makes any facile generalization unfeasible. One cannot but concur with scholars who insist that "it does not make much sense to simply characterize Sufism as Islamic mysticism"[18] and that "Islam's Sufi tradition cannot be equated simply with mysticism. Sufism includes many different practice regimes and their supporting social institutions, arts and scholarly justifications."[19] Indeed, in the terms suggested above, the very attempt by scholars, adherents (and, increasingly, scholars-adherents), mostly in the West, to foreground the mystical elements of Sufism in isolation from other traditional and cultural forms is a strongly discontinuous move. A perspective informed by both social science and more classical textual scholarship would lead to rather different conclusions. This being said, there is no doubt that modernizing political and technological developments, as in other traditions, have had a marked effect.[20]

Although the current state of kabbalistic thought and practice is largely covered in the article by Garb (as well as the more focused case study by Bilu and Mark, together with comments in Idel's article), one should note one significant cultural and geographical development but alluded to in the former. In recent years, continuous Haredi (so-called ultra-Orthodox) kabbalists have begun to rediscover and rehabilitate discontinuous mystics, most notably the socialist R. Yehuda L. Ashlag (often quoted by R. Yitzhak Meir Morgenstern, as well as American kabbalists influenced by him) and the Zionist R. Avraham Itzhaq Ha-Cohen Kook. Whilst the influence of the latter is less easily traceable, for reasons that can be defined as belonging to identity politics, one can offer a striking illustration: R. Moshe Weinberger, the founder and leader of the Aish Kodesh spiritual community in Woodmere, New York (and an admirer of R. Morgenstern), has now published the first part of his numerous classes on R. Kook's *The Lights of Repentance*, itself a gem of mystical writing.[21]

Within the mystical traditions of the Western church, mentioned here by Garb (and more briefly by Wexler), one should mention two major, at times overlapping, developments. The first, continuing the ever-unfolding legacy of Thomas Merton (himself a paragon of comparative concern), is the contemplative movement, most influentially expressed in the Centering Prayer school, whose most prominent exponent is Thomas Keating. Here one can discern a strong affinity with meditative traditions found in other contemporary mystical traditions, as well as "non-churched;" spiritual practices such as the Enneagram. A rather differently flavored and far more widespread development is that of "emergent Christianity," which is enjoying increasing scholarly interest. Against the background of the current global wave of social protest one should particularly note the radical socio-political stance of its Catholic parallels in the New Monasticism and Peter Rollins' highly creative Ikon group.[22] All of these discontinuous movements should be contrasted with the more "median" position of Richard Foster, as described in Garb's article.

In the case of the Buddhist world, the articles by Child and Loy (as well as that of Wexler to some extent), respectively, reflect two highly influential and complex trends; the first is that of Tantric Buddhism. Child's article continues her exploration of the implications of social theory for the study of Tantra in her earlier *Tantric Buddhism and Altered States of Consciousness: Durkheim,*

Emotional Energy, and Visions of the Consort. Alongside with her theoretical commitment to contextualism, this article contains illuminating comparison between Tantric Buddhism and anthropological findings from Papua New Guinea. This comparison to an archaic society underlines what we would term the continuous element in the Tantric discourse on secrecy. However, one must also consider the view of Hugh Urban, who stresses the "discontinuous" move towards what he terms exotericization through the recent and current transformations of Tantra within the social conditions of late capitalism. The second, in some ways similar to the New Monasticism, is that of "Engaged Buddhism," contrasting sharply with the commercialization often accompanying the propagation of Tantra. As in his other works, Loy moves beyond mere academic discussion to consider wider social, cultural and ecological issues. In many senses, Loy, a Buddhist thinker and practitioner as well as an academic scholar, can be seen as occupying a median position, rethinking continuous Buddhist themes in light of current challenges. It would not be overbold to conjecture that the highly active discussion of the Buddhist response to Occupy Wall Street movement led by Loy and others on the Internet will lead to both new literary as well as communal and institutional innovations. Indeed, moving back to the Jewish context, it would also not be farfetched to identify certain traces of "New Age" rhetoric and mentality in the 2011 social justice movement in Israel.[23]

This brings us to the "unchurched," "spiritual" or New Age manifestations addressed in Wexler's article. One salient case of the question of the relation between classical and contemporary forms, continuities, discontinuities and integrative efforts in both scholarship and practice is manifested in the relation between spirituality and mysticism. As Sutcliffe argues,[24] there has been a "discursive drift," from mysticism to spirituality. Without fully unpacking the historical career of the newer term, spirituality, and its roots in Christianity and Western esotericism, it is fair to argue, I think, that spirituality has become the popular, favored term to denote mystical experience and forms of life. At the practical level, however, the term has become linked to the "New Age," and has come to emphasize the inner, experiential aspect of what was always a core element in mysticism but without its social embodiment in more univocal sacred, religious traditions and institutions. "Spirituality" appeared in our initiating community of scholars, in connection to the New Age (as in a fieldwork based presentation by Véronique Altglas) but without a full interrogation of the character of this connection.

Sutcliffe wants to suggest that mysticism is a property of elites and that modern democratization leads to spirituality. Mathew Wood is less sanguine about the appearance of spirituality,[25] as a term in sociological discourse. It is not apparent how to disentangle the interweaving of two levels of spirituality, but their entanglement reflects a generic problem in social explanation. At one level, there are the popular social movements which describe themselves as "spiritual," and then there is use of the term in professional language by the experts in explanation. Wood criticizes any direct appropriation from practice to analysis, arguing that the sociologist of spirituality have uncritically adopted the individualistic ideology of the practitioners, in the notable example of Heelas' "self-spirituality" of "the New Age movement."[26] Wexler reinforces and elaborates the scientific limitation of the academic representatives of the spirituality movement, and its conceptual terms, mentioned by Wood, in their reliance on a *cultural* rather than a social interpretation of the popular spirituality movements.[27] Both Wood and Wexler want to re-contextualize spirituality in society, in dissent from a naïve, ideological replication of the spirituality movements' own limited, individualistic social self-awareness. Wood explains this social silence in part by suggesting that sociologies of spirituality have been conceptually overrun by Religious Studies' interest and linguistic hegemony over the New Age phenomenon. He writes: "Indeed, a raft of meta-narratives has been drawn upon in order to offer a sociological gloss to an increasingly Religious Studies oriented field: subjectivization, individualization, privatization, postmodernization and globalization."[28] The antidote, for him, is the analytical re-contextualization found in Anthroplogical ethnographies, which enables attention to religious "ritual and liturgical practices"[29] and social interactions and practices.

Our counterposition is analytically different, and in part based on a different assessment of the empirical phenomenon upon which these discursive assertions about spirituality and mysticism and the critique of sociologies of spirituality have been built. Analytically, beyond the individualist and culturalist bias, the sociological tradition has much more to offer in making sense of spirituality. Its re-contextualization is not only in relation to social practices and institutions, but more broadly and dynamically, as part of social *movement* processes, for which there are ample paradigmatic alternatives to the individualistic culturalism of academic replays of the popular discourse of spirituality; and of their critique, in general terms of a less socially abstracted institutional, Functionalist approach. Social movement theories are directed toward understanding processes of social dynamics, and they draw less upon the Durkheimian and Anthropological traditions, and more from Marx and Critical Theory. Spirituality is, of course, in part, about a historic commodification of religion, analogous to what occurs in every other social domain. The value-form of the commodity is abstract, monetizing, and disembodying.[30] A deeper critique is to argue that "spirituality," in popular practice, is the contemporary expression of the abstraction from social processes which Marx called the "fetishism of commodities." We might even simply say—almost as a provocation to further inquiry—that spirituality is the commodity fetish of religion.

What then is the relation between spirituality and mysticism? From this vantage point, spirituality abstracts, disembodies and commodifies, not simply the institutional rituals of religion, but it reifies the inwardness of mysticism—forgetting not only the external social context, but the depths and interior embodiment of traditions of belief and practice, reifying the experiential core of religion. Our scholarly interest also replicates in part at least, popular practice. Since, empirically, we see the New Age, dialectically, as also a portal, an opening to mystical "ancient heritages," in contemporary practice. It is, however, not any longer the case that spirituality and the New Age simply succeed and replace mysticism. On the contrary, there is a "new mysticism" in popular practice, which has itself needed to dig deeper to find more culturally and socially enduring roots.

The revitalization of mysticism in practice is one driving source for the renewal of mystical scholarship. We too are attentive to "discontinuities," to contemporary social appearances which instigate theoretical reflection and empirical exploration: from mystical practice to mystical theory. Yet, we argue against mere replication at the academic level, which is the work of ideologists. Rather, these changes are a spur to the sublimation of practice in intellectual work, to further scholarship and to studies of the archaic, yet continuing traditions of mystical practice. That is why we call this volume and the series which it begins, *"after* spirituality."

We would like to again thank the IAS and especially the director, Professor Eliezer Rabinovici, for wonderful support and research conditions during our exciting year. We are deeply grateful to the Jules and Gwen Knapp Charitable Foundation for their generous support for the series. We also wish to warmly thank Chris Myers, the managing director of Peter Lang Publishing, for his visionary and dedicated welcome to the series.

Notes

1. Moshe Idel, *Kabbalah: New Perspectives* (New Haven, CT: Yale University Press, 1988).
2. Gershom Scholem, "Mysticism and Society," *Diogenes* 15/58 (1967): 1–24.
3. Phillip Wexler, "Gershom Scholem's 'Mysticism and Society': Critique, Alternative, Text," *Kabbalah: Journal for the Study of Jewish Mystical Texts* (forthcoming).
4. Charles Lemert, *Sociology after the Crisis* (Boulder, CO: Westview, 1995).
5. Bryan S. Turner, *The New Blackwell Companion to the Sociology of Religion* (Chichester, West Sussex, UK: Wiley-Blackwell, 2010).
6. Paul Heelas and Linda Woodhead, *The Spiritual Revolution Why Religion Is Giving Way to Spirituality* (Malden, MA: Blackwell Publishers, 2005).
7. Alberto Melucci, *Challenging Codes: Collective Action in the Information Age* (Cambridge: Cambridge University Press, 1999).

8   See Jonathan Garb, *Manifestations of Power in Jewish Mysticism: From Rabbinic Literature to Safedian Kabbalah* (Jerusalem: Magnes Press, 2005) [Hebrew], as well as Jonathan Garb, "Powers of Language in Kabbalah: Comparative Reflections," in *The Poetics of Grammar and the Metaphysics of Sound and Sign*, ed. Sergio de La Porta and David Shulman, 230–69 (Leiden, The Netherlands: Brill, 2007).
9   See e.g., William Johnston, *Christian Zen: A Way of Meditation* (New York: Fordham University Press, 1997); Robert Powell, *Christian Zen: The Essential Teachings of Jesus Christ* (Berkeley, CA.: North Atlantic Books. 2003).
10 For Huss' approach, see his "The Mystification of the Kabbalah and the Modern Construction of Jewish Mysticism,' *Ben-Gurion University of the Negev Review* (2008), 1–14.
11 See David C. Greetham, *Textual Scholarship: An Introduction* (New York, Routledge, 2012); Daniel Abrams, *Kabbalistic Manuscripts and Textual Theory: Methodologies of Textual Scholarship and Editorial Practice in the Study of Jewish Mysticism* (Jerusalem and Los Angeles: Magnes Press and Cherub Press, 2010).
12 Compare to Jonathan Garb, *Shamanic Trance in Modern Kabbalah* (Chicago: University of Chicago Press), 2011, 4–6. For a similar approach to sociology of knowledge, see Randall Collins, *The Sociology of Philosophies: A Global Theory of Intellectual Change* (Cambridge, MA: Belknap Press of Harvard University Press, 1998).
13 Mircea Eliade, *Shamanism: Archaic Techniques of Ecstasy* (Princeton, MJ: Princeton University Press, 1964).
14 David Sorotzkin, *Orthodoxy and Modern Disciplination: The Production of the Jewish Tradition in Europe in Modern Times* (Ha-Kibbutz Ha-Mehuad, Tel Aviv, 2011) [Hebrew)].
15 Elliot Wolfson, *Open Secret: Post-Messianic Messanism and the Mystical Revision of Menahem. Mendel Schneerson* (New York: Columbia University Press, 2009); idem, *A Dream Interpreted Within a Dream: Oneiropoiesis and the Prism of Imagination* (New York: Zone Books, 2011). See also idem., *Through a Speculum That Shines: Vision and Imagination in Medieval Jewish Mysticism* (Princeton, NJ: Princeton University Press. 1994), 52–58, for a position close to the vision articulated here. Moshe Idel, *Old Worlds, New Mirrors: On Jewish Mysticism and Twentieth-Century Thought* (Philadelphia: University of Pennsylvania Press, 2010) (and see Idel, *Kabbalah: New Perspectives*, 22–25; Sorotzkin, *Orthodoxy and Modern Disciplination;* Abrams, *Kabbalistic Manuscripts and Textual Theory*; Shahzad Bashir, *Sufi Bodies: Religion and Society in Medieval Islam* (New York: Columbia University Press, 2011).
16 Zvi Mark, *Revelation and Rectification in the Revealed and Hidden Writings of R. Nahman of Breslav* (Jerusalem: Magnes Press, 2011) [Hebrew].
17 Aspects of these developments and surrounding methodological issues have been discussed in depth in the works of Jeffrey Kripal. See especially his *Roads of Excess, Palaces of Wisdom: Eroticism & Reflexivity in the Study of Mysticism* (Chicago: University of Chicago Press, 2001) and idem., *The Serpent's Gift: Gnostic Reflections on the Study of Religion* (Chicago: University of Chicago Press, 2007).
18 Oluf Schönbeck, "Sufism in the USA: Creolisation, Hybridization, Syncretisation?" in *Sufism Today: Heritage and Tradition in the Global Community*, ed. Catharina Raudvere and Leif Stenberg (London: I. B. Tauris, 2009), 183.
19 Julia Day Howell and Martin van Bruinessen, "Sufism and the 'Modern' in Islam," in *Sufism and the 'Modern' in Islam*, ed. by Julia Day Howell and Martin van Bruinessen (London: I. B. Tauris, 2007), 6.
20 In this context it is worth mentioning yet another recent study of the strongly discontinuous (though not described there in those terms) and rather influential Western center, with close ties to academia, Beshara. See Isobel Jeffery-Street, *Ibn Arabi and the Contemporary West: Beshara and the Ibn Arabi Society* (London & Oakville: Equinox Pub. Ltd., 2010).
21 Moshe Weinberger, *Song of Teshuva: A Commentary on Rav Avraham Yitzchak HaKohen Kook's Oros HaTeshuvah*, trans. by Yaacov Dovid Shulman (Penina Press, 2011).

22 See, most recently, Thomas Keating, *Intimacy with God: An Introduction to Centering Prayer* (New York: Crossroad Publishers, 1994); Jonathan R. Wilson, *Living Faithfully in a Fragmented World: From* After Virtue *to a New Monasticism* (Cambridge; Lutterworth Press, 2010); Peter Rollins, *Insurrection* (Nashville, TN: Howard Books, 2011), as well as http://www.contemplativeprayer.net and Richard Rohr, Andreas Ebert, and Peter Heinegg, *The Enneagram: A Christian Perspective* (New York: Crossroad Publishers, 2011). One informant in New York has told Garb that followers of Michael Laitman, of the R. Ashlag school of Kabbalah, attempted to propagate his teachings among the activists of the Occupy Wall Street movement.
23 Louise Child, *Tantric Buddhism and Altered States of Consciousness: Durkheim, Emotional Energy, and Visions of the Consort* (Farnham, England: Ashgate, 2007); Hugh Urban, *Tantra: Sex, Secrecy, Politics and Power in the Study of Religion* (Berkeley & Los Angeles: University of California Press, 2003), especially 227–63; idem, *Power of Tantra: Religion, Sexuality and the Politics of South Asian Studies* (London & New York: I. B. Tauris, 2009), especially 167–72, 178–86. For David Loy, see e.g., his collection *Awareness Bound and Unbound: Buddhist Essays* (Albany: State University of New York Press, 2009) that was concluded during his period at the IAS. On engaged Buddhism, see the recent reportage in Alan Senuake, *The Bodhisattva's Embrace: Dispatches from Engaged Buddhism's Front Lines* (Berkeley, CA: Clear View Press, 2010).
24 Steven J. Sutcliffe, "From Comparative Mysticism to New Age Spirituality: Teaching New Age as Raw Materials of Religion," in *Teaching Mysticism*, ed. William B. Parsons, 249–67 (New York: Oxford University Press, 2011).
25 Mathew Wood, "The Sociology of Spirituality: Reflections on a Problematic Endeavor," in *The New Blackwell Companion to the Sociology of Religion*, ed. Richard K. Fenn, 267–84 (Chichester, West Sussex, UK: Wiley-Blackwell, 2010).
26 Paul Heelas, *Spiritualities of Life: New Age Romanticism and Consumptive Capitalism* (Malden, MA: Blackwell Publishers, 2008); idem., *The New Age Movement: The Celebration of the Self and the Sacralization of Modernity* (Oxford: Blackwell, 1996).
27 Philip Wexler, *Mystical Sociology* (forthcoming).
28 Wood, "The Sociology of Spirituality," 275.
29 Ibid., 279.
30 Joseph W. H. Lough, *Weber and the Persistence of Religion: Social Theory, Capitalism and the Sublime* (London: Routledge, 2006).

Bibliography

Abrams, Daniel. *Kabbalistic Manuscripts and Textual Theory: Methodologies of Textual Scholarship and Editorial Practice in the Study of Jewish Mysticism* (Jerusalem & Los Angeles: Magnes Press & Cherub Press, 2010).

Bashir, Shahzad. *Sufi Bodies: Religion and Society in Medieval Islam* (New York: Columbia University Press, 2011).

Child, Louise. *Tantric Buddhism and Altered States of Consciousness: Durkheim, Emotional Energy, and Visions of the Consort* (Farnham, England: Ashgate, 2007).

Collins, Randall. *The Sociology of Philosophies: A Global Theory of Intellectual Change* (Cambridge, MA: Belknap Press of Harvard University Press, 1998).

Eliade, Mircea. *Shamanism: Archaic Techniques of Ecstasy* (Princeton, NJ: Princeton University Press, 1964).

Garb, Jonathan. "Powers of Language in Kabbalah: Comparative Reflections," in *The Poetics of Grammar and the Metaphysics of Sound and Sign*, ed. Sergio de La Porta and David Shulman, 230–69 (Leiden, The Netherlands: Brill, 2007).

Garb, Jonathan. *Manifestations of Power in Jewish Mysticism: From Rabbinic Literature to Safedian Kabbalah* (Jerusalem: Magnes Press, 2005) [Hebrew].

Greetham, David C. *Textual Scholarship: An Introduction* (New York: Routledge, 2012).
Heelas, Paul and Linda Woodhead. *The Spiritual Revolution: Why Religion Is Giving Way to Spirituality* (Malden, MA: Blackwell Publishers, 2005).
Heelas, Paul. *Spiritualities of Life: New Age Romanticism and Consumptive Capitalism* (Malden, MA: Blackwell Publishers, 2008).
Heelas, Paul. *The New Age Movement: The Celebration of the Self and the Sacralization of Modernity* (Oxford: Blackwell, 1996).
Howell, Julia Day and Martin van Bruinessen. "Sufism and the 'Modern' in Islam," in *Sufism and the 'Modern' in Islam*, ed. Julia Day Howell and Martin van Bruinessen (London: I. B. Tauris, 2007), 3–18.
Huss, Boaz. "The Mystification of the Kabbalah and the Modern Construction of Jewish Mysticism" *Ben-Gurion University of the Negev Review* (2008), 1–14.
Idel, Moshe. *Kabbalah: New Perspectives* (New Haven, CT: Yale University Press, 1988).
Idel, Moshe. *Old Worlds, New Mirrors: On Jewish Mysticism and Twentieth-Century Thought* (Philadelphia: University of Pennsylvania Press, 2010).
Jeffery-Street, Isobel. *Ibn Arabi and the Contemporary West: Beshara and the Ibn Arabi Society* (London & Oakville: Equinox Pub. Ltd., 2010).
Johnston, William. *Christian Zen: A Way of Meditation* (New York: Fordham University Press, 1997).
Keating, Thomas. *Intimacy with God: An Introduction to Centering Prayer* (New York: Crossroad Publishers, 1994).
Kripal, Jeffrey. *Roads of Excess, Palaces of Wisdom: Eroticism & Reflexity in the Study of Mysticism* (Chicago: University of Chicago Press, 2001).
Kripal, Jeffrey. *The Serpent's Gift: Gnostic Reflections on the Study of Religion* (Chicago: University of Chicago Press, 2007).
Lemert, Charles. *Sociology after the* Crisis (Boulder, CO: Westview, 1995).
Lough, Joseph W. H. *Weber and the Persistence of Religion: Social Theory, Capitalism and the Sublime* (London: Routledge, 2006).
Loy, David. *Awareness Bound and Unbound: Buddhist Essays* (Albany: State University of New York Press, 2009).
Mark, Zvi. *Revelation and Rectification in the Revealed and Hidden Writings of R. Nahman of Breslav* (Jerusalem: Magnes Press, 2011) [Hebrew].
Melucci, Alberto. *Challenging Codes: Collective Action in the Information Age* (Cambridge: Cambridge University Press, 1999).
Powell, Robert. *Christian Zen: The Essential Teachings of Jesus Christ* (Berkeley, CA.: North Atlantic Books. 2003).
Rohr, Richard, Andreas Ebert, and Peter Heinegg. *The Enneagram: A Christian Perspective* (New York: Crossroad Publishers, 2011).
Rollins, Peter. *Insurrection* (Nashville, TN: Howard Books, 2011).
Scholem, Gershom. "Mysticism and Society." *Diogenes* 15/58 (1967): 1–24.
Schönbeck, Oluf. "Sufism in the USA: Creolisation, Hybridization, Syncretisation?" in *Sufism Today: Heritage and Tradition in the Global Community*, ed. Catharina Raudvere and Leif Stenberg (London: I. B. Tauris, 2009), 177–88.
Senuake, Alan. *The Bodhisattva's Embrace: Dispatches from Engaged Buddhism's Front Lines* (Berkeley, CA: Clear View Press, 2010).
Sorotzkin, David. *Orthodoxy and Modern Disciplination: The Production of the Jewish Tradition in Europe in Modern Times* (Ha-Kibbutz Ha-Mehuad, Tel Aviv, 2011) [Hebrew)].
Sutcliffe, Steven J. "From Comparative Mysticism to New Age Spirituality: Teaching New Age as Raw Materials of Religion," in *Teaching Mysticism. William B. Parsons*, 249–67 (New York: Oxford University Press, 2011).
Turner, Bryan S. *The New Blackwell Companion to the Sociology of Religion* (Chichester, West Sussex, UK: Wiley-Blackwell, 2010).

Urban, Hugh. *Tantra: Sex, Secrecy, Politics and Power in the Study of Religion* (Berkeley & Los Angeles: University of California Press, 2003).
Weinberger, Moshe. *Song of Teshuva: A Commentary on Rav Avraham Yitzchak HaKohen Kook's Oros HaTeshuvah*, trans. by Yaacov Dovid Shulman (Penina Press, 2011).
Wexler, Philip. *Mystical Sociology* (forthcoming).
Wexler, Phillip. "Gershom Scholem's 'Mysticism and Society': Critique, Alternative, Text," *Kabbalah: Journal for the Study of Jewish Mystical Texts* (forthcoming).
Wilson, Jonathan R. *Living Faithfully in a Fragmented World: From* After Virtue *to a New Monasticism* (Cambridge: Lutterworth Press, 2010).
Wolfson, Elliot. *A Dream Interpreted Within a Dream: Oneiropoiesis and the Prism of Imagination* (New York: Zone Books, 2011).
Wolfson, Elliot. *Open Secret: Post-Messianic Messanism and the Mystical Revision of Menahem Mendel Schneerson* (New York: Columbia University Press, 2009).
Wolfson, Elliot. *Through a Speculum That Shines: Vision and Imagination in Medieval Jewish Mysticism* (Princeton, NJ: Princeton University Press).
Wood, Mathew. "The Sociology of Spirituality: Reflections on a Problematic Endeavor," in *The New Blackwell Companion to the Sociology of Religion*, ed. Richard K. Fenn (Chichester, West Sussex, UK: Wiley-Blackwell, 2010).

Part One

Jewish Mysticism

TWO

Contemporary Kabbalah and Classical Kabbalah
Breaks and Continuities

Jonathan Garb

The State of Research

In recent years, we have seen a striking increase in studies devoted to contemporary Kabbalah. Whilst in the past this rapidly growing phenomenon was addressed within the disciplines of sociology and anthropology, as in the pioneering studies of Yoram Bilu, today we can observe a convergence of interest on the part of historians of Jewish thought and culture as well as scholars concerned with contemporary mysticism and spirituality.[1] Though this is not the place to provide a comprehensive overview of the numerous important studies in this rapidly growing new field, one should briefly mention the following landmarks: Boaz Huss' research project on contemporary Kabbalah, funded by the *Israel Science Foundation*, which has resulted so far in several important edited volumes and articles (mentioned below) and an international conference, the proceedings of which have been published; the brief discussion of contemporary Sephardic Kabbalistic Yeshivas in Pinchas Giller's monograph on the fellowship of R. Shalom Shar'abi;[2] Jonathan Meir's critical studies of the R. Ashlag circle, which include several foundational discussions of other circles;[3] Zvi Mark's study of Bratzlav esotericism, which has resulted inter alia, in an extensive discussion included within his book *The Scroll of Secrets*;[4] Elliot Wolfson's incisive analysis of the thought of R. Menahem Mendel Shneurson, the seventh rebbe of Lubavitch.[5] Much of this innovative reflection was expressed and further refined during the felicitous meeting of disciplines within our *IAS* group, as reflected in this volume. The recognition of the new field on the part of academic institutions was reflected not only by the group, but also in repeated sessions on contemporary Kabbalah held at recent conferences convened by the *Association of Jewish Studies* and the *World Congress of Jewish Studies*.

My own overview of twentieth-century Kabbalah, *The Chosen Will Become Herds*,[6] though focused mostly on earlier developments, also provided an overview of several contemporary developments. Here one must mention, by way of introducing my theme, an astute observation by Zvi Mark, in his English-language review of the earlier Hebrew edition of my book, published in the journal *Kabbalah*.[7] Mark noted that this book focused mostly on more radical streams within twentieth-century Kabbalah, such as R. Kook and his circle, R. Ashlag and his followers, R. Yitzhaq Ginsburgh, and others. Mark claimed that this emphasis, coupled with the relative absence of more mainstream groups, such as the large Hasidic courts (and I myself might add, many Sephardic figures), enabled me to demarcate twentieth-century Kabbalah as a domain of inquiry distinct from earlier developments.

More pertinently for the present study, Mark correctly noted that this move enabled me to place contemporary Kabbalah in a wider cultural context, of the New Age and other non-traditional forms of spirituality, a move similar to that of Boaz Huss, in his foundational article "The New Age of Kabbalah."[8] Mark then went on to note that I diverged from this path in a short and rather personal piece in the magazine *Eretz Acheret*, which has subsequently been expanded in two academic articles.[9] There, I focused on the Haredi world, and especially on the Hasidic world, which was again far from central in my monograph. Mark concluded by correctly predicting that this will become the vector of my current research on contemporary Kabbalah. Mark's critique reflects the lively, yet collegial and sensitive, nature of debates within the new field of contemporary Kabbalah studies, which bodes well for the future of the emerging field.

Continuity and Discontinuity

I shall now reframe Mark's argument in new terms, incorporating it within a broader consideration of the relationship of contemporary and classical Kabbalah. Michel Foucault, especially in his inaugural lecture at the *Collège de France*, described the question of breaks versus continuities as a central quandary facing the historian of discourse.[10] Similarly, I believe that the central scholarly challenge facing the new field is that of determining its relationship to classical Kabbalah. Only once this issue is addressed can one move to what is in my mind an even more important question, which is nonetheless secondary from an analytical point of view, that of its relationship to global mystical culture. To rephrase this argument, to the extent that contemporary Kabbalah breaks with its origins, it is rendered freer to engage modernity (or what some describe as post-modernity), and thus extra-Jewish ideas and practices. To the extent that it maintains a strong connection to earlier forms of Kabbalah, it is impelled towards a more parochial and enclosed form of discourse. In other words, it is vital to distinguish between 'continuous' kabbalists, mostly but not entirely associated with Haredi (so-called Ultra-Orthodox) circles, whether Sephardic, Hasidic, or 'Lithuanian,' on the one hand and non-continuous groups on the other. The latter include the few adherents of this lore within Religious Zionism, most branches of the R. Ashlag school ranging to the neo-Kabbalistic followers of Philip Berg (subject of a recent monograph by Jody Myers) as well as followers of the Jewish renewal movement (which is studied by Shaul Magid and Rachel Werczberger).[11]

One must of course first clarify the precise meaning of the term 'classical Kabbalah.' As I have addressed this issue elsewhere,[12] here I will merely claim in a rather axiomatic manner that for contemporary kabbalists, the classics are not the twelfth century *Sefer Ha-Bahir*, nor the thirteenth-century writings penned in Catalonian and Castilian circles, nor fourteenth century classics such as *Sefer Ha-Temuna* and *Ma'arekhet Elohut*. Even the highly influential Zoharic literature, in and of itself, is not the classic that contemporary Kabbalah relates to.[13] Indeed, R. Yitzhaq Luria (1534–1572), the most authoritative of modern kabbalists, denied the authority of the great majority of medieval Kabbalistic works, and this position is still upheld at least by most Sephardic kabbalists.[14] One hint at the reason for this choice is that almost all of the above-mentioned works are anonymous or pseudo-epigraphic. Contemporary Kabbalah, in almost all of its forms, is first and foremost a cult of the exceptional individual and his mystical biography, in a manner, which recalls other recent and current mystical developments.[15] As a result, even such a venerated medieval kabbalist as Nahmanides (1194–1270), known almost entirely through his writings, could not serve as a model in later generations.

Rather, the classics for contemporary Kabbalah are the works composed by the great figures of modern Kabbalah, the age of the exceptional individual, namely Luria, R. Moshe Cordovero (1522–1570), R. Moshe Hayyim Luzzatto (1707–1746), R. Elijah of Vilna (1720–1797), the Besht (1698–1760), R. Shalom Shar'abi (1720–1777), and R. Shneur Zalman of Lyady (1745–1813). It is no coincidence that amongst the most widely circulated texts in contemporary circles, one must count the hagiographies composed around some of these figures. This, one should add, is the explanation for an intriguing phenomenon which was already noted by Huss: the one medieval writer who is central for almost all branches of contemporary Kabbalah is the most autobiographical and self-conscious of medieval kabbalists, the Castilian R. Abraham Abulafia (1240–1291?).[16]

Actually, this holds true for other realms in Jewish discourse. For legal halakhists and advocates of *mussar* (customarily translated as 'ethics'), the classics are also modern works. Thus, just as the *Zohar* is mediated for contemporary kabbalists through the commentaries of Luria, Cordovero, and Luzzatto, the medieval Halakhic classics, such as the *'Arb'a Turim* and the *Yad Ha-Hazaka* are mediated through later works, and especially the triad of works by sixteenth century R. Joseph Karo (1488–1575): *Sulkhan 'Arukh*, its main source, *Beit Yosef* on the *Turim*, and *Kesef Mishne* on the *Yad*. Likewise, although the modern *Mussar* movement does value the medieval works of R. Bahya Ibn Paquda (eleventh century) and especially those of R. Yonah Gerondi (died 1263), the major sourcebook by far is of course Luzzatto's *Mesilat Yesharim*, which is currently receiving an extensive Kabbalistic commentary.[17] Indeed it must be said here that those streams, which continue the traditions of classical Kabbalah also continue its organic connection to other branches of Jewish learning and practice.

It is true that several important and entirely continuous writers, such as R. Yitzhaq Moshe Erlanger (in his *Shiv'a 'Enayyim* and *Kabbalat Ha-Ge'onim* series, or R. Yitzhaq Maier Morgenstern in his *Yam Ha-Hokhma* series, do bypass the Lurianic interdict and return to neglected medieval texts which until then had largely been addressed by scholars (and one might add, do so while resorting to scholarly textual scholarship). These include the works of the Castilian *'Iyyun* circle, as well as the anonymous fourteenth-century *Brit Menuha* (which was singled out by Luria as being 'true'). However, in doing so, these two writers, who form part of a loose circle, declaredly chose to interpret earlier texts entirely through the lens of modern discourse and especially Hasidism.[18] For example, in introducing his commentary on *Brit Menuha*, Morgenstern warns that one should constantly connect the dangerous teachings of the earlier work, which deal with non-divine worlds, to the safer Lurianic teachings, which focus on the divine world of emanation.[19] Similarly, when Erlanger writes that "all the books require each other," including pre-modern works, nonetheless their gates were closed before the revelation which commenced with the founder of Hasidism, the Besht. Thus, only when studying the works of the *Rishonim*, or medieval kabbalists, through the lens of Luria and especially that of the Besht, then there can be no damage in interpreting these texts, even if erroneously so.[20]

These preliminary observations have already yielded three ways of differentiating continuous from discontinuous streams in contemporary Kabbalah: the very relationship, in exegesis as well as in self-modeling on biography, to the classical modern kabbalists, the connection to other branches of traditional

Jewish life and learning, and conversely the disengagement from non-Jewish discourse. I wish to add three more, which flow easily from the above: the degree of emphasis on theurgical practice of *kavvanot* and *yihudim* related to the traditional liturgy as opposed to anomian paths (such as Abulafian meditation and breathing techniques), which underscores the degree of connection to Halakha, as well as *minhag*, or custom; The degree of esotericism, as the classical approach of Luria, Sharʻabi and R. Elijah is certainly esoteric, whilst other figures such as Cordovero, Luzzatto, and the Besht also had to preserve some degree of esotericism.[21] And finally—and very importantly— the degree of response to current historical events: whilst Luzzatto, R. Elijah, and even Luria constructed theories of history, they did not really address specific historical events. Taking a positive interest in such events is really a function of relating to the non-Jewish world, or alternatively to the new forms of secular Jewish identity—a concern, which often goes together with a weakening of connection to classical forms of Jewish life such as Halakha. Thus, we shall soon see that non-continuous kabbalists such as R. Ashlag or R. Kook famously saw much that is beneficial in developments such as socialism, modern science, and Zionism. This was largely not the case for continuous mystics, such as R. Shlomo Elyashiv (1839–1926), the giant of Lithuanian Kabbalah, and R. Kook's erstwhile mentor.[22] In other words, this last criterion can also be shown to extend from those already mentioned. One may summarize this preliminary distinction by suggesting that while continuous Kabbalah relates 'vertically' to what Danièle Hervieu-Léger has termed the 'chain of memory,' discontinuous Kabbalah extends its vision 'horizontally' to the non-Orthodox or non-Jewish world.[23]

Periodization of Contemporary and Recent Kabbalah

The distinction developed above may now assist us in addressing the question of periodization, also raised by Mark: How should we envisage the relationship between the two parts of the twentieth century, or in other words, did contemporary Kabbalah start around 1900, as claimed in my monograph or around 1950, as suggested by Mark? Here a brief survey of major developments in twentieth-century Kabbalah is called for: Rabbi Avraham Yitzhaq Kook (1865–1935), arrived in Palestine in 1904, and this move catalyzed a profound break with classical Kabbalah, as well as *mussar* and Halakha, as part of his vision of renewal and the need for a new religious discourse in response to staggering modern developments.[24] This led him into several of the above forms of discontinuity: though a very prolific writer, as far as we know he composed hardly any commentaries on Kabbalistic works, he explicitly addressed non-Jewish thinkers such as Nietzsche and Bergson, he advocated a marked degree of exotericism, he espoused anomian and even antinomian moves—and most significantly—he discussed very specific historical events, both general and Jewish, rather positively, in mystical-messianic terms. Some of these characteristics were even more prominent in the life and works of his main student, R. David Ha-Kohen ("the Nazarite," 1887–1972), who teamed up with R. Kook already in the second decade of the twentieth century and subsequently relocated to Jerusalem. In other words, we are speaking here of a school, rather than an isolated figure.[25]

Soon after, R. Yehuda Petaya (1859–1942), an extremely exoteric writer (certainly relative to Sephardic kabbalists), also arrived in Jerusalem in 1934. Like R. Kook, R. Petaya responded, in Kabbalistic terms, to the First World War, albeit in the rather local frame of Baghdad.[26] Finally, in 1921, we have the immigration of R. Yehuda Ashlag (1884–1954), the most discontinuous and exoteric of the kabbalists of the first part of the century, who had little to say on other branches of Jewish life, but again much to say of Socialism, Zionism, evolution, and psychology. It is no coincidence that soon after arriving in Jerusalem, he clashed with the Sephardic kabbalists, seeking to substitute their highly traditionalist interpretation with his radically innovative one. Like R. Kook (but unlike R. Petaya), R. Ashlag established an ongoing school.[27]

We can see that already in the first part of the century, there were strong discontinuous moves among several figures, only some of whom have been mentioned here. Converging in the first part of the twentieth century in Palestine from locations as diverse as Latvia-Lithuania, Baghdad, and Poland, and together with academic researchers of Jewish mysticism (such as Gershom Scholem and Martin Buber), they synergistically formed the main center of discontinuous Kabbalah.[28] Discontinuity, then, was not created by the radical changes of the mid-century, as Mark would have it, but rather by the gradual dislocation of Jewish life from the Middle East, North Africa, and Europe to new centers such as Palestine. Even prior to the staggering waves of Jewish immigration during the late nineteenth and early twentieth centuries, we can discern a gradual re-location of Kabbalistic life, as evidenced in the surprising printing of works of Lithuanian Kabbalah (such as R. Yitzhaq Haver's *Ginzei Meromim*) in Johannesburg, far from a major center of Jewish printing, as early as the 1860s.

However, I will conclude the first part of this discussion adding that I do not completely set aside Mark's critique of my periodization, as the second part of the century did greatly enhance discontinuous elements. Assisted by globalization and later by new technologies, the chosen became herds, the elite fellowships morphed into mass movements, which had marked impact on the political life of Israel, especially after the watershed of 1967. Another major factor here was the development of the second discontinuous center:

the United States, and especially the rise, soon after 1950, of its most striking figure, R. Menahem Mendel Shneurson (1902–1994), who at least in simple terms advocated radical exotericism, for all of the subtle dialectic eloquently described by Elliot R. Wolfson in his *Open Secret*.[29] As a relatively discontinuous figure, Shneurson was extremely interested in the non-Jewish world, in current events, and in new technological media.

Both of these centers of discontinuity thrived precisely because of the collapse of the strongholds of more classical Jewish life and thus of continuous Kabbalah: Eastern Europe, which was devastated by the Holocaust, and the Middle Eastern communities which suffered the following fate after the establishment of Israel: removed from their original locations, which often included strong urban centers, such as Baghdad or Aleppo, mixed together in new peripheral locations, and in many cases forcibly secularized. At the very least, traditional forms of authority were shaken, and thus new forms of authority (including not only the Kabbalistic circles discussed here but also the neo-Sephardic and non-Kabbalistic R. 'Ovadyah Yosef), emerged.[30] As always, language played a key role in this process. The languages of continuous Kabbalah, Yiddish and *lashon ha-qodesh* or sacral Hebrew, were indigenous to the traditional Jewish world. The languages of discontinuous Kabbalah are Russian, as shown by Hamutal Bar-Yosef, the secularized neo-Hebrew developed by the famous linguist Eli'ezer Ben Yehuda (1858–1922), and other twentieth-century Zionists, and later English, French, and Spanish.[31] To conclude this part of the discussion, the bifurcation of Kabbalah into continuous and discontinuous streams cannot be seen in isolation, but rather as an expression of political, demographic, cultural, and linguistic processes which accelerated throughout the twentieth century.

Haredi Kabbalah: Earlier Stages

Continuous forms of Kabbalah, which shall concern us for the remainder of the article, are prevalent almost exclusively in the worlds least studied by scholars of contemporary Kabbalah and contemporary Jewish discourse in general, and as a result mostly covered by sociologists and anthropologists.[32] I am referring to the Haredi worlds (as opposed to the prevalent and undifferentiating term "world"). These also include Haredi-National (*le'umi*) groups, as exemplified by a central and eloquent opponent of exotericism and non-Jewish influence, R. Tzevi Yisra'el Tau (born 1936).[33]

Of course one should not expect every Haredi writer to avoid all six modes of discontinuity, as in the exceptional case of R. Ya'aqov Moshe Hillel (born 1945), a central Sephardic figure, just as there are few discontinuous thinkers who exhibit all six (unless one counts extremely discontinuous phenomena which in my view do not properly belong to the study of the history of Kabbalah, such as the *Kabbalah Center*), yet it would be rare to find even two or three discontinuous features in one Haredi writer.[34] Thus as a whole Haredi discourse takes the form of commentary on classical Kabbalistic works, is strongly connected to other forms of traditional Jewish discourse such as Talmudics, Halakha, *mussar* and traditional biblical exegesis, is largely disengaged from the non-Jewish world, emphasizes nomian practice and theurgy, maintains at least a rhetoric of esotericism, and usually does not explicitly address concrete historical events.

As a result, Haredi Kabbalah has to some extent resisted the two-pronged this-worldly reinterpretation of Kabbalah as either psychological or national-political, exemplified respectively by the Ashlag and Kook schools.[35] Another form of resistance blocks greater involvement of women in mystical life, as championed by discontinuous kabbalists such as R. David Kohen and R. Menahem Mendel Shneurson, a development which gained ground towards the end of the twentieth century.[36] Sociologically speaking, if one constructs an imaginary spectrum with secular forms of Jewish spirituality on the one side and the more austere and cloistered Haredi groups on the other, then the position of each group is somewhat determined by the degree of separation of men and women in public life, which is in turn related to economic and demographic factors such as the development of a leisure culture, family size etc.

As the primary distinction, which I have sharpened here as but a heuristic device, one can certainly point at gradients or degrees of continuity. As the Haredi worlds expand, and as a result become increasingly specialized, there is an ongoing proliferation of stances. However, there is usually at least a rhetorical obedience to a shared 'party line' vis-à-vis the non-Haredi worlds. In the first part of the century, when traditional forms of authority were stronger, this uniformity was actually more profound and as a result individualistic mysticism was less prominent in Haredi public life. Again, the roots of the relative rarity of Kabbalistic discourse in this period can be traced back to a somewhat earlier period (while bearing in mind the renaissance in Jerusalem described above). R. Yehuda Petaya, in his above-mentioned introduction, stressed the rarity of kabbalists in early twentieth-century Baghdad, even as he strove to remedy it. Likewise, the Hasidim greatly reduced their printing of Kabbalistic texts after the mid-nineteenth century, and as a whole, the Hasidic writings of subsequent decades indeed decreasingly refer to technical Kabbalistic terms. Although I do not share the opinion of Immanuel Etkes and Benjamin Brown as to the alleged 'indifference' to Kabbalah in the Lithuanian *Mussar*-movement, it is true that with the exception of R. Yehuda Leib Bloch of Telz (1860–1929), most *mussar* masters chose to conceal their esoteric knowledge, and later masters, such as R. Elijah Dessler (1892–1953), explicitly opposed the widespread study of Kabbalah.[37]

In addition, one should note the critique of exoteric Kabbalah voiced by two vastly influential Lithuanian figures active in the first part of the century: firstly R. Yisra'el Meir Kagan of Radin (1839–1933, the *Hafetz Hayyim*), wrote the following dismissal of Kabbalistic prayer meditations or *kavvanot* in his almost canonical *Mishna Berura*, (which did much to arrest the development of Halakha in the last century, even as theoretical, non-Halakhic Talmudic discourse went through an unprecedented revival in Lithuania):

> One should not intend (*yekhaven*) with names and *yihudim* [theurgical techniques], only pray simply to understand the words with intention of the heart, except for those who have entered the secret of God. . . for otherwise one damages exceedingly.[38]

Although this formulation, like practically everything else Kagan wrote, is based on earlier sources, its inclusion in an influential code is highly significant. According to this ruling, aside from a narrowly designated elite, Kabbalistic practice is harmful. Another Halakhic giant, R. Avraham Yesh'ayahu Karelitz (1878–1953), reputedly claimed that Kabbalah is in effect a lost art. Although his writings betray some semi-mystical experiences, in his classic critique of *mussar*, *Hazon 'Ish be-'Inyanei 'Emunah Ve-Bitahon*, he presents a rare return to faith based on observation of nature, in a medieval fashion, rather than on any supernal universes.[39]

Recent Discontinuities in Haredi Kabbalah

As the Haredim came to play an increasingly confident public role, both in Israel and the United States (as a result of demographic increase, proliferation, and growing economic and political clout), the place of Kabbalah in their worlds changed markedly towards the end of the last century and especially in the current decade. This striking process is greatly facilitated by recent technological developments. Of these I will note the following: the great popularity of MP3 recorders among Yeshiva students ensures that virtually every class on Kabbalah is instantaneously available in digital format. Almost all of these recordings soon make their way to vast audio collections accessible by various means and especially through websites such as *Kol Haloshon*, which offers over one hundred thousand talks.[40] Secondly, tens of thousands of Jewish books, including many thousands of Kabbalistic tomes, are accessible in ever-growing and increasingly sophisticated databases, such as *DBS* or *Otzar HaHochma*, the latter including some fifty thousand books.[41] Despite the increasing digitalization of Kabbalistic literature, desktop publishing has also made it easier to independently publish works of Kabbalah.[42] As part of the growing percentage of Haredi books within the Israeli publishing market, many mystical works are widely circulated in the huge new bookstores—such as *Manny's: Or Ha-Hayyim*—which have appeared in recent years in Haredi centers (even as they have been subject to attacks on the part of extremists resisting such modernizing trends).[43]

Within this rapidly proliferating market, one can observe the development of new specializations, such as works aimed at the separate world of Haredi women. Although books such as Tziporah Heller's and Sara Yoheved Rigler's *Battle Plans: How to Fight the Yetzer Hara According to Maharal, Ramchal, Chassidic and Mussar Masters*[44] do not include technical Kabbalistic discussions, the subtitle reveals the extent of exposure to sources which would not have been so freely available to large numbers of women as recently as the beginning of the current century. The rise of consumer culture in the Haredi world, as described in a slightly exaggerated fashion by Tamar Elor, merges with the continuing primacy of Torah learning, so as to create ever-increasing demand for new intellectual products.[45] This being said, I am far from a technological or economic determinist and these means of production and distribution are demanded by, rather than merely accelerating, cultural and social changes.

Paradoxically, as continuous Haredi Kabbalah became a legitimate form of public discourse, this very exposure, and indeed the very social and technological changes which enabled its rise, have moved this discourse further towards discontinuity. An amusing example of this paradox is that of Kabbalistically based attacks on the new 'machines' such as the internet (including identification of *Google* with the apocalyptic enemy *gog*), circulated via e-mail lists. In all of the parameters set out above, continuity is slowly but surely being eroded. Tellingly, senior Haredi kabbalists are now taking an interest in non-continuous kabbalists such as R. Kook and R. Ashlag. Although most Kabbalistic authorities, such as R. Ya'aqov Moshe Hillel and R. Yitzhaq Maier Morgenstern still represent the classical merger of Halakhic and Kabbalistic proficiency, there are now several Haredi authorities on Kabbalah who are not knowledgeable in other branches of Jewish lore. As we shall see, some kabbalists in these worlds secretly read books on Yoga or NLP as magical and ecstatic forms of Kabbalah are competing with theurgy for place of pride. Significantly, there are hints of antinomianism, as in the revival of the bold Hasidic practice of praying long after the set times mandated in Halakha. Finally, Kabbalistic analyses of events such as the Second Lebanon War and the 9/11 attacks (including the response of the non-Jewish world) have been composed.[46] These changes, in turn are part of a broader phenomenon of resurgence or revitalization, to employ Philip Wexler's analysis, in areas as diverse as Hasidic music, art and poetry inspired by Kabbalah and Talmudic learning.[47]

I wish to dedicate the rest of this section to a discussion of one such development, closely related to mystical experience and spirituality—Haredi psychology. In recent years, certain kabbalists have devoted entire works to this topic. These include R. Yitzhaq Ginsburgh (born 1944), the most discontinuous among thinkers operating—to any extent—within the Haredi worlds.[48] It is no coincidence that the latter is a *Ba'al Teshuva* of secular background who 'converted' to Haredi Judaism, as well as being an immigrant from the United States, as his interest in psychology reflects the influence of these two groups on the Haredi world. Indeed central Haredi psychologists, such as Yishai Shalif or Barukh Shulem, are either *Ba'alei Teshuva* or North Americans, or both, as in the case of the latter. The migration of new ideas from the United States to Israel further supports my thesis as to the role played by these post-Holocaust centers in the development of discontinuous Kabbalah. One result of this process is the growing influence of hypnosis among *Ba'alei Teshuva*, even as the practice of this method in the non-Haredi world is limited by Israel's restrictive laws (due to a residual law dating from the British mandate). Efim Svirsky, a student of the leading American hypnotherapist Gil Boyne, has written a manual of trance techniques and offers training in spiritual psychotherapy.[49] Likewise, NLP (Neuro-Linguistic Programming) techniques may be freely found in the *mussar*-oriented works of American-born Zelig Pliskin (born 1946). Here too, women play an increasingly important role, as reflected in the eclectic use of NLP methods, enegram diagnosis and other alternative therapies in the popular works of Miriam Adahan, yet another immigrant from the United States.

Within more continuous circles, the most prominent author on psychology is R. Itamar Schwartz, author of the series *Bi-Levavi Mishkan Evne*, an extremely prolific writer on Kabbalah and *mussar*, who has recently directed a series of seminars and books dealing with self-knowledge, marital relations and child rearing towards non-Haredi audiences.[50] Such open forays into the world of self-help and alternative therapies are paralleled in more traditionally framed discussions, such as the detailed treatment of trance states and techniques in the works of R. Yitzhaq Maier Morgenstern, Schwartz's former mentor.[51] This 'psychological turn' in Haredi spirituality should be viewed, looking ahead to my comparative conclusion, within a global frame. As Tanya M. Luhrmann has shown, psychological techniques, language, and experiences—including trance states—play a central role in the evangelical world in the United States, which she has also briefly compared to developments in the Jewish world.[52] Jeffrey Kripal has aptly summarized the role of psychology in this leading center of contemporary spirituality as follows: "Modern psychological theories and practices have become the basis for much of modern American spirituality in both many of its traditional Christian forms (psychological training and analysis are now standard features of pastoral training and counseling in most mainline denominations) and almost all of its alternative or emergent forms."[53] The rapid rise of psychology in various religious traditions is mirrored in the growing recourse to Buddhist ideas and techniques among American psychotherapists, as well as the proliferation of 'spiritual psychotherapy.'[54]

Both developments can be seen as reflecting a wider cultural shift, which as we have seen, has affected even the most insular of religious worlds. As a result, an entire new set of concepts and methods, in which external influences are far more clearly evident, has informed an extensive reinterpretation and updating of the rich reservoir of psychological theories and techniques found in classical Jewish spirituality. Consequently, the psychological dimension, though quite prominent even in earlier centuries, has gained still greater centrality in most continuous forms of Kabbalah, Hasidism and Mussar, while more abstract theosophical speculations on the one hand, and mythical imagery, on the other, have receded to a more marginal position.[55]

The State of Research Revisited

Haredi Kabbalah must surely be regarded as one of the most widespread and rapidly growing intellectual and spiritual phenomena in contemporary Jewish life. Libraries, databases, and audio collections give us some sense of the scope of this discourse, however I believe that it should also be directly accessed through fieldwork. During 2006–2011 I conducted weekly participant observations in one Kabbalistic Yeshiva (one of at least ten of this kind in Jerusalem alone), together with less regular visits to other institutions (including comparisons with Yeshivas in which Kabbalah is not officially part of the curriculum). Although some of the approximately fifteen thousand lectures given at this one site over those years have been recorded or printed, many others have not, especially as the official classes are joined by an inestimable number of other sessions held for restricted groups in the house of the *r'osh yeshiva*. To this one should add his *havrut'a* sessions of joint study of texts, day and night, with other kabbalists (only one of which I was able to observe), which are of course paralleled by those of the students, who operate in shifts around the clock. It is of sociological curiosity that this sheer volume of learning is all but ignored in the teaching and writing of most university scholars located literally minutes away, who are often engaged in studying the very same texts.[56] Paradoxically, these same scholars increasingly rely on the above-described databases, as well as increasingly accurate textual editions produced within the Haredi world, and available only in the dozens of Judaica bookstores found in the Haredi sections of Jerusalem and in the Haredi city of Bnei Brak, as the non-Haredi bookshops are increasingly dominated by a limited number of publishers, who have merged with monopolistic chains of retailers.[57]

The dismissal of continuous Kabbalah in the present is reflected in studies of the past: discontinuous groups, such as Habad or Bratzlav, or the antinomian theories of R. Mordekhai Yosef Leiner of Izbicha (1800–1854) are accorded a disproportional portion of current research, whilst the Sephardic world or large parts of nineteenth-century Lithuanian Kabbalah, are only now beginning to be studied to a significant extent.[58] A similar phenomenon can be discerned in research on twentieth-century Halakha—discontinuous but minor figures, such as R. Hayyim Hirschenson (1857–1935) and R. Hayyim David Ha-Levi (1924–1998), receive far more attention than more stolid authorities, such as R. Hayyim 'Ozer Grodzinsky (1863–1940) or R. Yitzhaq 'Elhanan Spector (1817–1896).[59]

As I have suggested elsewhere, academia in Israel is very much part and parcel of a society increasingly fragmenting into rival 'sectors' (*migzarim*). This loaded identity politics orients certain scholars towards a secular or religious-Zionist agenda, which accounts for stereotypical descriptions of the Haredi worlds as 'ultra-orthodox,' 'fundamentalist,' and otherwise defensive, uniform, and devoid of spiritual and intellectual vitality.[60] Rather than being entirely spontaneous, such scholarly moves enjoy massive financial backing from agents such as the *Posen Foundation*, as part of the rapid privatization of academia, in Israel and elsewhere.[61] Whilst some social scientists, most notably Wexler and Bilu, view the Haredi world within more global frames of reference, historical studies of the Haredim and their intellectual origins tend to express their Israeli context in which they were composed, comparing them to the sectors in Israeli society to which they themselves belong rather than to other religious traditions.[62] While awareness of the role of identity politics in scholarly choices, such as one finds in fields such as gender, queer, and minority studies, is a prerequisite for a critical evaluation of the state of research, another way forward is offered by a wider comparative perspective, as offered briefly in the following section.

Comparative Reflections

I believe that similar distinctions between continuous and discontinuous streams could be suggested with regard to Sufism, Tantra, and other traditions. Although of course, the definition of continuity with the classical as opposed to breaks with tradition need to be re-defined anew for each respective religious context. Nonetheless, especially in the era of globalization, some comparative reflections are called for, especially in terms of the current state of research. A good example of a similar anachronistic projection by scholars who are strongly oriented towards the discontinuous, may be found in the case of the widely prevalent portrayal of Sufism as consisting mainly of two figures, Ibn 'Arabi and Rumi, who have inspired the rapidly growing discontinuous Sufi circles in the West.[63] The increasingly dominant role of such Western Sufis in scholarly circles could yield fascinating comparisons to the role of identity politics in the study of contemporary Jewish thought. Here, however, I must confine my comments to the vast world of Christian mysticism and spirituality. Prevalent scholarly attitudes are rather similar here, as in the inordinate emphasis on discontinuous figures, such as Teilhard De Chardin (1881–1955) or Thomas Merton (1915–1968).[64] Likewise, one of the most strikingly discontinuous developments within the Christian world, Pentecostalism, though indeed impressive in its rapid numerical increase, has been accorded a somewhat excessive portion of academic attention, as in entire scholarly societies. The infinite variety of continuous forms of Protestant, Catholic, and Orthodox mysticism that may be found throughout the globe have not been accorded such enviable resources, unless designated to frameworks such as the 'fundamentalism project' and viewed within a frame which essentially belongs to the study of religion as it impacts on political life, rather than that of mysticism, spirituality, or psychology of religion. The sheer scope of Christian worlds suggests a more extensive variety of stances than one may find in the Jewish world (especially in Israel), as, for instance, numerous evangelical groups can be said to be situated in median positions between the continuous and the discontinuous.

From this staggering range of cases, many of which have not yet been researched, I have selected the influential works of Richard Foster, founder of the international 'spiritual formation' movement *Renovaré*, which trains spiritual directors. His revised best seller *Celebration of Discipline: The Path to Spiritual Growth*, begins with an opposition of the "classical disciplines" to the "curse of our age"—the "doctrine of instant satisfaction."[65] In other words, classical and continuous forms are opposed to what the author diagnoses as the prevalent forms of superficial spirituality. Although Foster's writing reflects awareness of current scientific and psychological trends, in a manner similar to Haredi rhetoric, he opposes "obedient living" to a "sin racked world."[66] While rejecting the "absurd political clichés and propaganda fed us today," also by "shallow and slanted" newspapers, Foster calls on his readers to "hold the events of our time before God and ask for prophetic insight" in order to be "salt and light in our decaying and dark world."[67] In other words, just like more explicitly political groups such as the Ordinary Radicals, or highly independent thinkers such as Walter Wink, Foster adopts a consciously oppositional stance vis-à-vis the prevailing cultural and political forces.[68] His position should be contrasted with the general acceptance of the prevailing order in New Age circles, which I have critiqued elsewhere.[69] As he simply puts it, "conformity to a sick culture is to be sick," while '"the modern counter-culture is hardly an improvement. It is a superficial change in life style without dealing seriously with the root problems of a consumer society."[70] Therefore, he repeatedly critiques the pragmatist attempts of this movement to describe spiritual practice in quasi-scientific terms:

> If you feel that we live in a purely physical universe, you will view meditation as a good way to obtain a consistent alpha-wave pattern. But if you believe that we live in a universe created by the infinite-personal God who delights in our communion with him, you will see meditation as communication between the Lover and the one beloved.[71]

At the same time, Foster avoids the reduction of the spiritual quest to socio-political critique and resistance. As he writes, "Focus on the kingdom [of God] produces the inward reality... nothing else can be central. The desire to get out of the rat race... the redistribution of the world's wealth... the concern for ecology cannot be central. Seeking *first* God's kingdom... is the only thing that can be central."[72]

The various quotations in Foster's book, though drawn from the entire history of Christian spiritual writing, can be shown to be significantly indebted to the 'religion of the heart' of the seventeenth and eighteenth centuries, as well as earlier texts, especially Thomas à Kempis, and later writers (especially Dietrich Bonhoeffer and Thomas Merton).[73] Here, over and above its value for the history of the present, following the avenues of continuity in Western spirituality may yield valuable historical insights. Whilst most researchers of contemporary spirituality have concentrated on its Renaissance and Romantic origins, a perspective, which includes the entire scope of modernity, would point at the importance of this median chapter in the history of modern religion.[74] In texts belonging to the various persuasions of 'the religion of the heart,' one may find the following statements (adduced from Jaroslav Pelikan's multi-series masterpiece on the Christian tradition): the evidence for the validity of religion is "being so affected by all the sayings of Jesus that it would be clearly impossible for Jesus to be speaking this way if the Christian religion were false;" doctrine is "confirmed by your experience and mine," it "passes... directly from God into the believing soul;" the Holy Spirit is "the feeling that lies naturally in the human heart."[75] Placing contemporary subjectivist spirituality, both continuous and discontinuous within this wider frame would also mitigate the tendency to describe it in terms of the "Easternization of the West" (a move which also ignores the role played by Kabbalah or Sufism).[76]

To conclude, the exercise of distinguishing between continuous and discontinuous forms of spirituality, especially within a comparative framework, can be seen as a valuable corrective to prevalent tendencies in the study of contemporary spirituality. Dominant cultural and economic forms, which academia is increasingly dependent on and far from immune from, have dictated a disproportionate stress on the latter. The spiritual logic of late capitalism, as one sharp observer has put it, favors transient and globalized trends over traditional and parochial forms of life.[77] Although the sympathies of progressive academics might well lie with the former, we would do well to recall that continuous religion can also be a form of resistance to the tyranny of the present. I believe that it is in this spirit that Michel Foucault, with whom we commenced our reflections on continuity and change, found much to admire even in the Iranian revolution. It is well worth sealing this essay (in both senses), by quoting at length from a recently published interview:

> I am astonished by the connections. . . that exist between Shi'ism and some of the religious movements in Europe at the end of the Middle Ages, up to the seventeenth or eighteenth centuries. These were great popular movements against feudal lords, against the first cruel formations of bourgeois society, great protests against the all-powerful control of the state. In Europe in the late eighteenth and early nineteenth centuries, before they adopted a directly political form, all such movements appeared as religious movements. Take for example the Anabaptists. . . . It was a movement which rejected the power of the state, government bureaucracy, social and religious hierarchies. . . . This movement supported the right to individual conscience and the independence of *small religious groups* (my italics, J. G). . . these movements are religious because they are political and political because they are religious.. . . I therefore think that the history of religions, and their deep connection to politics ought to be thought anew.[78]

Notes

This writing of this article was facilitated by the generous support of the Jules and Gwen Knapp Charitable Foundation. My thanks to Tanya Luhrmann, for her helpful comments on an earlier version.

1. See e.g., Yoram Bilu, *The Saints' Impresarios: Dreamers, Healers and Holy Men in Israel's Urban Periphery* (Haifa: Haifa University Press, 2005) [Hebrew].
2. Pinchas Giller, *Shalom Shar'abi and the Kabbalists of Beit El* (New York: Oxford University Press, 2008); Boaz Huss (ed.) *Kabbalah and Contemporary Spiritual Revival* (Beer Sheva: Ben Gurion University of the Negev Press, 2011).
3. Jonathan Meir, "The Revealed and the Revealed within the Concealed: On the Opposition to the 'Followers' of Rabbi Yehuda Ashlag and the Dissemination of Esoteric Literature," *Kabbalah* 16 (2007): 151–258; idem., "Wrestling with the Esoteric: Hillel Zeitlin, Yehuda Ashlag and Kabbalah in the Land of Israel," in *Judaism, Topics, Fragments, Faces, Identities: Jubilee Volume in Honor of Rivka Horwitz*, ed. Haviva Pedaya & Ephraim Meir, 585–647 (Beer Sheva: Ben Gurion University Press, 2007) [Hebrew].
4. Zvi Mark, *The Scroll of Secrets: The Hidden Messianic Vision of R. Nachman of Breslav* (Brighton, MA.: Academic Studies Press, 2010).
5. Elliot Wolfson, *Open Secret: Post-Messianic Messanism and the Mystical Revision of Menahem. Mendel Schneerson* (New York: Columbia University Press, 2009). See also the discussions of this figure within Dov Schwartz, *Habad's Thought from Beginning to End*, (Ramat Gan: Bar-Ilan University Press, 2011) [Hebrew].

6   Jonathan Garb, *The Chosen Will Become Herds: Studies in Twentieth-Century Kabbalah* (New Haven, CT & London: Yale University Press, 2009).
7   Zvi Mark, "Review of Jonathan Garb, *The Chosen Will Become Herds*," *Kabbalah* 17 (2008): 89–99.
8   Boaz Huss, "The New Age of Kabbalah: Contemporary Kabbalah, the New Age, and Postmodern Spirituality," *Journal of Modern Jewish Studies* 6/2 (2007): 107–25.
9   See Jonathan Garb, "Mystical and Spiritual Discourse in the Contemporary Ashkenazi Haredi Worlds," *Journal of Modern Jewish Studies* 9 (2010): 29–48; idem., "Towards the Study of the Spiritual-Mystical Renaissance in the Contemporary Ashkenazi Haredi World in Israel," in *Kabbalah and Contemporary Spiritual Revival*, ed. Boaz Huss, 117–40.
10 Michel Foucault, *The Archeology of Knowledge* trans. A. M. Sheridan-Smith (New York: Pantheon Books, 1972), especially 21–23. Compare to idem., *L'Ordre du discours* (Paris: Gallimard, 1971).
11 See Jody E. Myers, *Kabbalah and the Spiritual Quest: The Kabbalah Centre in America* (Westport, CT: Praeger Publishers, 2007); Shaul Magid, "Rainbow Hassidism in America—The Maturation of Jewish Renewal," *The Reconstructionist* 68 (2004): 34–60; Rachel Werczberger, "Memory, Land, and Identity: Visions of the Past and the Land in the Jewish Spiritual Renewal Movement in Israel," *Journal of Contemporary Religion* 26 (2011): 269–289; idem., "Self, Identity, and Healing in the Ritual of Jewish Spiritual Renewal in Israel," in *Kabbalah and Spiritual Revival: Historical, Sociological and Cultural Perspectives*, ed. Boaz Huss, 75–100 (Beer Sheva: Ben Gurion University of the Negev Press, 2011).
12 See Garb, "Mystical and Spiritual Discourse."
13 A very central contemporary Sephardic kabbalist, R. Ya'aqov Moshe Hillel (*Petah Sha'ar Ha-Shamayim* (Jerusalem: 'Ahavat Shalom: 2008), 67–68), cites an earlier text (by the Hasidic master R. Barukh of Kossov) requiring study of Lurianic texts prior to beginning Zoharic studies in order to avoid error. Hillel then significantly expands this rule, in stipulating that the *Zohar* should only be studied after many years of immersion in Luria's works, and even then only as mediated by the latter. Indeed, the works of Sephardic Kabbalah studied in both Sephardic and Ashkenazi Yeshivas, especially those originating from the school of Shar'abi, are almost always commentaries on the writings of Luria, rather than on the *Zohar* itself—as one finds in the more discontinuous case of R. Yehuda Petaya, to be discussed below). This is only to be expected, as the centre of the spiritual life of these groups is the *kavvanot* or meditations on prayer (See Pinchas Giller, *Shalom Shar'abi*, 19–53) and these are sparse in the *Zohar* and voluminous in Luria. One should also note, in passing, that the canonization of the *Zohar* is itself largely a modern phenomenon. See idem., *Reading the Zohar: The Sacred Text of the Kabbalah* (New York: Oxford University Press, 2001), Boaz Huss, *Like the Radiance of the Sky: Chapters in the Reception History of the Zohar and the Construction of its Symbolic Value* (Jerusalem: Ben-Zvi Institute and Bialik Institute, 2008) [Hebrew].
14 See the introduction of his main student, R. Hayyim Vital, to the canonical 'Etz Hayyim (Jerusalem, 1910), fol. 5a.
15 Jonathan Garb, *The Chosen Will Become Herds*, 73–74, 108–9; Hugh Urban, "An Avatar for our Age: Sathya Sai Baba and the Cultural Contradictions of Late Capitalism," *Religion* 33 (2003): 73–93; idem., "The Cult of Ecstasy: Tantrism, the New Age and the Spiritual Logic of Late Capitalism," *History of Religions* 39 (2000): 268–304.
16 See Boaz Huss, "The Formation of Jewish Mysticism and Its Impact on the Reception of Rabbi Abraham Abulafia in Contemporary Kabbalah," in *Religion and Its Other*, ed. Heike Bock, Jörg Feuchter, and Michi Knechts, 142–62 (Frankfurt: Campus Verlag, 2008).
17 Including Mordekhai Chriqui, *Sod le-Yesharim—Mesilat Yesharim in the Light of Ramhal's Writings* (Jerusalem, 2000) [Hebrew]; Alexander Aryeh Mendelbaum, *Be-Mesila Na'ale: Be-'Inyanei Sefer Mesilat Yesharim* (Jerusalem, 2005); David Shalem Ben Shlomo, *Yihud ha-Hatava* (Jerusalem, 2009); David Tzevi Hoffman, *'Orot Genuzim* (Jerusalem, 2009), as well as two volumes of an ongoing and undated commentary, *Bi-Levavi Mishkan 'Evne*,

by R. Itamar Schwartz, which appeared in 2009–2010. I shall discuss this literature in my intellectual biography of Luzzatto.

18 On their relationship see Garb, "Mystical and Spiritual Discourse." In doing so, they are following in the footsteps of the early nineteenth-century Hasidic master R. Yisra'el Hopstein of Kuznitz, whose works are enjoying a vogue for this reason among others. See e.g., the meticulous ten-volume commentary *Petilot Yisra'el* by 'Amram Offman.

19 See the 2006 volume of the annual *Yam ha-Hokhma*, 353–54.

20 See Yitzhaq Moshe Erlanger, *Shiv'a 'Enayim*, vol. 1 (Jerusalem 1992), 5 and 160. See also at length in his *Kabbalat ha-Ge'onim*, 2 vols. (Jerusalem, 2006–7).

21 This stress again relates to Halakha, as esotericism in matters of mysticism is also a legal issue, as clearly stated in *Shulkhan 'Arukh, Yor'e De'ah*, 246, 4, and its glosses and commentaries (*Nos'ei Kelim*).

22 See Garb, *The Chosen Will Become Herds*, 40, 118–19. On this figure see also Eliezer Baumgarten, "History and Historiosophy in the Doctrine of R. Shlomo Elyashiv," (M.A. thesis, Ben Gurion University, 2006) [Hebrew]. For critiques of these and other modern developments in the works of what I would term a continuous thinker, R. Yo'el Teitelbaum of Satmar, see the fascinating discussion by David Sorotzkin, *Tradition, Orthodoxy and Modernity* (Tel Aviv: Ha-Kibbutz ha-Meuhad, 2011) [Hebrew]. While Sorotzkin correctly emphasizes the radical and innovative dimensions of Teitelbaum's thought, the latter's vehement critique of virtually all forms of twentieth-century Jewish thought was founded on a rhetoric of total faithfulness to the hallowed past.

23 For the implications of Hervieu-Léger's theory for Kabablah research see Jonathan Garb, "Moshe Idel's Contribution to the Study of Religion," *Journal for the Study of Religions and Ideologies* 18 (2007): 116–29.

24 See e.g., Garb, *The Chosen Will Become Herds*, especially 23–24, 28–29, 43, 77–78, 84–93, and see also Neria Gutel, *Innovation in Tradition: The Halakhic-Philosophical Teachings of Rabbi Kook* (Jerusalem: Magnes Press, 2005) [Hebrew], Shlomo Fischer, "Self-Expression and Democracy in Radical Religious Zionist Ideology" (PhD diss., The Hebrew University of Jerusalem, 2007). On Rav Kook and *mussar*, a topic which I shall address in my monograph on kabbalistic psychology, see Smadar Cherlow, "Boldness and Modesty: R. Kook's Ethical System versus The Power Morality of Nietzsche," in *Nietzsche, Zionism and Hebrew Culture*, ed. Jacob Golomb, 347–74 (Jerusalem: Magnes Press, 2002) [Hebrew]; Yehudah Mirsky, "An Intellectual and Spiritual Biography of Rabbi Avraham Yitzhaq Ha-Cohen Kook from 1865–1904" (PhD diss., Harvard University, 2007), 187–95, 229–35 (this fine study sensitively addresses the question of discontinuity in R. Kook's own trajectory, as reflected in the consequences of his move to Palestine. However the Kabbalistic-mystical dimension is not its focus). Beyond the sources cited here, there is a vast literature (mostly in Hebrew) on these topics, reflecting the centrality of non-continuous Kabbalah, especially in its religious Zionist forms, in current research, as critiqued below.

25 See Dov Schwartz, *Religious Zionism Between Logic and Messianism* (Tel Aviv, 1999) [Hebrew]; idem., *Challenge and Crisis in Rabbi Kook's Circle* (Tel Aviv, 2001) [Hebrew]; Uriel Barak, "New Perspectives on R. Kook and His Circle: Rabbi Abraham Yitzhaq Ha-Cohen Kook and his Principal Disciples through the Prism of an Integrated Methodology" (PhD diss., Bar Ilan University, 2009) [Hebrew]. Kook's few known kabbalistic commentaries have now been printed in *Pinkasei ha-Reaya* (Jerusalem 2011).

26 See R. Yehuda Petaya's Introduction to *Beit Lehem Yehuda—Commentary on 'Etz Hayyim* (Jerusalem, 1936) [Hebrew], which also contains relatively strong statements on exotericism and subverts traditionalist views of Kabbalistic authority. This kabbalist has mainly been discussed from a social science angle. See e.g., Yoram Bilu, "Sigmund Freud and Rabbi Yehudah: On a Jewish Mystical Tradition of 'Psychoanalytic' Dream Interpretation," *The Journal of Psychological Anthropology* 2 (1979): 443–63.

27 See Garb, *The Chosen Will Become Herds*, 29–32, 52–57; Huss, "The New Age of Kabbalah;" Jonathan Meir, "The Revealed and the Revealed within the Concealed." Generally

speaking, as reflected in Meir's analysis, the Sephardim represent the more continuous part of the spectrum. See also my study "Kabbalah Outside the Walls: The Response of Rabbi Haddayah to the State of Israel," in *Rabbi Uziel and his Peers: Studies in the Religious Thought of Oriental Rabbis in 20th-Century Israel*, ed. Zvi Zohar, 13–27 (Tel Aviv: Tel Aviv University, 2009) [Hebrew], where I show that even a dramatic historical change such as the establishment of the state of Israel did little to disturb continuity within one important Sephardic school in Jerusalem. The theoretical contents of Ashlag's dispute with the Shar'abi-centered form of Kabbalah shall be discussed in a monograph of mine on kabbalistic psychology.

28 See also Boaz Huss, "'Authorized Guardians': The Polemics of Academic Scholars of Jewish Mysticism against Kabbalah Practitioners," in *Polemical Encounters: Esoteric Discourse and Its Others*, ed. K. von Stuckrad & O. Hammer, 104–26 (Leiden, The Netherlands: Brill, 2007). The recent historical study by Jonatan Meir, *Rehovot ha-Nahar: Kabbalah and Exotericism in Jerusalem (1896–1948)* (Jerusalem: Ben Zvi Institute and Mandel Institute, 2011), discusses the influx of kabbalists to Jerusalem in the late nineteenth and early twentieth centuries in detail. Meir addresses the question of continuity and discontinuity (though not in those terms), mostly through the question of esotericism versus exotericism.

29 See above. For a historical-sociological study of Shneurson which fails to integrate his life and thought, see Samuel Heilman and Menachem Friedman, *The Life and Afterlife of Menachem Mendel Schneerson* (Princeton, NJ: Princeton University Press, 2010). On the relative roles of Israel and the United States in twentieth-century Jewish history, see the interesting, but wide-sweeping claims of Yuri Slezkine, *The Jewish Century* (Princeton, NJ: Princeton University Press, 2004).

30 The best study on Yosef is Ariel Picard, *The Philosophy of Rabbi 'Ovadya Yosef in an Age of Transition: Study of Halakhah and Cultural Criticism* (Ramat-Gan: Bar-Ilan University Press, 2007) [Hebrew]. It is highly significant that Yosef developed his new vision of Sephardic Halakha as a critique of the positions of one major halakhist-kabbalist (Petaya's teacher, R. Yosef Hayyim of Baghdad, 1834–1909) and in opposition to another (the above-mentioned R. 'Ovadia Haddaya, 1891–1969).

31 Hamutal Bar-Yosef, *Mysticism in Modern Hebrew Poetry* (Boston: Academic Studies Press, 2010). Russian also plays a major role in the dissemination of Michael Leitman's strongly discontinuous version of R. Ashlag's teachings. On the distinction between *lashon ha-qodesh* and Israeli Hebrew in Haredi discourse, see Dalit Assouline, "The Haredi Distinction between *Ivrit* and *Loshn-Koydesh*," in *Hebrew as a Cultural Language*, ed. Yotam Benziman (Jerusalem: Van Leer Institute, forthcoming) [Hebrew]. For a literary expression of the dislocation from Hebrew to English in discontinuous American receptions of Kabbalah, see Myla Goldberg, *Bee Season: A Novel* (New York, 2001). Famously, the extremely discontinuous *Kabbalah Center* claims that the knowledge of Hebrew is unnecessary for the study and practice of Kabbalah.

32 See David Lehman and Batia Siebzehner, *Remaking Israeli Judaism: The Challenge of Shas* (New York: Oxford University Press, 2006) for a fine English-language representative of recent work, which includes relatively updated references to earlier studies. For exceptions to the neglect of the Haredi world in research on contemporary Kabbalah, see the above-mentioned studies by Jonathan Meir and me. See anon for examples of Benjamin Brown's erudite studies (almost entirely in Hebrew) of twentieth-century Haredi thought, which consciously minimize the role of Kabbalah and generally do not include recent or contemporary developments.

33 See Garb, *The Chosen Will Become Herds*, 9, 18–19, 35–36, 94, 117, 145 n 63, and 182 and especially Tzevi Yisra'el Tau's *Tzaddiq Be-Emunato Yihye* (Beit Shemesh, 2004). This intriguing figure, who like other Haredi-National figures has received relatively little scholarly attention, will be discussed at greater length in a PhD dissertation currently being written by Udi Abramovitz.

34 On Ya'aqov Moshe Hillel and his circle, see Jonathan Meir, "The Revealed and the Revealed within the Concealed," 241–58; idem, "The Boundaries of the Kabbalah: R. Yaakov Moshe Hillel and the Kabbalah in Jerusalem," in *Kabbalah and Contemporary Spiritual Revival*, in *Kabbalah and Contemporary Spiritual Revival*, ed. Boaz Huss, 163–80 (Beer Sheva: Ben Gurion University of the Negev Press, 2011). R. Ben Zion Rabinovitch, the Rebbe of Biale-Lugano, whom Meir associates with Hillel, cannot be regarded as an entirely continuous figure, due to his explicit discussions of current political developments. See e.g., the discussions of the Arab-Israeli conflict and the attack on left-wing positions in his *Mevaser Tov: Yesodot Kabbalat Ha-Torah* (Jerusalem, 2008), 149, 156–7, 182–3.

35 See Garb, *The Chosen Will Become Herds*, especially 37–38, 52–53; idem., "Rabbi Kook and his Sources: From Kabbalistic Historiosophy to National Mysticism," in *Studies in Modern Religions, Religious Movements and the Babhi-Bahai Faiths*, ed. M. Sharon, 77–96. (Leiden, The Netherlands: Brill, 2004).

36 See Schwartz, *Religious Zionism*, 321–31 (as well as the recently published *Zakhu Shekhina Beneyihem* (Jerusalem, 2006) by David Kohen); Naftali Loewentahl, "Women and the Dialectic of Spirituality in Hasidim," in *Within Hasidic Circles: Studies in Hasidism in Memory of Mordecai Wilensky*, ed. David Assaf, Israel Bartal, and Elchanan Reiner, 7–65 (Jerusalem: Mosad Bialik, 1999), Ada Rapoport-Albert, "The Emergence of a Female Constituency in Twentieth-Century Habad Hasidism," in *Let the Old Make Way for the New: Studies in the Social and Cultural History of Eastern European Jewry Presented to Immanuel Etkes*, ed. David Assaf and Ada Rapoport-Albert, vol. 1, 7–68 (Jerusalem: Zalman Shazar Center for Jewish History, 2009) and cf. Wolfson, *Open Secret*, 209–23.

37 Immanuel Etkes, *Rabbi Israel and the Mussar Movement* (Philadelphia & Jerusalem: Jewish Publication Society, 1993), 92–97, and cf. Hillel Goldberg, *Israel Salanter: Text, Structure, Idea* (New York: Ktav, 1982), 209–20. Brown has rephrased this view in a more considered and textually grounded manner in a forthcoming article in a *Festschrift*. On this issue and especially on Bloch see Mordechai Pachter, "The Musar Movement and the Kabbalah," in *Let the Old Make Way for the New: Studies in the Social and Cultural History of Eastern European Jewry Presented to Immanuel Etkes*, ed. David Assaf and Ada Rapoport-Albert, vol. 1, 223–50 (Jerusalem: Zalman Shazar Center for Jewish History, 2009) [Hebrew]. Cf. Garb, *The Chosen Will Become Herds*, 16, 130 n 27, 173 n 61.

38 R. Yisra'el Meir of Radin, *Mishna Berura* on *Orakh Hayyim* 98, par. 1. Kagan's approach has been discussed at length by Benjamin Brown, "Soft stringency" in the Mishnah Brurah: jurisprudential, social, and ideological aspects of a halachic formulation," *Contemporary Jewry* 27 (2007): 1–41.

39 See Benjamin Brown, *The Hazon Ish: Halakhist, Believer and Leader of the Haredi Revolution* (Jerusalem: Magnes Press, 2011), 171–92 [Hebrew]. Compare however to *Hayyei 'Olam* (Bnei Brak, 2006) by his son-in-law and successor in the leadership of the Lithuanian world, R. Ya'aqov Kanievsky, who merges this naturalistic approach with Kabbalistic views. A parallel successor, R. 'Eli'ezer Shach, certainly avoided Kabbalah and persecuted those who openly included it in their teaching (see Benjamin Brown, "The Rav Shach: Spiritual Admiration, Criticism of Nationalism, and Political Rulings in the State of Israel," in *Religion and Nationalism in Israel and the Middle East*, ed. Neri Horowitz, 278–342 (Tel Aviv: 'Am Oved, 2002) [Hebrew]; "Garb, "Mystical and Spiritual Discourse").

40 http://www.kolhashiurim.com/showdoc.asp?id=924. See also the clear yet scholarly explanations of classical Kabbalistic texts on *The Jewish Heritage Foundation* website: http://www.jewishheritagefoundation.org/

41 http://www.otzar.org/otzaren/indexeng.asp

42 Of course the fact that traditionalist Halakha prohibits use of electronic devices for around twenty percent of the year ensures the continued demand for non-digital material.

43 Cf. the figures presented by Ze'ev Gries, "The Printing of Kabbalistic Literature in the Twentieth Century," *Kabbalah* 18 (2008): 113–32, which are based on library holdings and thus are neither updated nor complete. Fieldwork, as described below, grants access to

numerous internal publications, which never make their way to Israel's National Library. According to the report in *Haaretz* (02 June 2010), 33 percent of Hebrew books published in Israel in 2009 belong to the Orthodox worlds.

44 Yoheved Rigler, *Battle Plans: How to Fight the Yetzer Hara* (New York: Mesorah Publications, 2009).

45 See Tamar El-Or, "The Length of the Slits and the Spread of Luxury: Reconstructing the Subordination of Ultra-Orthodox Jewish Women through the Patriarchy of Men Scholars," *Sex Roles* 29/9–10 (1993): 585–98, especially 591–92.

46 For some of these developments, see Garb, "Mystical and Spiritual Discourse," 29–48 as well as Yehiel M. Hendler, *Barukh u-Mevurakh: Bi'ur al Metbe'a Shel Brakha la Rashash* (Jerusalem, 2011), 14–15, itself part of a new wave of writing on Kabbalah in Haredi circles in New York that is heavily influenced by R. Morgenstern's works.

47 See Phillip Wexler, *The Mystical Society: An Emerging Social Vision* (Boulder, CO: Westview Press, 2000), 27–32; idem., "Toward a Social Psychology of Spirituality," in *Kabbalah and Contemporary Spiritual Revival*, ed. Boas Huss, 213–31 (Beer Sheva: Ben-Gurion University of the Negev Press, 2011). For poetry and art, see *Closure: A Visual Poetic Journey* (Jerusalem: Mahrwood Press, 2009) by Ezra Jacob—a student in the veteran Ashkenazi Kabbalistic Yeshiva *Sha'ar Ha-Shamayyim*. Compare to the turn of some Hasidic writers, such as Erez Moshe Doron, to the genre of fantasy. See his *The Warriors of Transcendence* (Brooklyn: Moznaim, 2008). The transformation and popularization of Hasidic music, obviously accelerated by the technological devices mentioned above, were discussed in a special issue of the mass-circulation Haredi magazine *Mishpaha* (13 May 2010), dedicated to the resurgence of Hasidism. In and of itself, *Mishpaha* reflects the consumerization of the Haredi public, together with the resilience of the written word in the age of digitalization (though some Halakhic authorities may frown, it is well known that such magazines are mostly read during the Sabbath afternoon rest).

48 On this kabbalist in the context of twentieth-century Kabbalistic psychology see Garb, *The Chosen Will Become Herds*, 58–59 as well as Huss, "The New Age of Kabbalah." For Ginsburgh's English-language works on this topic, see his *Transforming Darkness into Light: Kabbalah and Psychology* (Rehovot: Gal Einai, 2002); *Body, Mind and Soul: Kabbalah on Human Physiology, Disease, and Healing* (Rehovot: Gal Einai, 2003) (which can be described as a Hasidic variation on the body/mind psychology of the New Age); as well as *Consciousness and Choice: Finding your Soulmate* (Rechovot: Gal Einai, 2004); *The Mystery of Marriage: How to Find True Love and Happiness in Married Life* (Rehovot: Gal Einai, 1999) (note also the four-volume Hebrew work *Yayin ha-Mesameah*, which includes detailed treatments of sexual issues). Such books reflect the increase of interest in the issue of *shalom bayit*—or marital harmony—in the Haredi world. Compare to the very popular book *The Garden of Peace: A Martial Guide for Men Only* (Jerusalem: Diamond Press, 2008), penned by R. Shalom 'Arush, the head of a Bratzlav Yeshiva, yet another *ba'al teshuva*. One should also note a volume of collected talks on *shalom bayit* (*Tif'eret 'Avot: Ha-Bayit Ha-Yehudi* (Jerusalem, 2002)) by R. Shimshon Pinkus (student of the "Lithuanian" kabbalist R. Elijah Weintraub, of whom I have written elsewhere), a greatly popular figure whose criticism of Haredi society marginalized him in his lifetime but who is currently enjoying a vogue (see Garb, "Mystical and Spiritual Discourse").

49 Efim Svirsky, *Connection: Emotional-Spiritual Growth through Experiencing God's Presence* (Jerusalem, 2004).

50 On Itamar Schwartz, see Elliot Wolfson, "Building a Sanctuary of the Heart: The Kabbalistic-Pietistic Teachings of Itamar Schwartz," in *Kabbalah and Contemporary Spiritual Revival*, ed. Boaz Huss, 141–62 (Beer Sheva: Ben Gurion University of the Negev Press, 2011); Garb, "Mystical and Spiritual Discourse;" Itamar Schwartz, *D'ah et 'Atzmekha: Le Hakarat Kohot HaNefesh* (Israel, circ. 2008); idem., *D'ah et Beitekha: Binyan Habayit Hayehudi* (Israel, circ. 2009); idem., *D'ah et Yaldekha: Hinukh Yeladim* (Israel, circ. 2009). It is noteworthy that the English version of his latest book on psychology, *Get-*

ting to Know Your Soul: Gateway to Understanding Your Personality (Jerusalem: BiLvavi Books, 2010), appeared in advance of the Hebrew edition (For English versions of some of Schwartz's other writings and talks see http://bilvavi.net/content/view/311/57/). Child rearing is another extremely popular subject of books and lectures, a foundational text being *Planting and Building in Education* (Jerusalem: Feldheim Publishers, 1995), by R. Shlomo Wolbe, a *mussar* teacher who reputedly studied psychology at university (on his psychological theories see for now Garb, *The Chosen Will Become Herds*, 58–59).

51 See especially the "*Quntres Derekh ha-Yihud*" sections in the 2006, 2007 and 2009 volumes of *Yam Ha-Hokhma*. On trance in contemporary Haredi spirituality, see Jonathan Garb, *Shamanic Trance in Modern Kabbalah* (Chicago: University of Chicago Press), 2011, 117–18.

52 See Tanya M. Luhrmann, "Metakinesis: How God Becomes Intimate in Contemporary U.S. Christianity," *American Anthropologist* 106/3 (2004): 518–28; Tanya M. Lhurmann, *When God Talks Back: Understanding the American Evangelical Relationship with God*, New York: Alfred A. Knopf, 2012. One should also compare Haredi psychology to the vast literature on self-help and family relations produced in various parts of the Christian world, including markedly continuous circles.

53 Jeffrey Kripal, *Esalen: America and the Religion of No Religion* (Chicago: University of Chicago Press, 2008), 141–42. See also Jeffrey Kripal, *Authors of the Impossible: The Paranormal and the Sacred* (Chicago: University of Chicago Press, 2010), 42.

54 See e.g., Len Sperry and Edward P. Shafrankse (eds.), *Spiritually Oriented Psychotherapy* (Washington, DC: American Psychological Association, 2005), as well as Polly Young-Eisendrath and Shoji Muramoto (eds.), *Awakening and Insight: Zen Buddhism and Psychotherapy* (New York: Routledge, 2002). One should especially note the emergence of spiritual teachers who are trained as psychotherapists, such as Barry Magid, founder of the *Ordinary Mind Zendo*.

55 For classical kabbalistic psychology, see for now Jonathan Garb, "The Psychological Turn in Sixteenth-Century Kabbalah" (forthcoming).

56 An important exception is Haviva Pedaya. See for now, her astute comments in the interview published as "The Peak of Thirst for Memory," *Eretz Acheret* 50 (2009): 18–25 [Hebrew].

57 As sadly noted by Daniel Abrams, *Kabbalistic Manuscripts and Textual Theory: Methodologies of Textual Scholarship and Editorial Practice in the Study of Jewish Mysticism* (Jerusalem and Los Angeles: Magnes Press and Cherub Press, 2010), 10, 22, 35–36, 63–65, 67–68, the study and editing of manuscripts has dramatically decreased in graduate training and scholarly practice in universities, both in Israel and abroad. At the same time one should add that the initial move of the Haredi scholars into this enterprise was assisted by academic scholars and scholarship.

58 As in the above-mentioned works of Pinchas Giller and Jonathan Meir, as well as Eliezer Baumgarten, "Kabbalah Within the Circle of the Vilna Gaon's Disciples: Torah in the thought of R' Menachem Mendel of Shklov and R' Isaac Eisik Heber (!) Wildmann" (PhD diss., Ben Gurion University, 2010) [Hebrew]. For an important recent study of a continuous group which I have touched on in Garb, "Towards the Study of the Spiritual-Mystical Renaissance"—that of Sanz-Klausenberg—see Tamir Granot, "The Revival of Hasidism in the Land of Israel after the Holocaust: The Ideological, Halachic and Social Doctrine of the Admor Rabbi Yequtiel Yehuda Halberstam of Sanz-Klausenberg" (PhD diss., Bar Ilan University, 2008) [Hebrew].

59 Compare to a similar critique in Benjamin Brown, "The Eastern Scholars and Religious Zealotry: Points Towards a New Examination," *Akdamot* 10 (2000): 289–324 [Hebrew].

60 See Granot, "The Revival of Hasidism," especially 355, and compare to the incisive critique of the term fundamentalism and its application in the study of contemporary Judaism in Fischer, "Self-Expression and Democracy,." For critiques of the retroactive projection

of this bias, see Garb, *Shamanic Trance*, 96–97, 99, 136, as well as Sorotzkin, *Tradition, Orthodoxy and Modernity*.
61 For the extent of the influence of this well-funded foundation on Jewish studies, see http://www.posenfoundation.com. Tellingly, though its rhetoric was toned down after a recent managerial change, the website still prominently features an op-ed by a Tel Aviv University professor of psychology, entitled "Dear Haredim, while you were sleeping, secular Jewish culture was thriving." For Israel see http://www.posenfoundation.com/organizations/posenfoundationisrael.html.
62 See also Nurit Stadler, *Yeshiva Fundamentalism: Piety, Gender, and Resistance in the Ultra-Orthodox World* (New York: New York University Press, 2009), 14, 61, 117–18. However this study is clouded by its uncritical and total acceptance of the "fundamentalism" paradigm, even though I believe that it is "resisted" by her own ethnographic material.
63 Accordingly, two important and lengthy studies of the reception of Sufism in the West, Fraklin Lewis, *Rumi—Past and Present, East and West: The Life, Teaching, and Poetry of Jalâl al-Din Rumi* (Oneworld Publications, 2000), and Suha Taji-Farouki, *Beshara and Ibn 'Arabi: A Movement of Sufi Spirituality in the Modern World* (Oxford: Anqa Publishing, 2007), have focused on these figures. For an important recent corrective, see Sara Sviri, *The Sufies: An Anthology* (Tel Aviv: Tel Aviv University Press, 2008) [Hebrew], especially 21, 40. Compare to the critique of prevalent descriptions of Tantra in David G. White, "Tantra in Practice: Mapping a Tradition," in *Tantra in Practice*, ed. David G. White, 41–51 (Princeton, NJ: Princeton University Press, 2000), especially 4–5, 18, 35–36.
64 An interesting example can be found in the insightful and pioneering work by Harold Bloom, *The American Religion: The Emergence of the Post-Christian Nation* (New York: Simon & Schuster, 1992), which foregrounds discontinuous moves.
65 Richard Foster, *Celebration of Discipline: The Path to Spiritual Growth* (London: Hodder and Stoughton, 1989), 1.
66 Ibid., 12.
67 Ibid., 36. Compare to 74–75 on "fasting from the media," 93 on "mind pollution," and to 92 on the critical function of "Christian prophets in our day."
68 On the related phenomenon of the 'emerging churches,' see Eddie Gibbs and Ryan K. Bolger, *Emerging Churches: Creating Christian Community in Postmodern Cultures* (Grand Rapids, IA: Baker Academic, 2005); James Bielo, *Emerging Evangelicals: Faith, Modernity and the Desire for Authenticity* (New York: New York University Press, 2011).
69 See Garb, *The Chosen Will Become Herds*, 123, as well as the more popular version in Jonathan Garb, "The Power and the Glory: A Critique of 'New Age' Kabbalah," http://zeek.net/604garb (Hebrew original in *Eretz Aheret* 26 (2005): 30–34).
70 Foster, *Celebration of Discipline*, 101.
71 Ibid., 26–27.
72 Ibid., 107 and compare to 151–52.
73 See the important monograph Ted A. Campbell, *The Religion of the Heart: A Study of European Religious Life in the Seventeenth and Eighteenth Centuries* (Eugene, OR: Wipf and Stock, 2000). In addition, Foster refers his readers to various works providing an entrée into the world of the Desert Fathers.
74 Walter Hanegraaff, *New Age Religion and Western Culture: Esotericism in the Mirror of Secular Thought* (Albany: State University of New York Press, 1998); Paul Heelas, *Spiritualities of Life: New Age Romanticism and Consumptive Capitalism* (Oxford amd Malden, MA: Blackwell, 2008), especially 25–46.
75 Jaroslav Pelikan, *Christian Doctrine and Modern Culture (Since 1700)* (Chicago: Chicago University Press, 1989), 167, 171, 122. For similar developments in eighteenth-century Sufism, see Bernd Radtke, "Sufism in the Eighteenth Century: An Attempt at a Provisional Appraisal," *Die Welt des Islam* 36 (1996): 326–64.
76 See Colin Campbell, *The Easternization of the West: A Thematic Account of Cultural Change in the Modern Era* (Boulder, CO: Paradigm Publishers, 2007).

77 Hugh Urban, *Tantra: Sex, Secrecy, Politics and Power in the Study of Religion* (Berkeley and Los Angeles: University of California Press, 2003), 203–64.
78 Dialogue between Michel Foucault and Baqir Parham, translated and cited in Janet Afary and Kevin B. Anderson, *Foucault and the Iranian* Revolution: Gender and the Seductions of Islamism (Chicago and London: The University of Chicago Press, 2005), 186–87, and compare to Foster, *Celebration of Discipline*, 227–28, on the revolutionary role of one eighteenth-century American Christian group. Sorotzkin's above-mentioned work, which is rather influenced by Foucault, can be seen as a fine example of the re-thinking demanded here. On Haredi critiques of nationalism and militarism, see Garb, "Mystical and Spiritual Discourse."

Bibliography

Abrams, Daniel. *Kabbalistic Manuscripts and Textual Theory: Methodologies of Textual Scholarship and Editorial Practice in the Study of Jewish Mysticism* (Jerusalem and Los Angeles: Magnes Press and Cherub Press, 2010).

Afary, Janet and Kevin B. Anderson. *Foucault and the Iranian Revolution: Gender and the Seductions of Islamism* (Chicago and London: The University of Chicago Press, 2005).

'Arush, Shalom. *The Garden of Peace: A Martial Guide for Men Only* (Jerusalem: Diamond Press, 2008).

Assouline, Dalit. "The Haredi Distinction between *Ivrit* and *Loshn-Koydesh*," in *Hebrew as a Cultural Language*, ed. Yotam Benziman (Jerusalem: Van Leer Institute, forthcoming). [Hebrew].

Barak, Uriel. "New Perspectives on R. Kook and his Circle: Rabbi Abraham Yitzhaq Ha-Cohen Kook and his Principal Disciples through the Prism of an Integrated Methodology" (PhD diss., Bar Ilan University, 2009) [Hebrew].

Bar-Yosef, Hamutal. *Mysticism in Modern Hebrew Poetry* (Boston: Academic Studies Press, 2010).

Baumgarten, Eliezer. "History and Historiosophy in the Doctrine of R. Shlomo Elyashiv," (M.A. thesis, Ben Gurion University, 2006) [Hebrew].

Baumgarten, Eliezer. "Kabbalah Within the Circle of the Vilna Gaon's Disciples: Torah in the thought of R' Menachem Mendel of Shklov and R' Isaac Eisik Heber (!) Wildmann" (PhD diss., Ben Gurion University, 2010) [Hebrew].

Ben Shlomo, David Shalem. *Yihud ha-Hatava* (Jerusalem, 2009).

Bielo, James. *Emerging Evangelicals: Faith, Modernity and the Desire for Authenticity* (New York: New York University Press, 2011).

Bilu, Yoram. "Sigmund Freud and Rabbi Yehudah: On a Jewish Mystical Tradition of 'Psychoanalytic' Dream Interpretation," *The Journal of Psychological Anthropology* 2 (1979): 443–63.

Bilu, Yoram. *The Saints' Impresarios: Dreamers, Healers and Holy Men in Israel's Urban Periphery* (Haifa: Haifa University Press, 2005) [Hebrew].

Bloom, Harold. *The American Religion: The Emergence of the Post-Christian Nation* (New York: Simon & Schuster, 1992).

Brown, Benjamin, *The Hazon Ish: Halakhist, Believer and Leader of the Haredi Revolution* (Jerusalem: Magnes Press, 2011), 171–92 [Hebrew].

Brown, Benjamin. "Soft stringency" in the Mishnah Brurah: Jurisprudential, social, and ideological aspects of a halachic formulation," *Contemporary Jewry* 27 (2007): 1–41.

Brown, Benjamin. "The Rav Shach: Spiritual Admiration, Criticism of Nationalism, and Political Rulings in the State of Israel," in *Religion and Nationalism in Israel and the Middle East*, ed. Neri Horowitz, 278–342 (Tel Aviv: 'Am Oved, 2002) [Hebrew].

Brown, Benjamin. "The Eastern Scholars and Religious Zealotry: Points Towards a New Examination," *Akdamot* 10 (2000): 289–324 [Hebrew].

Campbell, Colin. *The Easternization of the West: A Thematic Account of Cultural Change in the Modern Era* (Boulder, CO: Paradigm Publishers, 2007).
Campbell, Ted A. *The Religion of the Heart: A Study of European Religious Life in the Seventeenth and Eighteenth Centuries* (Eugene, OR: Wipf and Stock, 2000).
Cherlow, Smadar. "Boldness and Modesty: R. Kook's Ethical System versus The Power Morality of Nietzsche," in *Nietzsche, Zionism and Hebrew Culture*, ed. Jacob Golomb, 347–74 (Jerusalem: Magnes Press, 2002) [Hebrew].
Chriqui, Mordekhai. *Sod le-Yesharim — Mesilat Yesharim in the Light of Ramhal's Writings* (Jerusalem, 2000) [Hebrew].
Doron, Erez Moshe. *The Warriors of Transcendence* (Brooklyn: Moznaim, 2008).
El-Or, Tamar. "The Length of the Slits and the Spread of Luxury: Reconstructing the Subordination of Ultra-Orthodox Jewish Women through the Patriarchy of Men Scholars," *Sex Roles* 29/9–10 (1993): 585–98.
Erlanger, Yitzhaq Moshe. *Kabbalat ha-Ge'onim*, 2 vols. (Jerusalem, 2006–7).
Erlanger, Yitzhaq Moshe. *Shiv'a 'Enayim*, vol. 1 (Jerusalem 1992).
Etkes, Immanuel. *Rabbi Israel and the Mussar Movement* (Philadelphia & Jerusalem: Jewish Publication Society, 1993).
Fischer, Shlomo. "Self-Expression and Democracy in Radical Religious Zionist Ideology" (PhD diss., The Hebrew University of Jerusalem, 2007).
Foster, Richard. *Celebration of Discipline: The Path to Spiritual Growth* (London: Hodder and Stoughton, 1989).
Foucault, Michel. *L'Ordre du discours* (Paris: Gallimard, 1971).
Foucault, Michel. *The Archeology of Knowledge* trans. A. M. Sheridan-Smith (New York: Pantheon Books, 1972), especially 21–23.
Garb, Jonathan, "Moshe Idel's Contribution to the Study of Religion," *Journal for the Study of Religions and Ideologies* 18 (2007): 116–29.
Garb, Jonathan, "Kabbalah Outside the Walls: The Response of Rabbi Haddayah to the State of Israel," in *Rabbi Uziel and his Peers: Studies in the Religious Thought of Oriental Rabbis in 20th-Century Israel*, ed. Zvi Zohar, 13–27 (Tel Aviv: Tel Aviv University, 2009) [Hebrew].
Garb, Jonathan. "Mystical and Spiritual Discourse in the Contemporary Ashkenazi Haredi Worlds," *Journal of Modern Jewish Studies* 9 (2010): 29–48.
Garb, Jonathan. "Rabbi Kook and His Sources: From Kabbalistic Historiosophy to National Mysticism," in *Studies in Modern Religions, Religious Movements and the Babhi-Bahai Faiths*, ed. M. Sharon, 77–96. (Leiden, The Netherlands: Brill, 2004).
Garb, Jonathan. "The Power and the Glory: A Critique of 'New Age' Kabbalah," http://zeek.net/604garb (Hebrew original in *Eretz Aheret* 26 (2005): 30–34).
Garb, Jonathan. "The Psychological Turn in Sixteenth-Century Kabbalah" (forthcoming).
Garb, Jonathan. "Towards the Study of the Spiritual-Mystical Renaissance in the Contemporary Ashkenazi Haredi World in Israel," in *Kabbalah and Contemporary Spiritual Revival* (Beer Sheva: Ben Gurion University of the Negev Press, 2011), 117–40.
Garb, Jonathan. *Shamanic Trance in Modern Kabbalah* (Chicago: University of Chicago Press, 2011).
Garb, Jonathan. *The Chosen Will Become Herds: Studies in Twentieth-Century Kabbalah* (New Haven, CT and London: Yale University Press, 2009).
Gibbs, Eddie and Ryan K. Bolger. *Emerging Churches: Creating Christian Community in Postmodern Cultures* (Grand Rapids, IA: Baker Academic, 2005).
Giller, Pinchas, *Reading the Zohar: The Sacred Text of the Kabbalah* (New York: Oxford University Press, 2001).
Giller, Pinchas, *Shalom Shar'abi and the Kabbalists of Beit El* (New York: Oxford University Press, 2008).
Ginsburgh, Yitzhaq. *Body, Mind and Soul: Kabbalah on Human Physiology, Disease, and Healing* (Rehovot: Gal Einai, 2003).

Ginsburgh, Yitzhaq. *Consciousness and Choice: Finding your Soulmate* (Rechovot: Gal Einai, 2004).
Ginsburgh, Yitzhaq. *The Mystery of Marriage: How to Find True Love and Happiness in Married Life* (Rehovot: Gal Einai, 1999).
Ginsburgh, Yitzhaq. *Transforming Darkness into Light: Kabbalah and Psychology* (Rehovot: Gal Einai, 2002).
Goldberg, Hillel. *Israel Salanter: Text, Structure, Idea* (New York: Ktav, 1982).
Goldberg, Myla. *Bee Season: A Novel* (New York, 2001).
Granot, Tamir. "The Revival of Hasidism in the Land of Israel after the Holocaust: The Ideological, Halachic and Social Doctrine of the Admor Rabbi Yequtiel Yehuda Halberstam of Sanz-Klausenberg" (PhD diss., Bar Ilan University, 2008) [Hebrew].
Gries, Ze'ev. "The Printing of Kabbalistic Literature in the Twentieth Century," *Kabbalah* 18 (2008): 113–32.
Gutel, Neria. *Innovation in Tradition: The Halakhic-Philosophical Teachings of Rabbi Kook* (Jerusalem: Magnes Press, 2005) [Hebrew].
Hanegraaff, Walter, *New Age Religion and Western Culture: Esotericism in the Mirror of Secular Thought* (Albany: State University of New York Press, 1998).
Heelas, Paul. *Spiritualities of Life: New Age Romanticism and Consumptive Capitalism* (Oxford and Malden, MA Blackwell, 2008).
Heilman, Samuel and Menachem Friedman. *The Life and Afterlife of Menachem Mendel Schneerson* (Princeton, NJ: Princeton University Press, 2010).
Hendler, Yehiel M. *Barukh u-Mevurakh: Bi'ur al Metbe'a Shel Brakha la Rashash* (Jerusalem, 2011).
Hillel, Ya'aqov Moshe, *Petah Sha'ar Ha-Shamayim* (Jerusalem: 'Ahavat Shalom: 2008).
Hoffman, David Tzevi, *'Orot Genuzim* (Jerusalem, 2009).
Huss, Boaz (ed.) *Kabbalah and Contemporary Spiritual Revival* (Beer Sheva: Ben Gurion University of the Negev Press, 2011).
Huss, Boaz. "'Authorized Guardians': The Polemics of Academic Scholars of Jewish Mysticism against Kabbalah Practitioners," in *Polemical Encounters: Esoteric Discourse and Its Others*, ed. K. von Stuckrad & O. Hammer, 104–26 (Leiden, The Netherlands: Brill, 2007).
Huss, Boaz. "The Formation of Jewish Mysticism and Its Impact on the Reception of Rabbi Abraham Abulafia in Contemporary Kabbalah," in *Religion and Its Other*, ed. Heike Bock, Jörg Feuchter, and Michi Knechts, 142–62 (Frankfurt: Campus Verlag, 2008).
Huss, Boaz. "The New Age of Kabbalah: Contemporary Kabbalah, the New Age, and Postmodern Spirituality," *Journal of Modern Jewish Studies* 6/2 (2007): 107–25.
Huss, Boaz. *Like the Radiance of the Sky: Chapters in the Reception History of the Zohar and the Construction of Its Symbolic Value* (Jerusalem: Ben-Zvi Institute and Bialik Institute, 2008) [Hebrew].
Jacob, Ezra. *Closure: A Visual Poetic Journey* (Jerusalem: Mahrwood Press, 2009).
Kanievsky, Ya'aqov. *Hayyei 'Olam* (Bnei Brak, 2006).
Kohen, David. *Zakhu Shekhina Beneyihem* (Jerusalem, 2006).
Kook, Avraham Yitzhaq Ha-Cohen. *Pinkasei ha-Reaya* (Jerusalem 2011).
Kripal, Jeffrey. *Authors of the Impossible: The Paranormal and the Sacred* (Chicago: University of Chicago Press, 2010).
Kripal, Jeffrey. *Esalen: America and the Religion of No Religion* (Chicago: University of Chicago Press, 2008).
Lehman, David and Batia Siebzehner. *Remaking Israeli Judaism: The Challenge of Shas* (New York: Oxford University Press, 2006).
Lewis, Fraklin. *Rumi — Past and Present, East and West: The Life, Teaching, and Poetry of Jalâl al-Din Rumi* (Oneworld Publications, 2000).
Loewentahl, Naftali. "Women and the Dialectic of Spirituality in Hasidim," in *Within Hasidic Circles: Studies in Hasidism in Memory of Mordecai Wilensky*, ed. David Assaf, Israel Bartal, and Elchanan Reiner, 7–65 (Jerusalem: Mosad Bialik, 1999).

Luhrmann, Tanya M. "Metakinesis: How God Becomes Intimate in Contemporary U.S. Christianity," *American Anthropologist* 106/3 (2004): 518–28.
Lhurmann, Tanya M. *When God Talks Back: Understanding the American Evangelical Relationship With God*, New York: Alfred A. Knopf, 2012.
Magid, Shaul. "Rainbow Hassidism in America—The Maturation of Jewish Renewal," *The Reconstructionist* 68 (2004): 34–60.
Mark, Zvi, "Review of Jonathan Garb, *The Chosen Will Become Herds*," *Kabbalah* 17 (2008): 89–99.
Mark, Zvi. *The Scroll of Secrets: The Hidden Messianic Vision of R. Nachman of Breslav* (Brighton, MA: Academic Studies Press, 2010).
Meir Jonathan. "Wrestling with the Esoteric: Hillel Zeitlin, Yehuda Ashlag and Kabbalah in the Land of Israel," in *Judaism, Topics, Fragments, Faces, Identities: Jubilee Volume in Honor of Rivka Horwitz*, ed. Haviva Pedaya & Ephraim Meir, 585–647 (Beer Sheva: Ben Gurion University Press, 2007) [Hebrew].
Meir, Jonatan. *Rehovot ha-Nahar: Kabbalah and Exotericism in Jerusalem (1896–1948)* (Jerusalem: Ben Zvi Institute and Mandel Institute, 2011).
Meir, Jonathan. "The Boundaries of the Kabbalah: R. Yaakov Moshe Hillel and the Kabbalah in Jerusalem," in *Kabbalah and Contemporary Spiritual Revival*, ed. Boaz Huss, 163–80 (Beer Sheva: Ben Gurion University of the Negev Press, 2011).
Meir, Jonathan. "The Revealed and the Revealed within the Concealed: On the Opposition to the 'Followers' of Rabbi Yehuda Ashlag and the Dissemination of Esoteric Literature," *Kabbalah* 16 (2007): 151–258.
Meir, Yisra'el of Radin. *Mishna Berura* on *Orakh Hayyim* (n.a.).
Mendelbaum, Alexander Aryeh. *Be-Mesila Na'ale: Be-'Inyanei Sefer Mesilat Yesharim* (Jerusalem, 2005).
Mirsky, Yehudah, "An Intellectual and Spiritual Biography of Rabbi Avraham Yitzhaq Ha-Cohen Kook from 1865–1904" (PhD diss., Harvard University, 2007).
Morgenstern, Yitzhaq Maier. *Yam ha-Hokhma* (Jerusalem, 2006).
Myers, Jody E. *Kabbalah and the Spiritual Quest: The Kabbalah Centre in America* (Westport, CT: Praeger Publishers, 2007).
Offman,'Amram. *Petilot Yisra'el* (n.a.).
Pachter, Mordechai. "The Musar Movement and the Kabbalah," in *Let the Old Make Way for the New: Studies in the Social and Cultural History of Eastern European Jewry Presented to Immanuel Etkes*, ed. David Assaf and Ada Rapoport-Albert, vol. 1, 223–50 (Jerusalem: Zalman Shazar Center for Jewish History, 2009) [Hebrew].
Pedaya Haviva. "The Peak of Thirst for Memory," *Eretz Acheret* 50 (2009): 18–25 [Hebrew].
Pelikan, Jaroslav. *Christian Doctrine and Modern Culture (Since 1700)* (Chicago: Chicago University Press, 1989).
Petaya, Yehuda. Introduction to *Beit Lehem Yehuda — Commentary on 'Etz Hayyim* (Jerusalem, 1936) [Hebrew].
Picard, Ariel. *The Philosophy of Rabbi 'Ovadya Yosef in an Age of Transition: Study of Halakhah and Cultural Criticism* (Ramat-Gan: Bar-Ilan University Press, 2007) [Hebrew].
Pinkus, Shimshon. *Tif'eret 'Avot: Ha-Bayit Ha-Yehudi* (Jerusalem, 2002).
Rabinovitch, Ben Zion. *Mevaser Tov: Yesodot Kabbalat Ha-Torah* (Jerusalem, 2008).
Radtke, Bernd. "Sufism in the Eighteenth Century: An Attempt at a Provisional Appraisal," *Die Welt des Islam* 36 (1996): 326–64.
Rapoport-Albert, Ada. "The Emergence of a Female Constituency in Twentieth-Century Habad Hasidism," in *Let the Old Make Way for the New: Studies in the Social and Cultural History of Eastern European Jewry Presented to Immanuel Etkes*, ed. David Assaf and Ada Rapoport-Albert, vol. 1, 7–68 (Jerusalem: Zalman Shazar Center for Jewish History, 2009).
Rigler, Yoheved. *Battle Plans: How to Fight the Yetzer Hara* (New York: Mesorah Publications, 2009).
Schwartz, Dov. *Challenge and Crisis in Rabbi Kook's Circle* (Tel Aviv, 2001) [Hebrew].

Schwartz, Dov. *Habad's Thought from Beginning to End*, (Ramat Gan: Bar-Ilan University Press, 2011) [Hebrew].
Schwartz, Dov. *Religious Zionism Between Logic and Messianism* (Tel Aviv, 1999) [Hebrew].
Schwartz, Itamar. *Bi-Levavi Mishkan 'Evne* (n.a.).
Schwartz, Itamar. *D'ah et 'Atzmekha: Le Hakarat Kohot HaNefesh* (Israel, circ. 2008).
Schwartz, Itamar. *D'ah et Beitekha: Binyan Habayit Hayehudi* (Israel, circ. 2009).
Schwartz, Itamar. *D'ah et Yaldekha: Hinukh Yeladim* (Israel, circ. 2009)
Schwartz, Itamar. *Getting to Know Your Soul: Gateway to Understanding Your Personality* (Jerusalem: BiLvavi Books, 2010).
Slezkine, Yuri. *The Jewish Century* (Princeton, NJ: Princeton University Press, 2004).
Sorotzkin, David. *Tradition, Orthodoxy and Modernity* (Tel Aviv: Ha-Kibbutz ha-Meuhad, 2011) [Hebrew].
Sperry, Len and Edward P. Shafrankse (eds.). *Spiritually Oriented Psychotherapy* (Washington, DC: American Psychological Association, 2005).
Stadler, Nurit. *Yeshiva Fundamentalism: Piety, Gender, and Resistance in the Ultra-Orthodox World* (New York: New York University Press, 2009).
Sviri, Sara. *The Sufies: An Anthology* (Tel Aviv: Tel Aviv University Press, 2008) [Hebrew].
Svirsky, Efim. *Connection: Emotional-Spiritual Growth through Experiencing God's Presence* (Jerusalem, 2004).
Taji-Farouki, Suha. *Beshara and Ibn 'Arabi A Movement of Sufi Spirituality in the Modern World* (Oxford: Anqa Publishing, 2007).
Tau, Tzevi Yisra'el. *Tzaddiq Be-Emunato Yihye* (Beit Shemesh, 2004).
Urban, Hugh. "An Avatar for Our Age: Sathya Sai Baba and the Cultural Contradictions of Late Capitalism," *Religion* 33 (2003): 73–93.
Urban, Hugh. "The Cult of Ecstasy: Tantrism, the New Age and the Spiritual Logic of Late Capitalism," *History of Religions* 39 (2000): 268–304.
Urban, Hugh. *Tantra: Sex, Secrecy, Politics and Power in the Study of Religion* (Berkeley and Los Angeles: University of California Press, 2003).
Vital, Hayyim. 'Etz Hayyim (Jerusalem, 1910).
Werczberger, Rachel. "Self, Identity, and Healing in the Ritual of Jewish Spiritual Renewal in Israel," in *Kabbalah and Spiritual Revival: Historical, Sociological and Cultural Perspectives*, ed. Boaz Huss, 75–100 (Beer Sheva: Ben Gurion University of the Negev Press, 2011).
Werczberger, Rachel. "Memory, Land, and Identity: Visions of the Past and the Land in the Jewish Spiritual Renewal Movement in Israel," *Journal of Contemporary Religion* 26 (2011): 269–289.
Wexler, Phillip. "Toward a Social Psychology of Spirituality," in *Kabbalah and Contemporary Spiritual Revival*, ed. Boaz Huss, 213–31 (Beer Sheva: Ben Gurion University of the Negev Press, 2011).
Wexler, Phillip. *The Mystical Society: An Emerging Social Vision* (Boulder, CO: Westview Press, 2000).
White, David G. "Tantra in Practice: Mapping a Tradition," in *Tantra in Practice*, ed. David G. White, 41–51 (Princeton, NJ: Princeton University Press, 2000).
Wolbe, Shlomo. *Planting and Building in Education* (Jerusalem: Feldheim Publishers, 1995).
Wolfson Elliot. *Open Secret: Post-Messianic Messanism and the Mystical Revision of Menahem. Mendel Schneerson* (New York: Columbia University Press, 2009).
Wolfson, Elliot. "Building a Sanctuary of the Heart: The Kabbalistic-Pietistic Teachings of Itamar Schwartz," in *Kabbalah and Contemporary Spiritual Revival*, ed. Boaz Huss, 141–62 (Beer Sheva: Ben Gurion University of the Negev Press, 2011).
Young-Eisendrath, Polly and Shoji Muramoto (eds.), *Awakening and Insight: Zen Buddhism and Psychotherapy* (New York: Routledge, 2002).

THREE

Between Tsaddiq and Messiah
A Comparative Analysis of Chabad and Breslav Hasidic Groups

Yoram Bilu and Zvi Mark

The dynamism and salience of Chabad (Lubavitch) and Breslav Hasidim make them highly noticeable in the diversified mosaic of Jewish religious communities in contemporary Israel. Their vibrant religious activities make them a common topic in public discourse and the media, and leave their mark on the local landscape. The historical trajectories of Chabad and Breslav have been quite divergent, and in terms of institutional organization they were located at the opposing poles of the Hasidic spectrum. Chabad—a central, influential, and highly organized Hasidic group, with branches all over the globe—has been dubbed by historian Jacob Katz "the first order in Jewish history."[1] Breslav, in contrast, remained mostly small, marginal, and highly polarized and was often discriminated against by other Hasidic groups. Chabad, the name of which is an acronym for wisdom, intellect and understanding, has been the Hasidic epitome of scholarship and cultivated introspection and meditation as a means of the mystical negation of the self[2]; whereas Breslav glorified pure ignorance and the struggle against enlightenment and commended ecstasy and acts of repudiating the intellect ("השלכת השכל") as Hasidic ideals.[3]

These differences notwithstanding, comparing Chabad and Breslav is a task worth pursuing for reasons that transcend their common visibility and popularity in the Israeli public sphere. Since the death of the seventh president of Chabad, Rabbi Menachem Mendel Schneerson (hereafter the "Rebbe") in 1994 the movement has remained leaderless, a situation which has been Breslav's way for the last 200 years, since the death of its first and only master, Rabbi Nachman. This commonality raises an intriguing issue. The living *tsaddiq*, acting as an intermediary between the Hasidim and the Divine, is a *sine qua non* of Hasidism, and yet Chabad and Breslav are thriving in Israel and abroad without a presiding master.[4] How should we explain the growing popularity of these "oxymoronic" communities? Is the fact that Chabad and Breslav are leaderless relevant to their present success? Is it conducive to it?

In the following comparative analysis, we seek to map and explore the major parallels between Chabad and Breslav, focusing on their common inclination to undermine established boundaries in the orthodox world and expand them in various domains. Our preliminary comparison is based on the following rationale: border-crossing in Chabad and Breslav is intimately related to the messianic orientation which informs both groups. More specifically, it is related to the sublime messianic status ascribed to the Rebbe, and less explicitly so to Rabbi Nachman. The identification of the *tsaddiq* as a messianic figure capable of transforming history is incompatible with a routine succession of leadership in the community; therefore both Chabad and Breslav are devoid of a presiding *tsaddiq*. We would like to argue that this absence, which ostensibly deprives the Hasidic community of its very essence, turns into a virtue in the current historical period, when rank and file Hasidim have more elbow room to initiate autonomous activities. Epistemologically, boundary crossing in various domains might be conducive to making the absent *tsaddiq* present, that is, palpable and accessible in the lives of the followers, who can enjoy his bliss without the constraints of a hierarchical mediation system.

Before elaborating on these arguments, we present in brief the divergent historical trajectories of Chabad and Breslav.

Chabad

Chabad was shaped as a distinct Hasidic group under the leadership of the "Alte Rebbe," Schneur Zalman, at the beginning of the 19th century in Lyady and later in Lubavitch in Belorussia. For almost 200 years it was headed by an unbroken succession of seven presidents from the Schneerson family. Chabad accommodated to the modern world more successfully than other Hasidic groups, and in the second half of the 20th century it established itself as a leading movement in the Jewish world. Under the charismatic leadership of Menachem Mendel Schneerson, Chabad established a global network of educational and religious institutions, catering to the needs of all Jews. Chabad Houses in many cities across the globe are run by emissaries (*shluchim*) unconditionally devoted to the Rebbe.[5]

Early scholarship on Hasidism has maintained that Chabad was less amenable to messianic tension given its radical mystical doctrine promulgated by the Alte Rebbe and further cultivated by his successors.[6] This a-cosmic doctrine[7] divests the material world of any ontological validity as it views empirical reality as an illusion sustained by human shortsightedness.[8] The dialectical logic of Chabad's mysticism posits absence and nothingness as the real essence, suffused with divine spirituality, with which the Hasid is to merge himself in a contemplative process of self abnegation. The uncompromisingly individual nature of Chabad's mysticism seemed to constitute a deterrent to messianic eruption[9] More recently, however, scholars have presented a more complex picture, highlighting Chabad's ongoing interest in eschatological issues as a source of potential for messianic orientation,[10] yet most of them agree that early Chabad was not gripped by messianic tension.[11]

The messianic turn in Chabad stemmed from a confluence of historical, theosophical, and personal-biographical factors. At the end of the 19th century, Chabad's fifth Grand Rabbi, Rabbi Shalom Dov-Baer began promoting messianic ideas to counterbalance the Zionist ideology which was alluring to many young Hasidim with its quasi-messianic notions of national revival and redemption.[12] His son and successor, Rabbi Yoseph Yitzhak, resorted to a messianic rhetoric in order to account for the horrors of the Holocaust, which he presented as messianic tribulations.[13] The messianic idea has become a major tenet of Chabad under the leadership of the seventh Grand Rabbi of the movement, Rabbi Menachem Mendel Schneerson, the son-in-law of Rabbi Yoseph Yitzhak. Even though he always presented himself as his predecessor's emissary, the Rebbe was an authoritative and charismatic leader, who transformed Chabad into a transnational movement. From the outset he viewed the elaborate system of religious-educational activities he initiated as a vehicle for promoting redemption and its impressive success—as a clear indication that the "work (to bring forth the Messiah) has been completed." In one of his last speeches he asserted that "we have already reached the very end, the people of Israel have already repented and completed all that was required. . ."[14] In another talk he declared that the messianic reality (מציאות דמשיח) which already enshrouds us includes also the "revelation of the Messiah (התגלות דמשיח)." "All that is left is to welcome the Messiah in actuality (לקבל פני משיח צדקנו בפועל ממש)."[15]

Unlike the catastrophic messianism of his predecessor, the Rebbe cultivated a messianism of success.[16] Momentous historical events such as the Six Day War, the collapse of the Soviet Union and the exodus of its Jews, the first Gulf War and the efforts to end the global arms race, were interpreted by him as miraculous signs that redemption was imminent.[17] Although he had never explicitly identified himself as the designated Messiah, as he grew older his Hasidim did not fail to point to him as the chosen one. This conclusion was reinforced by the lineage of the Schneerson family which connected him to the House of David as well as by the mythical tradition predicting that Chabad will be led by a sequence of seven spiritual leaders culminating in the arrival of the Messiah.[18] It is not far-fetched to assume that at the zenith of his power, reflecting upon his impressive achievements, he might have acquiesced to the insistence of his followers that he could well be the chosen one.[19] Following the Rebbe's deteriorating health in the early 1990s and his death in June 1994, the messianic tension reached a new climax,[20] but it also aggravated the frictions within the movement.

In popular discourse post-Schneerson Chabad is divided into two camps, a moderate mainstream and a vocal minority of radical messianists (*meshichistim*). This dichotomy overshadows more nuanced distinctions. The *meshichistim* include extremists who flatly deny the Rebbe's death asserting that he continues to reside, "in body and soul," in his former abode and headquarters of the movement, on 770 Eastern Parkway, in Crown Heights, Brooklyn.[21] Dubbed "Seven Seventy" or the "House of the Messiah" by the *meshichistim* the house is viewed by them as a temple of utmost holiness. A small peripheral group among the *meshichistim* even endows the Rebbe with an explicit divine stature.[22] Most of the other Hasidim are in fact moderate messianists who accept that the Rebbe has passed away and pay frequent visits to his tomb, though without giving up the hope for his resurrection as the designated Messiah who will lead the people of Israel to redemption.

The death of the childless Rebbe left Chabad without a successor. But the movement's institutions, particularly the worldwide network of emissaries, continue their activities with the same vigor and devotion as before, while the number of its followers and supporters seems to be growing.

Breslav

Rabbi Nachman of Breslav (1772–1810), a descendant of the founder of Hasidism, Rabbi Israel Ba'al Shem Tov (Besht) and the *tsaddiq*, Rabbi Nachman of Horodenka, was born in Medzhybizh, Ukraine, and grew up in a Hasidic ambience. Already at a tender young age, he engrossed himself in prayers, fasts, and seclusions in pursuit of spiritual enlightenment. Following his marriage at age 14 he lived with his father-in-law in Ossatin, in the Kiev district, but after the latter's death he moved to Medvedevka where he started to make a name for himself as a Hasidic master. After a short, difficulty-ridden visit to Eretz Israel, he moved to Zlatopol, where he became the center of a heated controversy regarding his agenda and character. The bone of contention was his claim that in terms of grandeur and virtuousness he was above and beyond all past and present *tsaddiqim*. In his own words: "I am walking on a new path that no one has trod before, not even the Besht, since the giving of the Torah."[23] Also: "Now I know for sure that I am the only world leader of this generation. . . there is no other leader like me."[24] On various occasions he presented himself as the soul root of the Messiah and his harbinger, if not as the Messiah himself.[25]

Given his presumptuousness he was persecuted by other Hasidic leaders, particularly by Rabbi Aryeh Leib, "the Grandfather of Shpola," and had to move again, this time to Breslav. There he associated himself with his senior student, Rabi Nathan Sternhartz, who promulgated his Rabbi's teachings and was instrumental in their distribution. In 1805 Rabbi Nachman's son Shlomo Ephrayim was born, but the messianic hopes he associated with the "holy boy" (note that his name refers to the two Messiahs, son of Joseph and son of David) evaporated following the baby's death. Rabbi Nachman's messianic vision is enfolded in his cryptic text, *megilat starim* ("the secret scroll"), in which the figure of the child-messiah bears a clear resemblance to his own.[26] He passed away in 1810 as a result of tuberculosis and was buried in Uman.

Rabbi Nachman was one of the most creative and original scholars in Hasidic history and his works clearly belong at the summit of Hasidic literature. His sermons are imaginative and creative and his fanciful and inspiring stories are unique in Jewish religious thought and scholarship. Rabbi Nachman attributed great importance to *tikkunim* (rectifications)—ritual practices designed to rectify weaknesses and vices. His doctrine fuses an essentially pessimistic view of reality with an optimistic belief that all states of pain and distress can be transformed into states of happiness, joy, and elation. Since God is omnipresent and can be found even in the heart of darkness, even arch-sinners can repent and gain expiation. In his own words: "No one should fall into despair as a result of his vices and blemishes. If you believe that things can be spoiled, you should also believe that they can be repaired."[27] The rituals and practices he and his students instituted, designed to help the believer reach spiritual devotion and a state of cleaving to the Divine, put great store in the power of unconditional faith, imagination, and emotional arousal while disdaining knowledge and scholarships as aids for reaching mystical fulfillment.

Rabbi Nachman's sense of grandeur did not leave much leeway for a successor, and his followers have remained "orphans," without a presiding *tsaddiq*, since their Rabbi's death. The Breslav communities were led by Rabbi Nathan and by other Rabbis, but none of them ever presented himself as Rabbi Nachman's heir. Rabbi Nathan played a decisive role in preserving Breslav's literature and shaping its practices, the most significant of which was the gathering at the Rabbi's grave in Uman on the *Rosh Hashana* (New Year) festival. Notwithstanding these efforts, Breslav remained small and peripheral, and its followers were often persecuted by other Hasidic groups.[28] The community dwindled in the first half of the 20th century, with only a few dozen Hasidim remaining by the middle of the century, mostly in Jerusalem.

This decline was reversed in the 1970s. Since then Breslav has begun to expand by unprecedented proportions. From a negligible group it became a large and influential movement, though sharply divided into rival factions. At the same time Rabbi Nachman's emerging status as a cultural hero in Israeli society and in Jewish communities abroad began to attract attention. Thousands of newcomers joined the movement, and many others began to view themselves as Rabbi Nachman's students and admirers. In most of Breslav's factions today, newcomers constitute the majority of Hasidim. Among these newcomers, returnees to Judaism (*Ba'alei Teshuva*) are clearly overrepresented. One small but highly visible group comprises the followers of Rabbi Israel Odesser, "the owner of the note," known as *"Na-Nachim."* This group subscribes to a manifest messianic agenda, as does the group led by Rabbi Eliezer Shlomo Shick, whose community is divided between New York and Yavne'el in Israel.[29] It should come as no surprise that these communities are the most conspicuous in terms of public visibility and involvement in the distribution of Rabbi Nachman's books. Still, the conviction that the key to redemption is enfolded within Rabbi Nachman's teachings is common to all the factions of Breslav.

The main event in Breslav is the pilgrimage on *Rosh Hashana* to Rabbi Nachman's tomb in Uman. Following the fall of the Soviet Union, the pilgrimage tradition was resumed with full force, and the number of congregants at this event has been systematically growing. Most of the tens of thousands of pilgrims have been Israelis coming from varied backgrounds, far beyond the core of Brelsav Hasidim.

Comparative Background

The supposition underlying our comparative analysis relates the growing popularity of Chabad and Breslav to their messianic orientation and, somewhat counterintuitively, to the absence of a presiding *tsaddiq*. Methodologically, the time frame of the comparison may appear to detract from its effectiveness: Breslav Hasidim are "orphaned" or "dead" (as they have been mockingly designated in the Hasidic world) for more than 200 years, while Chabad's Hasidim were without a leader only for the last 17. Still, it should be noted again that for most of its existence Breslav was insignificantly small, struggling for mere survival; only in the last generation has it become a popular movement. Chabad had been a dominant group in Hasidism from the outset, but in complete defiance of scholarly predictions, its growth has been facilitated rather than halted by the Rebbe's disappearance.[30] We argue that the reluctance of the

Hasidim in either group to nominate successors to the Rebbe and Rabbi Nachman, respectively, stems from the messianic stature of these leaders; as we will show, this stature and reluctance has had significant implications. It should be noted though, that the messianic screenplay is "hotter" in Chabad. Beyond the prevalent belief that the Rebbe is the Messiah, many *meshichistim* unequivocally deny that he has ever passed away. Despite the debate over the Rebbe's ontological status, both moderates and extremists aspire for his revelation as the redeemer. Most Breslav Hasidim resemble the moderates in Chabad. While not denying Rabbi Nachman's death, they look forward in expectation of his revelation as the Messiah's harbinger or teacher, and they view his teachings as the key for universal redemption.[31]

Both Rabbi Nachman and the Rebbe were born into aristocratic families in the Hasidic milieu. We have noted Rabbi Nachman's noble ancestry which includes the founder of Hasidism. The Rebbe was a direct descendant and a namesake of *the Zemah Zedeq*, the third leader of Chabad. More pertinently, in both cases this noble pedigree was further aggrandized by linking it to the House of David, from which the Messiah is predicted to come. Note also that the common root of their names—N.Kh,M, to comfort or console, in Hebrew—bears clear messianic connotations.[32] In this messianic context, it is crucially significant that neither Rabbi Nachman nor the Rebbe had male offspring when they passed away.[33] The Rebbe was childless, a situation perfectly matching the prevalent myth in Chabad of a sequence of seven (or ten) *tsaddiqim* culminating in the arrival of the Messiah.[34] There are scholars who even claim that the Rebbe patterned himself on this myth by design. Rabbi Nachman, who maintained that the Messiah would come from his seed, was outlived by seven daughters; but his two sons, including Shlomo Ephraim "the holy boy," died before him.

Both Rabbi Nachman and the Rebbe enjoyed exalted status, far beyond other *tsaddiqim*. Rabbi Nachman's elevated self-image, as *"tsaddiq* for generations" (צדיק לדורות), and *"tsaddiq* of truth" (צדיק האמת), was enthusiastically embraced by his followers. The Rebbe was viewed by his followers as the leader, in a movement where "the leader is everything" (הנשיא הוא הכל) and as Rabbi (רב"י), acronym for "the head of the people of Israel" (ראש בני ישראל), the spiritual leader of all Jews. Given his messianic stature the Rebbe was compared to Moses, "the first redeemer," and dubbed "the ultimate redeemer." This holds true for Breslav too where Rabbi Nachman, on whose shoulders rests the ultimate redemption, is likened to Moses as well. Unlike the doctrine of partial redemption pertinent to "ordinary" *tsaddiqim*, locked in historical dynasties and limited to their own followers of their redemptive projects, Chabad and Breslav embrace a universal and cosmic notion of redemption. Admittedly, the individual rectification rituals in Breslav, based as they are on seclusion and intimate dialogue with the Creator, are more geared to personal rather than collective redemption. But the mass pilgrimage to Uman on *Rosh Hashana* has given rise in the last decade to the "general global rectification," which clearly reflects an extension of the idea of personal redemption to the collective plane.[35]

This comparative background is the springboard for the analytic core of the comparison—an examination of selected domains in which Chabad and Breslav tend to cross established boundaries in the orthodox and Hasidic worlds.

Border Crossing

The discourse on boundaries in the social sciences highlights their dialectical and ambivalence-raising character.[36] The basic tenets of human functioning—organizing space, time and social reality, imposing meaning and order on inchoate experiences and puzzling events, constituting a coherent sense of self and a distinctive group identity—are dependent on the cognitive capacity to establish boundaries through demarcation, categorization, and classification. At the same time, crossing and collapsing boundaries are no less vital to human existence. Human development presupposes a cognitive penchant for transforming chaos into cosmos, for establishing meaning through structure and frame; but it also relies on openness to creativity and innovation predicated on line-crossing cognitive flexibility. Unlike established religious systems, which subscribe to strict hierarchical divisions of the universe and to binary demarcations between in-group and out-group, believer and apostate, pure and impure,[37] mystical orientations tend to prefer a more holistic and fluid perception of reality to strict analytic distinctions between domains and objects.[38]

Messianic visions, which tend to germinate in mystical ambiance, inescapably entail the undermining of borders[39] which makes the religious establishment ambivalent and wary. Jewish history has been dotted with notorious messianic figures such as Jesus, Sabbatai Zvi and Jacob Frank who established novel, subversive doctrines that generated an irreparable gulf between normative Jewry and the new messianic communities. Such a gulf has not been created in the case of Chabad, but amid the radically messianic groups one can find extremists (viewed from inside as "lunatic fringes") who endow the Rebbe with explicit divine attributes or seek to abolish the minor fasts in the name of a "New Torah." But even without embarking on the issue of heresy enfolded in messianic visions, the notion of boundaries appears advantageous for studying the distinctive aspects of Chabad and Breslav that distinguish them from other Hasidic groups and contribute to their growing popularity.[41]

Boundary crossing in Hasidism is compatible with the idea of "spreading the wellsprings" (הפצת המעיינות חוצה), that is, the outwardly distribution of the Hasidic mystical doctrine. After all, this activity was presented as a prerequisite for redemption by the Messiah when the Besht met him during a trance state in which his soul ascended to Heaven. Still, in the history of Hasidism no leader has been as active and effective as the Rebbe in realizing this tenet. His assertive and expansive manner of "break through" (ופרצת), characterized by "breaking the established orthodox structure," and in "shattering traditional dogmas," was articulated in military idioms;[42] he encouraged his Hasidim to use the tools provided by modern science and technology to kindle the Jewish spark in the souls of all Jews in order to expedite redemption.

In his seminal work on Breslav, Yoseph Weiss devoted a special chapter to the alluring power of the border as a major attribute of this Hasidic group.[43] He described Rabbi Nachman as "someone who viewed himself as standing on the border, within the domain of life, but nevertheless committed to take care of those who are already beyond the border."[44] Weiss maintained that "this sense of open border is a fundamental feeling in Hasidic religiosity,"[45] but Rabbi Nachman cultivated this feeling and was attracted to physical and spiritual places he defined as "the edge and the end of Israel. . ."[46] His haunting interest in issues of heresy and apostasy and his decision to reside in Uman in the house of a Jewish intellectual, point to this tendency. Weiss views Rabbi Nachman's messianic self-consciousness as related to his belief that he could rectify human conduct and fate without limiting himself to Jews.[47] The life circumstances of young Menachem Mendel during his stay in Berlin and Paris, when he distanced himself from the court of his father-in-law and studied engineering and science also bespeaks of an inclination to test established limits and broaden one's horizons. The romantic halo that enshrouds the Rebbe in this period in the Hasidic literature accentuates the dialectical tension between this inclination and his ability to ignore the temptations of the outer world, and to subject the external knowledge he gained to the vision of the coming redemption.[48]

The most encompassing boundary crossing is informed by the universality of the messianic vision. It seems that the messianic orientation propels Chabad and Breslav Hasidim to exhaust the Hasidic notion of "break through" (ופרצת) as a precondition for the coming of the Messiah. The redemptive messages dispatched by Chabad are designed for all human beings, though the difference between Jews and non-Jews is meticulously kept. Addressing non-Jews in Chabad is a relatively limited project intended to urge them to keep the seven Noahide commandments. But the very fact that such an address is part of the movement's agenda and finds explicit expression in Chabad's publications is quite exceptional. The tenor of Rabbi Nachman's "secret scroll" is decidedly universal, and its redemptive vision is oriented to humanity at large culminating in world peace. Converting non-Jews to Judaism and affecting other nations are matters dealt with repeatedly by Rabbi Nachman. It is not surprising therefore, that a Breslav global internet site dedicates a special section to the sons of Noah.[49]

The universal scope of the messianic vision perforce encompasses other, less inclusive types of boundary crossing. Initially, Chabad and Breslav view all Jews—Orthodox, traditional and secular—as their target. This inclusive orientation stems from the Rebbe's and Rabbi Nachman's self-images as leaders of all Jews, as opposed to the bounded, sectarian authority of the traditional *tsaddiq*. The military idioms employed in Chabad, glorifying, for example, "the soldiers of the armies of the Lord," mounted on "mitzvah tanks" and conducting "operations" to dispatch "weapons" (*Neshek*, acronym of "candles for the holy Sabbath"), attest to the active and assertive character of the Hasidim's activities. These activities are addressed to secular Jews who are cajoled to put on phylacteries (*teffilin*) and to light Sabbath candles in order to animate their hidden Jewish spark. The most impressive manifestation of this extravert modality is the global activities of the emissaries seeking to cultivate Jewish life wherever Jews reside or visit, from Tashkent to Marrakesh, from Cusco to Varanasi.[50] Given the insulated and inward-oriented lifestyle of most ultra-orthodox communities, the revolutionary nature of this project cannot be overstated. The rationale of this project is twofold: first, all Jews are inherently linked with the "general soul," of the Rebbe. Second, kindling the dormant divine spark in the soul of each and every Jew generates a collective messianic awareness thus paving the road to redemption. It is not surprising therefore that for many Jews and non-Jews Chabad is representative of the Jewish people and the keeper of its legacy. Breslav Hasidim also actively seek to distribute Rabbi Nachman's teachings in the widest circles possible.[51] The two groups are engaged in publishing and aggressive marketing of their leaders' teachings, and both design their publications for a broad spectrum of readers, far beyond hard-core Hasidim. Apparently the messianic literature published and distributed by Chabad in the last generation exceeds the entire messianic literature produced in all of Jewish history.[52]

Given the inclusive orientation toward all Jews, it should not come as a surprise that the two groups stand out in their unqualified readiness to absorb returnees to Judaism (*Ba'alei Teshuva*). These newcomers have further reinforced the processes of boundary crossing and expansion through their impact on the absorbing communities.[53] Despite the absence of reliable data, it appears likely that in the present moment most of the Hasidim in Chabad were not homegrown. This supposition is all the more true for Breslav. Aside from their easier access to skills and practices imported from the secular world (particularly in the domains of art, media and technology), these new Hasidim are motivated by religious enthusiasm and intensive search for spiritual and mystical experiences, tending to downplay routine and conformist observant behavior. These preferences have clearly fortified the messianic redemptive climate in Chabad and Breslav.[54] Since these new Hasidim did not grow up amid the hierarchically rigid frameworks of the ultra-orthodox communities, they tend to look up to the Rebbe and Rabbi Nachman as exemplary models,[55] seeking to emulate them and identify with them without the assistance of mediators; they find a convenient avenue for articulating experiences of spiritual search and fulfillment by addressing these sublime figures directly and intimately.

The vigorous outwardly oriented activity of Chabad and Breslav renders geographical boundary crossing in the two groups highly significant (with all the cultural passages this entails). Within Israel, Chabad's emissaries can be found engaged in operations in public spaces addressing passers-by to put on *teffilin* or light Sabbath candles. Their counterparts in Breslav are dancing and chanting at crossroads in order to draw attention to Rabbi Nachman's teachings. Chabad Houses are scattered all over the globe. In South East Asia and South America they provide assistance in varied matters, material as well as spiritual, to young Israeli backpackers and are much frequented by them. The "Jewish House" centers erected by Breslav Hasidim in India, Thailand, and South America, cater to the needs of the same concentrations of young Israelis. Common to both establishments is the ambition to create Jewish enclaves in places quite remote from Israel and the Jewish world.[56]

The holy centers of Chabad and Breslav are far removed from the Land of Israel. The holiness of Rabbi Nachman's tomb in Uman—in the midst of a Ukrainian territory deemed by the Hasidim tainted and impure—stems from Rabbi Nachman's lively presence there.[57] In the same vein, "770" is saturated with holiness, despite its location in a neighborhood dominated by Afro- and Hispanic Americans, because it was the Rebbe's abode. In either case, it is the sublime figure of the *tsaddiq* who endows the site with a sacred aura.[58] The appeal of these remote places bespeaks of a centrifugal orientation competing with the notion of the holiness of the Land of Israel. Note that the Rebbe refused to visit Israel, firmly resisting repeated petitions to do so. Rabbi Nachman did spend a few months in the Holy Land, but refrained from visiting Jerusalem.

The uncontested sanctity of the diasporic centers of Chabad and Breslav supports Yoni Garb's assertion that "20th century Kabbalistic discourse internalized the concept of the holy place substituting it with the holy man."[59] From a prosaic point of view the rise of these holy centers outside Israel was facilitated by their relatively easy accessibility due to mass locomotion and the rise of tourism in the age of globalization. But from an ideological vantage point it resonates with the universal messianic vision of Chabad and Breslav. For the *meshichistim*, 770, dubbed "the House of the Messiah" or "the House of our lives" (בית חיינו) is the diasporic equivalent of the Temple, enjoying Divine bliss. In depicting his vision of redemption, the Rebbe maintained that the Third Temple will descend first in Crown Heights then taking off to Jerusalem jointly with 770, followed by all Jews, living and dead. In a similar vein, the pilgrimage to Rabbi Nachman's tomb was equated in Breslav with visiting the Foundation Stone in the Temple, the starting point of creation and an *axis mundi* par excellence. Some sources even consider Rabbi Nachman's tomb holier than Jerusalem and the Temple's inner sanctum,[60] just as 770 was viewed by some *meshichistim* as holier then the Western Wall. According to Rabbi Israel Odesser, Breslav's "owner of the note," the era of redemption will start when the child-Messiah will arrive at the tomb in Uman, resurrect Rabbi Nachman, guide him to the Temple in Jerusalem, and situate him to serve in the inner sanctum.[61]

Gender is another domain where a significant boundary crossing and expansion has been taking place in both groups. In Chabad the Rebbe led a systematic process of female empowerment, encouraging women to study Torah, Kabbala and Hasidism, and to become full-fledged Hasidim and emissaries. He had generated the infrastructure for organized female activism in Chabad even before women's organizations emerged in American society and accorded them a key role in hastening redemption.[62] Following the teachings of the Alte Rebbe he claimed that the hidden source of the material and ostensibly inferior female domain is spiritual and supernal. Once this female spiritual element will be exposed in the era of redemption, it will sublimate the lower spirituality of the male domain. Moreover, women's activities designed for maintaining the Jewish house in mundane reality are but a resonance of preparing the world as God's "lower abode" (דירה בתחתונים), which is the ultimate aim of creation in Chabad's theosophy. This argument supposes an intimate linkage between redemption and women.[63] Hence, it is not surprising that women are strongly represented among the messianic activists.

Rabbi Nachman for his part amply urged his followers to let their wives become full-fledged Hasidim. Indeed, the female voice is loud and clear in Breslav's public gatherings and internet sites. Rivaling noted female emissaries in Chabad such as Nechama Greisman,[64] are Breslav women such as Tehilah Berland, the spouse of Rabbi Eliezer Berland, head of Breslav's famous Yeshiva, *Shuvu Banim*, whose books, including commentaries on Rabbi Nachman's teachings, can be found side by side with those of her husband. Women in Breslav claim their right to maintain "seclusions" (התבודדויות), practices of solitary devotion, as men do, and to go on pilgrimage to Rabbi Nachman's tomb; the controversy stirred by these demands do not deter them from realizing their wish to approach their master and God without male mediation.

Chabad and Breslav are the only Hasidic groups that unconditionally accept Mizrahi Jews (Jews of Middle Eastern and North African descent) to their ranks, thus facilely crossing the (intra-Jewish) ethnic boundary. To date, newcomers of Mizrahi background constitutes the majority in most of Breslav's factions. In Chabad too Hasidim of Mizrahi extraction are highly represented.[65] In both groups the number of Mizrahi Rabbis is growing steadily. Beyond the ethnic issue per se, it should be noted that since Chabad and Breslav address all Jews, they constitute categories of identity which are less exclusive than in other Hasidic groups.[66] One can be attached to Chabad even if one is not observant "for the time being" (in Chabad's euphemistic lingo). Analogously, one can have a high regard for Rabbi Nachman, delve deeply into his writings and go on pilgrimage to his grave on *Rosh Hashana*, thus becoming a "part-time" Breslaver, while still maintaining another primary religious identity, related to another Hasidic or non-Hasidic group. These expansive identities associated with Chabad and Breslav reflect and at the same time reinforce the growing religious diversification in Israeli society and the weakening of sectarian demarcations within its orthodox sector.[67] It might not be accidental, therefore, that the first two letters in the acronym *Havakuk*, referring to the composite identity of neo-Hasidic youth in contemporary Israel, correspond to Chabad and Breslav.[68] The non-sectarian character of the two Hasidic groups, sharply contrasted with the segregated image of ultra-orthodox society, adds to their popularity. Chabad and Breslav are "Israelis" despite the Hasidic attire of their members, and their appeal is bolstered by their universal vision and transnational flavor (more evident in Chabad but present in Breslav too, given the popularity of the voyage to Uman and the emergence of branches of the "Jewish House" in various places around the world).

Another boundary crossing typical of Chabad and Breslav has to do with their readiness to adopt innovations related to applied science, technology, and art, and to harness them to their needs. In Chabad this openness stems directly from its a-cosmic theology, according to which all progress in science, medicine, and the media is just the manifestation of God's will and presence.[69] Chabad and Breslav are ahead of other groups in the ultra-orthodox camp in employing visual media, the internet, and digital technologies,[70] though the former is more advanced and sophisticated than the latter in these respects. Note, however, that embracing advanced technologies does not entail the adoption of the disenchanted modern ethos and its underlying scientific paradigms. On the contrary, the technological frontier is re-delineated in mystical terms associated with the idea of the holy and a hyper-enchanted world.[71] Note that Chabad and Breslav's openness to modern technology has intriguing ramifications on the epistemological level: in the current historical moment (late or post-modern), the seemingly intolerable void created by the *tsaddiq*'s absence may open new horizons of mystical-religious imagination and experience.

In both Chabad and Breslav this epistemological boundary crossing entails creative efforts to make the absent *tsaddiq* present through incessant maneuverings between actual and virtual reality. Religious belief systems are by definition virtual heeding to latent (transcendent) aspects of the universe and existence; this virtuality is all the more enhanced in Chabad and Breslav. As noted, Chabad subscribes to a-cosmic naturalism which altogether denies the ontological validity of sense-informed reality relegating such validity exclusively to the invisible divine essence. Breslav Hasidim are urged by Rabbi Nachman's teachings to abandon their critical-rational faculties in favor of innocent awareness guided by imagination, creativity and unbounded faith; Breslav's doctrine is dialectical too, seeking to transform episodes of helplessness and hopelessness into states of joy and elation.

Most significantly, both groups are adept in transforming their respective virtual *tsaddiq* into a close, palpably-felt figure in both the private and public life spheres. This transformation is particularly remarkable among Chabad's *meshichistim*, who deny that the Rebbe had ever died. The *mesichistim*'s daily routine revolves around the Rebbe and is shaped by their efforts "to live with the Rebbe" and "to be with the Rebbe." Contacting the absent Rebbe through the oracle of "the Holy Letters," which enables any supplicant to receive immediate and direct feedback from him in the form of specific instructions and advice, is quite widespread in messianic Chabad. Based on the easy availability of the Rebbe's responses, the *meshichistim* claim that he is more accessible now then he had ever been before.[72] Hasidim outside the U.S. try to visit the Rebbe in his abode during Tishrei, the month of the High Holidays, or on other festive occasions. Some of the visitors even manage to see him there.[73] It seems that Chabad in particular has been invigorated by the alchemic magic of turning the invisible leader into a closely felt figure through a rich ecology of indexical signs[74] and ritual practices of embodiment, that is, ritual activities in which the Rebbe is accorded a central role as an active participant. Thus, the Rebbe is called to the prayers in 770 synagogue three times a day and receives *aliyot* (for reading the Torah) every Sunday, Thursday and Saturday; on Sundays, he continues to distribute dollar bills for charity; and at the end of each Sabbath and major holiday—pieces of cake and glasses of wine. This embodiment is supported by visual technologies which continually reproduce pictures of the Rebbe, and video cassettes and CDs of his *farbrengens* (gatherings).[75] Chabad's unprecedented visual culture, amounting to iconophilia, has been informed by the ocular-centric American society in which Chabad was reshaped in the second half of the 20th century. The Rebbe's still and moving pictures, the crux of Chabad's visual culture, clearly assist in "reviving" him.

Consequently, the virtual Rebbe has become more visible—due to his omnipresent portraits—more accessible—due to the widespread use of the oracle of the Holy Letters—and also portable and embodied—due to the fact that his portrait appears on various artifacts, from key chains to visa cards and watches, carried by believers. The Rebbe's virtuality renders his glorification easier—allowing him to be viewed even as a demi-God by some fringe groups of extremists.

Rabbi Nachman was also glorified by some of his followers; he too has become the object of a widespread personality cult. But alongside this aggrandizement, both Rabbi Nachman and the Rebbe are experienced as present, accessible and intimately close to their Hasidim. Note the absence in Chabad and Breslav of an elaborate hierarchical organization that may serve as a buffer between the master and his disciples. All of the Hasidim have equal opportunity to visit their leaders' tombs and to utter or leave their petitions there. The *meshichistim* who refrain from visiting the Rebbe's tomb, can come any time to be with him in his abode at 770. Coming to the *tsaddiq* for confession had become an established practice in Breslav already in Rabbi Nachman's lifetime, and after his death the practice was maintained at his tomb.[76]

The easy mingling of exaltation and intimate bonding with the *tsaddiq* among the *Na-Nachim* (Rabbi Odesser's Hasidim) is reflected in Rabbi Shalom Arush's internet question and answer forum[77] titled "Seclusion (התבודדות) before the Lord/ our Holy Rabbi." The discussion here and in other Breslav sites indicates that the practice of addressing Rabbi Nachman directly during daily seclusion is tinged with ambivalence, as some Rabbis have limited it to the tomb in Uman and the Western Wall. But the prevalent opinion allows such address, provided the *tsaddiq* is not the object of prayer. "But it is permitted to talk and ask for (his intercession) as one begs a living person." Rabbi Arush sums up the discussion by asserting that "if someone feels a natural urge to talk to our Rabbi he is allowed to do it." Given the strong wish expressed by the discussants to pour their hearts out to Rabbi Nachman, it seems safe to conclude that personal attachment to Rabbi Nachman that involves an intimate conversation with him is a widespread practice in Breslav. This practice reaches its zenith at Rabbi Nachman's tomb on *Rosh Hashana*. It might not be accidental that in Breslav, with its reigning individualistic ethos and its resistance to institutionalization, we do not find an equivalent to the oracle of the Holy Letters, Chabad's structured device for addressing the Rebbe. Yet a thorough search of Rabbi Nachman's writings for orientation and advice is a very common practice in Breslav.

Rabbi Nathan, Rabbi Nachman's senior disciple and the disseminator of his teachings, was aware of the fact that the figure of his admired master, strongly inscribed in his mind, was out of reach for the younger Hasidim who never met Rabbi Nachman. Therefore he invested much effort in making the *tsaddiq* present in the life of the new generation of followers. Indeed, the different historical periods in which Rabbi Nachman and the Rebbe were active— the former in the late 18th century and the latter in the second half of the 20th century—present a dramatic gap in the potentials for their remembrance and commemoration. This gap was generated by the "epistemological revolution" brought about by the invention of the camera.[78] While the Rebbe's pictures are ubiquitous, pre-photography Breslav lacks a visual representation of Rabbi Nachman. Other, non-iconic means had to be employed to render him present. Thus, Rabbi Nathan devoted much effort to enrich each and every commandment with meanings associated with Rabbi Nachman's spiritual essence, thus making him closer and more tangible. Various ritual practices were endowed with new interpretations that made it easier to incorporate them in the mythical life cycle of the *tsaddiq*. For example, the "descent" (ירידה) and diminution (קטנות) of the *tsaddiq* were integrated into the ritual cycle of the fateful days of Yom Kippur and the Ninth of Av (commemorating the destruction of the two Temples). More important, other rituals were coated with a new layer of meaning to assist in substituting the lost visual memory with embodied memory, more resistant to extinction. For example, Rabbi Nathan suggested that the close presence of the *tsaddiq* could be sensed by fixing one's gaze on the light of the *Hanukkah* candles.[79]

Rabbi Nachman's evocative stories and sermons have been conducive to turning him into a close, engaging figure. Moreover, the style he used in his talks and conversations was very personal. Rabbi Nachman was willing to expose the fluctuations of his inner world to his followers. He was quite outspoken regarding the spiritual summits he conquered yet he did not hesitate to share with his Hasidim his doubts and failings as well. He related to them his personal and national lofty hopes and his assurance that they would be realized in his lifetime but was also willing to share with them his anguish and disappointment when these hopes were bitterly crushed; nor did he hide his painful awareness that he would not be blessed by seeing these hopes realized. He related even nightmares, replete with doubts, anxiety, and distress to the Hasidim. All in all, he refrained from keeping a distance from his followers using in his discourses a direct and intimate parlance based on a singular voice as if engaged in an informal face-to-face conversation. In his texts his parlance conveys a sense of directness and closeness that readers do not fail to note. The intimate nature of Rabbi Nachman's writings enables the reader to derive personal advice from them, thus displaying their similarity in function to the oracle of the "Holy Letters" in Chabad, despite the divergence of literary genre. It should be noted that the edited letters of the Rebbe constitute a huge corpus of instructions, practical advice, blessings and encouragements addressed to specific supplicants; those reading them in the context of the oracle of the Holy Letters firmly believe that they have received a personal answer from the Rebbe.

In Breslav, the intense bonding of the Hasidim with Rabbi Nachman has received formal expression in a standard version of devotion which is used before each and every prayer. In this version, they associate themselves with all the *tsaddiqim* of the generations, but the only *tsaddiq* mentioned by name and praised as "the foundation of the world" (וצדיק יסוד עולם) is Rabbi Nachman, the prime object for bonding.[80]

In recent years a new line of communication with Rabbi Nachman was opened following Rabbi Israel Odesser's announcement that he had received heavenly notes from the *tsaddiq*. The most famous among these notes was the one with Rabbi Nachman's mantra for redemption—"*Na-Nach-Nachma-Nachman of Uman.*" This slogan, based on the letters of Rabbi Nachman's name, became, in Israel, the textual equivalent of the Rebbe's iconic portrait. This battle cry appears in gigantic format on buildings, fences, and other landscape markers all over the country as well as on stickers adorning thousands of cars. Many Breslav Hasidim of this faction carry the formula on a chain around their necks. The *meshichistim* in Chabad are equipped with their own mantra: "Long live our Master, King and Rabbi, the King Messiah for ever." The two slogans are embroidered on the black head coverings of the *meshichistim* and adorn the white crocheted head coverings of the Na-Nachim, respectively, adding to the distinctive habitus of each group. Radical *meshichistim* have added the "long live" to their liturgy. They open and end each and every prayer with this declaration of commitment to the King-Messiah.

It is interesting to note that some Breslav Hasidim have recently sought to fill in the visual void and to provide a portrait of Rabbi Nachman. The portrait was made by a returnee (*ba'al teshuva*) of Mizrahi extraction who had a revelation of Rabbi Nachman during his stay in Uman. The authenticity of the portrait was validated by another Hasid who reported a near-death experience and later a dream in which Rabbi Nachman was revealed to him.[81]

The virtual *tsaddiqim* are reproduced time and again through visual and textual means, but for their Hasidim this invisibility does not situate them in the realm of virtual reality as ordinarily conceived, that is, as inferior and lacking compared with actual reality.[82] More compatible with their perspective is the notion of virtuality as conceptualized by Deleuze and Guattari: a liminal domain of emergence, an abstract realm of imminent potential that might be enhanced and become an actual event. This conceptualization resonates with the dialectical contemplation of the universe and existence. Given that the major aspect of the Hasidic community, the bonding with the living *tsaddiq*, is lacking in Chabad and Breslav, the Hasidim in both groups have managed to establish alternative means to communicate with their absent leaders.[83] In Chabad the prime locus for direct and intimate contact with the Rebbe is 770, while in Breslav it is Rabbi Nachman's tomb in Uman. The Hasidim articulate the experiences of their visits to the two sites with idioms that connote an encounter with a present living being and not with a holy site per se. *Meshichistim* in Chabad are coming to 770 "to see the Rebbe and be seen by him;" while in Uman the pilgrimage discourse includes phrases such as "Rabbi Nachman accepted me" (or did not). There too it is Rabbi Nachman whom one visits and from whom one departs. An interesting illustration of the sense of personal closeness to Rabbi Nachman is provided by the letters sent by Rabbi Yitzhak Breiter (1886–1943) to Rabbi Nachman.[84] Whenever Rabbi Yitzhak, one the leaders of the Breslav community in Poland, could not visit the tomb, he would send Rabbi Nachman personal letters containing his confessions.

To summarize, the glowing messianic vision that activates Chabad and Breslav Hasidim endows them with a sense of mission and direction. The personal initiative and responsibility undertaken by the Hasidim are enhanced by the awareness that they act in the world on behalf of their absent leaders. In messianic Chabad the disappearance of the *tsaddiq* is taken as the ultimate test of faith. Some Rabbis in their midst even interpret this absence as intended to expose the dormant messianic spark in each and every Hasid.[85] In the "order" of Chabad the sense of mission is formulated in collectivistic terms and military jargon, but the work of the emissaries is conducted in splendid isolation, far away from the support systems of family and community, and entails stamina, personal initiative and sacrifice, autonomy, and unbounded commitment. Breslav survived two hundred years without a living *tsaddiq*. During these years an individualistic ethos emerged with semi-anarchistic hues, entirely at odds with the organized framework and military language of Chabad.[86]

The smiling faces of Hasidim in both groups are informed by their messianic visions and further reinforce them. Unlike the nostalgic yearning for the past, typical of ultra-orthodox society, the future-oriented messianic messages provide the Hasidim of Chabad and Breslav with an optimistic, quasi-utopian worldview. Unlike traditional conceptions of apocalyptic messianism, emerging from catastrophe, in these two groups the era of redemption will be realized through a "messianism of success."[87] In Chabad the signs of imminent redemption are deciphered from events in history such as the collapse of the Soviet Union, the exodus of its Jews, the first Gulf War, and the accords for limiting nuclear proliferation. In Breslav the ascent from summit to summit on the way to redemption is based on the global dissemination of Rabbi Nachman's name and teachings and informed by the dramatic transformation of Breslav and Rabbi Nachman in Jewish society from a marginal, near-pariah group to a central and dominant movement.

The crux of our comparative analysis is the argument that in both Chabad and Breslav the absence of the *tsaddiq* does not prevent the Hasidim from bonding with him and seeking to emulate him. In fact, they are equipped with varied tools for transforming the absent *tsaddiq* into a present one, accessible and communicable.[88] The painful absence of the saint is mitigated and may even become an advantage due to these tools, some of which are clearly associated with modern technology. The significant gap between the Hasid and the *tsaddiq* may be looked upon as another boundary, and it can be more easily traversed when the *tsaddiq* is virtual. Such a virtual Rabbi is shared by all Hasidim.

In both Chabad and Breslav the individual Hasid's sense of personal responsibility and commitment is grounded in an all-encompassing system of meaning. In Chabad it is the dialectical theosophical doctrine according to which the material world and the symbolic-spiritual world are fused together, to the extent that there is no difference between the symbol and the symbolized: all that exists in the world carries a symbolic significance. In Breslav it is the corpus of Rabbi Nachman's sermons, stories, and parables, suffused with metaphors and allusions and providing idioms for articulating a wide spectrum of human experiences.[89] In addition, Rabbi Nachman's *Likutei Halachot* (Collected Injunctions) bestows on each and every commandment in the *Shulhan Aruch* a specific significance associated with Breslav. The underlying principle is that all the commandments are associated with the *tsaddiq*, Rabbi Nachman. That the believer is armed with a comprehensive system of meaning may appear clichéd. Yet, no other Hasidic group studies its own specific canon as Chabad and Breslav do. Rabbi Shach's sarcastic remark that Chabad is the religion closest to Judaism becomes more than a joke if one takes into account that Chabad Hasidim enjoy their own Temple (770), Holy Scripture (Tania), ritual calendar (related to significant events in the lives of Chabad's leaders), distinctive iconic symbols and melodies, and their own Messiah. But this bounded universe is open to all. The redemptive message of Chabad as well as of Breslav is decidedly universal.

The major price paid by both groups for being leaderless is the weakening of its unity as factionalism grows. During most of its history, Breslav was heavily fragmented, and in its glorious present it is composed of many rival factions. Chabad, a centralized and highly controlled organization, is gradually turning into a global federation of scattered communities. The growing cleavages in Chabad, particularly between *meshichistim* and their opponents, indicate that "the first order in Jewish history" has been recently undergoing a process of "Breslavization." This is a steep price yet it can be tolerated and even transformed into a virtue at the present time, which can be defined as the "Era of the Hasidim." The pendulum is moving from the *tsaddiqim* towards the Hasidim, accentuating the wide margins of autonomy and personal accountability of the latter.

The Rebbe himself asserted that "each and every Jew in our generation, the last for exile and the first for redemption, is part of the mission to prepare the soil for redemption."[90] We mentioned before the argument that the Rebbe's disappearance was deliberately engineered to generate for each Hasid the potential space for expressing his own messianic spark. This radical idea resonates with the Lurianic idea of contraction (צמצום). Hence, it might not be accidental that Rabbi R. Yitzhaq Ginzburg, who articulated this idea, holds a radical conception of the *tsaddiq* as the material realization of God.[91] Note, however, that the glorification of the Rebbe is now projected onto the Hasidim. Ginzburg claimed that in one of the last Hasidic gatherings initiated by the Rebbe, he said explicitly that any one of the congregants could obtain the title Hasidic Master (*Admor*).[92] Elliot Wolfson has claimed that the Rebbe's powerful vision of redemption was misunderstood by his Hasidim. Rather than perceiving himself as the Messiah in the personal sense, he sought to generate a collective messianic arousal that would encompass all Hasidim, and in fact each and every Jew, as emissaries, kindling the messianic spark in their souls. This arousal will constitute a special state of awareness thus paving the way to redemption.[93] In this vein, Alon Dahan maintains that the Rebbe's messianic doctrine led to "a radical democratization of the supreme status of *tsaddiqim*."[94] Paradoxically, "more and more people become quasi-Messiahs for themselves and for others, and the Messiah who is awaited, no longer has a monopoly on the status of *tsaddiq*."[95]

The recent trend to identify oneself generically as a Hasid, without commitment to one specific Hasidic group and without binding oneself to a presiding *tsaddiq* is congruent with the shift of the center of gravity from the *tsaddiq* to ordinary Hasidim. This pattern is compatible with the emergence of Chabad and Breslav as less binding categories of religious identity. The two groups profit from this new openness, while simultaneously strengthening it.

The Link between Chabad and Breslav

Thus far, the focus of our comparison was the phenomenological similarities between Chabad and Breslav generated by a universal messianic ideology and the absence of a presiding *tsaddiq*. Yet, the possibility of a real link between the two groups, entailing reciprocal influence, should not be ruled out. Light should be shed first on the possible influence of Breslav on Chabad, since the Hasidim of the former were orphaned of their *tsaddiq* 200 hundred years ago. According to some inner sources the Rebbe believed he was a descendant of

Rabbi Nachman.[96] Is it possible that he viewed Breslav's survival as a model for securing the survival of the transnational movement he had erected?

Note that the Rebbe "revived" his predecessor, presenting him as the present-day leader of Chabad and the Jewish world and reducing his own position to the role of deputy and intermediary. He encouraged his Hasidim to frequent his predecessor's tomb in the same way that Rabbi Nachman had urged his followers to visit his tomb after his death. It is not far-fetched to assume that the global network of emissaries that the Rebbe established, nurtured by the Rebbe's messianic vision, was designed, among other things, to make sure that his *shluchim*, his symbolic children, would continue to lead their communities after his death. Breslav sources accentuate the long and intimate association between the Rebbe and Rabbi Zvi Aryeh Rosenfeld, a central figure in the Breslav community in the U.S. The Rebbe was always happy to meet with him, would urge him to visit him more often, and gave instructions to escort him in without delay whenever he appeared. He also asked him to keep the contents of their meetings private.[97] Is it possible that during these meetings the Rebbe was interested in learning how a Hasidic group maintains itself without a living *tsaddiq*?[98]

Summary

If indeed the messianic orientation of Chabad and Breslav contributes to their mounting popularity as we proposed, it might also lend support to the general argument that the messianic idea has remained at the core of Jewish life and thought in late modernity. The two critical events that shaped Jewish history in the 20th century, the Holocaust and the establishment of the state of Israel, were understood meta-historically as part of a universal messianic scheme by various orthodox camps.[99] The glamour of the Zionist vision of redemption in its secularized form, either in its pre-state socialist-collectivist version or in its later national version of state-building, has been significantly dimmed in the last generation. The void created by the fall of the old Zionist dream was filled by the ultra-Zionist national-religious vision (*Gush Emunim*), and also by the classic pattern of turning to charismatic individuals such as Rabbi Nachman and the Rebbe as messianic figures. It seems that the optimistic hope for a utopian future that feeds Chabad and Breslav is all the more enticing against the background of gloomy scenarios and a general sense of malaise that pervades the various camps and factions of present-day Israeli society and politics.

By way of conclusion, we would like to sharpen the argument that the mediating variable between the messianic agenda of Chabad and Breslav and their recent proliferation is the peculiar phenomenon of present-absent leadership in both groups. This is a virtual leadership, present enough to offer an orientation point and a spiritually rewarding system of meaning, and absent enough to leave significant leeway for personal action. It seems that in the current religious atmosphere, in which the pendulum sways from the rabbinical leadership to rank and file Hasidim, leaving latitude for individual initiative and autonomous activities, the liability of absent leadership can become a virtue. Anybody can receive inspiration from Rabbi Nachman's teachings or specific advice from the Rebbe's Holy Letters. Without a rabbi, each and every Hasid may become a rabbi. The uncompromising readiness for initiative and energetic action derives from the embodiment work (that is, the incessant attempts to revive the invisible Rabbi), from the intensive imaginative work it entails, from the "democratic" dimension of the messianic project—and also from the autonomy that absence engenders, cumulatively strengthening "the era of the Hasidim." The *tsaddiq*'s virtual position in both groups does not distance him from the Hasidim nor does it make him vague and opaque. On the contrary, a diversified system of means of embodiment, including technologically sophisticated practices of production, reproduction, and distribution of metonymic and iconic manifestations of the Rebbe and Rabbi Nachman, largely non-existent before late modernity, assists in transforming the *tsaddiq* into a living essence, close, accessible and palpable. The model of present-absent leadership, providing inspiration and orientation while at the same time urging the individual Hasid to initiative and autonomous action, appears to be working quite effectively in the current historical moment.

Notes

1   Joseph Dan, *Modern Jewish Messianism: From Safed to Brooklyn* [Hebrew] (Tel Aviv 1999).
2   On the theosophy of Chabad *see*, Rachel Elior, *Unity of Opposites: The Mystical Theosophy of Habad* [Hebrew] (Jerusalem 1992); Dov Schwartz, *Habad's Thought: From Beginning to End* [Hebrew] (Ramat Gan 2010); Naftali Lowenthal, *Communicating the Infinite: The Emergence of the Habad School* (Chicago 1990).
3   Zvi Mark, *Mysticism and Madness: The Religious Thought of Rabbi Nachman of Bratslav* (London 2009); on "casting away the intellect" *see*, Ibid pp. 13–24.
4   Jonathan Garb, *The Chosen Will Become Herds: Studies in Twentieth-Century Kabbalah* [Hebrew] (Jerusalem 2005) pp. 2–31; Kimmy Caplan, *Internal popular Discourse in Israeli Haredi Society* [Hebrew] (Jerusalem 2007).
5   For how Chabad has adapted to the modern world and on the institution of emissaries in Chabad *see*, Menachem Friedman, "Messiah and Messianism in Chabad-Lubavitch Hassidism," in *The War of Gog and Magog: Messianism and Apocalypse in Judaism in the Past and Present*, David Ariel-Joel and others, eds. [Hebrew] (Tel Aviv 2001) pp. 174–229; Yitzchak Krauss, *The Seventh: Messianism in the Last Generation of Chabad* [Hebrew] (Tel Aviv 2007); Aviezer Ravitzky, *Messianism, Zionism and Jewish Religious Radicalism* [Hebrew] (Tel Aviv 1993); *Freedom Inscribed: Diverse Voices of the Jewish Religious Thought* [Hebrew] (Tel Aviv 1999); Sue Fishkoff, *The Rebbe's Army: Inside the World of Chabad Lubavitch*, (New York 2003); Menachem Friedman, "Habad as Messianic Fundamentalism: From Local Particularism to Universal Jewish Mission," in *Accounting for*

Fundamentalism: The Dynamic Character of Movements, Marty E. Martin and R. Scott Appleby, eds., pp. 328–357 (Chicago 1994); Samuel Heilman and Menachem Friedman, *The Rebbe: The Life and Afterlife of Menachem Mendel Schneerson*, (Princeton, NJ 2010).

6   See mainly, Rivka Schatz Uffenheimer, *Hasidism as Mysticism: Quietistic Elements in Eighteenth-Century Hasidic Thought* [Hebrew] (Jerusalem 1968); Gershom Scholem, *Elements of the Kabbalah and Its Symbolism* [Hebrew] (Jerusalem 1976); *Major Trends in Jewish Mysticism* (London 1955) pp. 325–350.

7   Elior, Unity of Opposites; Aviezer Ravitzky, "The Contemporary Lubavitch Hasidic Movement: Between Conservatism and Messianism," in *Fundamentalism Observed*, Martin E. Marty and R. Scott Appleby, eds., pp 303–327 (Chicago 1991).

8   It is noteworthy that not all of the scholars agree that this extreme a-cosmic formulation is representative of Chabad thought. Elliot Wolfson suggests an alternative conceptualization which he calls apophatic panentheism. *See*, Elliot R. Wolfson, *Open Secret: Postmessianic Messianism and the Mystical Revision of Menahem Mendel Schneerson* (New York 2009). Dov Schwartz suggests "paradoxical dialectics" (*see*, Schwartz, *Habad's Thought*, pp. 35–46).

9   Dan, *Modern Jewish Messianism*, p. 200.

10 The scholars who have identified messianic trends in Hasidism include Benzion Dinur (*Historical Writings* [Hebrew], (Jerusalem 1955)), Isaiah Tishby ("The Messianic Idea and Messianic Trends during the Flowering of Hasidism," [Hebrew] *Zion* 32 (1967) pp. 1–45) and Mor Altshuler (*The Messianic Secret of Hasidism* [Hebrew] (Haifa 2002)). Simon Dubnow (*The History of Hasidism* (Tel Aviv 1960)), and Martin Buber (*The Hassidic "Garden of Knowledge" Studies in Hassidism* [Hebrew] (Tel Aviv 1945) emphasized the decline of the messianic trend in Hasidism following the return to the personal sources of religious life. This position was further strengthened by Scholem (*Major Trends*) who analyzed the neutralization of the mystical impulse, and by Schatz Uffenheimer (*Hasidism as Mysticism*). Idel opposed Scholem's position with his claim that mysticism, including Hasidism, is a breeding ground for messianic ideas (Moshe Idel, *Messianic Mystics* (New Haven, CT 1998)).

11 Naftali Lowenthal, "Contemporary Habad and the Paradox of Redemption," in *Perspectives on Jewish Thought and Mysticism*, Alfred I. Ivry, Elliot R. Wolfson, and Allan Arkush, eds., pp. 381–402 (Sidney 1994); see also, Jacob Gotlieb, *Rationalism in Hasidic Attire: Habad's Harmonistic Approach to Maimonides* [Hebrew] (Ramat Gan 2009) p. 173.

12 *See*, Friedman, "Habad as Messianic Fundamentalism;" Ravitzky, "The Contemporary Lubavitch Movement."

13 *See*, Rachel Elior, "Lubavitch Messianic Resurgence: The Historical and Mystical Background 1939–1996," in: *Toward the Millennium*, P. Schafer and M.R. Cohen, eds, pp. 383–408 (Leiden 1999); Friedman, "Habad as Messianic Fundamentalism." Rabbi Yoseph Yitzhak's choice of a teleological interpretation may be attributed to Habad's extreme a-cosmic approach, which views all aspects of physical reality (including the Holocaust) as reflecting the divine presence—"there is no place devoid of Him"—as well as to his own traumatic encounters with the two most ruthless regimes of the twentieth century, Communism and Nazism, escaping both only by the skin of his teeth. *See also*, Ravitzky, *Messianism*, p. 264.

14 *Dvar Malchus* [Words of the King], [weekly Torah portion] *Shemot* (22 Tevet 5752) [1992].

15 *Dvar Malchus* [Words of the King], [weekly Torah portion] *Vayera* (18 Mar-Chesvan 5752) [1992].

16 A dialectical connection exists between these two seemingly contradictory approaches, for it is written, "trouble shall not rise up a second time (Nahum 1:9);" *see also*, Ravitzky, *Messianism*, pp. 265–267.

17 *See*, Yori Yanover and Nadav Ish-Shalom, *Dancing and Crying: The Truth about the Chabad Movement* [Hebrew] (Jerusalem 1994); William Shaffir, "Jewish Messianism—Lubavitch Style: An Interim Report," *Jewish Journal of Sociology* 35 (1993), pp. 115–128;

Martin Katchen, "Who Wants Moshiach Now? Pre-Millennialism and Post-Millennialism in Judaism," *Australian Journal of Jewish Studies* 5 (1991), pp. 59–76.

18 *See,* Dan, *Modern Jewish Messianism,* p. 195. According to a more complex version of this tradition, the dynastic lineage begins with Rabbi Israel Ba'al Shem Tov, the founder of Hasidism, continuing with the Magid of Mezritch, and following him, Schneur Zalman and his descendants, the leaders of Chabad. Since, with his ascent to the leadership of Chabad, Rabbi Schneerson appointed his predecessor to a second term of leadership, his own term became the tenth and final one—corresponding to the *Sefirah* of *Malkhut,* the last *Sefirah* which heralds the end of the exile and the coming redemption (*see,* Alon Dahan, "A Final Redeemer without Heirs: Did Rabbi Menachem Mendel Schneerson (The Lubavitcher Rebbe) Choose neither Heirs nor Successors for Messianic Reasons?" *Kabalah* [Hebrew] 17 (2008), pp. 289–309.

19 *See,* Gotlieb, *Rationalism in Hasidic Attire,* pp. 174–178; Alon Dahan, "A Dwelling Below: Menachem Mendel Schneerson's Messianic Doctrine," Doctoral Thesis [Hebrew] submitted to the Hebrew University in Jerusalem (2006); Dahan, "A Final Redeemer;" Dan, *Modern Jewish Messianism,* pp. 194–196.

20 Leon Festinger's theory of cognitive dissonance, Leon Festinger, Henry W. Riecken, and Stanley Schachter, *When Prophecy Fails* (Minneapolis 1956), served as a central source of inspiration for the study of messianic tension in Chabad. *See,* Simon Dein, "What Really Happens When Prophecy Fails?" *Sociology of Religion* 62 (2001), pp. 383–401; "Moshiach Is Here Now: Just Open Your Eyes and You See Him," *Anthropology and Medicine* 9 (2002), pp. 25–36; Simon Deine and Lorne L. Dawson, "The Scandal of the Lubavitch Rebbe: Messianism as a Response to Failed Prophecy," Journal of Contemporary Religion 23 (2), pp. 163–180; William Shaffir, "Interpreting Adversity: Dynamics of Commitment in a Messianic Redemption Campaign," *Jewish Journal of Sociology* 36 (1994), pp. 43–53; "When Prophecy Is Not Validated: Explaining the Unexpected in a Messianic Campaign," *Jewish Journal of Sociology* 37 (1995), pp. 119–135.

21 Michal Kravel-Tovi and Yoram Bilu, "The Work of the Present: Constructing Messianic Temporality in the Wake of Failed Prophecy among Chabad Hasidim," *American Ethnologist* 35 (2008), pp. 1–17.

22 In a publication of this group from 5756 [1995], the Rebbe is referred to by the title "His Royal Holiness our Master, Teacher and Rabbi, May He Live Long and Prosper, Eternal King Messiah, the Essence and Being, Blessed be He, our Creator, Designer and Redeemer."

23 *Chayei Moharan* [The Life of our Teacher Rabbi Nachman] with restored omissions [Hebrew] (Jerusalem [5760] 2000) "On the controversy surrounding him," 392 (1), p. 338.

24 Ibid., "The great awesomeness of his understanding," 258 (18), p. 267.

25 Zvi Mark, *The Scroll of Secrets: The Hidden Messianic Vision of R. Nachman of Breslav* (Brington 2010).

26 Ibid.

27 *Likutei Moharan, Tanina,* 112 [Collected Works of our Teacher Rabbi Nachman].

28 David Assaf, "Happy are the persecuted: The struggle against the Hasidim of Breslav," in *Caught in the Thicket, Crisis & Discontent in the History of Hasidism* [Hebrew] (Jerusalem 2006), pp. 179–234.

29 Zvi Sobel, *A Small Place in the Galilee: Religion and Social Conflict in an Israeli Village* (New York 1993).

30 Krauss points to two indices of the strengthening of Chabad following the death of the Rebbe: "The considerable increase (by hundreds of percent) in the number of international emissaries, and the great number of books on the teachings and personality of the Rebbe published by Chabad." *See,* Krauss, *The Seventh,* p.16. Statistics that he presented in a July 6 2008 article on the Ynet internet site ("The Rebbe is Gone, Chabad is Alive and Kicking"), showed an estimated 600–700 emissaries worldwide at the time of the Rebbe's death in 1994, while the participants of an emissary conference organized in 2007 numbered

3500. This number did not account for emissaries of the radical messianic groups who are organized independently. A November 8, 2010 article in the Ha'aretz newspaper reported that the number of emissaries had grown to 4000. *See also,* Jeffrey Shandler, *Jews, God, and Videotape: Religion and Media in America* (New York 2009), pp. 255–256.
31 *See,* Garb, *The Chosen,* p. 131.
32 According to one Talmudic source, the name of the messiah is Menachem (TB San. 98b). The correlation between name and messianic enlightenment is discussed in relation to Jesus (Yehuda Liebes, "Brings Forth the Horn of Redemption [*Yeshuah*]," *Mekhqarei Yerushalayim beMakhshevet Yisrael* [Jerusalem Studies in Jewish Thought] [Hebrew] 3 (1984) pp. 313–348), Sabbatai Zvi (Moshe Idel, "Sabbatai (Saturn) the Planet and Sabbatai Zvi: a new approach to Sabbateanism," *Mada-ei haYahadut* [Judaic Studies] [Hebrew] 37, (1997), pp. 161–184), Maimonides (Israel Jacob Yuval, "Moses Redivivus: Maimonides as an Assistant of the King Messiah," *Zion* [Hebrew] 82 (2007), pp. 161–188) and Rabbi Moshe Haim Luzzato (Dan, *Modern Jewish Messianism,* p. 100).
33 Dan, *Modern Jewish Messianism,* p. 195.
34 Ibid.
35 Zvi Mark, *le-Akhar Matayim Shana—miTikkun Ishi leTikkun Olam, Hitgalut veTikkun* [Two Hundred Years Later—from Personal Rectification to Universal Rectification, Revelation and Rectification], [Hebrew] Jerusalem (Jerusalem 2011), pp. 253–282.
36 A number of landmark studies in the conceptualization of "boundary" in the social sciences: Georg Simmel's study of social boundary and the processes of endosmosis and exosmosis. Georg Simmel, "The Social Boundary," *Theory, Culture & Society* 24 (2007), pp. 53–56; Fredrik Barth's pioneering study of ethnic boundaries, *see,* Fredrik Barth, *Ethnic Groups and Boundaries* (Boston 1969); Erving Goffman's Gregory Bateson-inspired suggestion of "frame analysis," *see,* Erving Goffman, *Frame Analysis* (New York 1974); ; Don Handelman, "Framing," in *Theorizing Rituals: Issues, Topics, Approaches, Concepts,* Jens Kreinath, Jan Snoek & Michael Stausberg, eds., pp. 571–582 (Leiden, The Netherlands 2006); Victor Turner's Arnold Van Gennep-influenced conceptual system involving anti-structure and liminality, *see,* Victor Turner, *The Ritual Process, Structure and anti-Structure* [Hebrew] (Tel Aviv 2004); *The Forest of Symbols* (Ithaca 1970); and studies on "border" from a post-colonial orientation, e.g.,: Donald Weber, "From Limen to Border," *American Quarterly* 47 (1995), pp. 526–536. Some scholars have identified a distinctive discipline of "boundary studies," *see,* Reece Jones, "Categories, Borders and Boundaries," *Progress in Human Geography* 33 (2009), pp. 174–189; The work of Eviatar Zerubavel summarizes many of these concepts: Eviatar Zerubavel, *The Fine Line: Making Distinctions in Everyday Life* (Chicago 1991); Lamont, Michele and Virag Mollnar, "The Study of Boundaries in the Social Sciences," *Annual Review of Sociology* 28 (2002), pp. 167–195.
37 Mary Douglas, *Purity and Danger* (London 1966).
38 Zerubavel, *The Fine Line,* p. 84.
39 Elliot Wolfson emphasizes that messianic enlightenment means being delivered of all conceptual limitation. *See,* Wolfson, *Open Secret.*
41 On the veiled threat of blasphemy in Chabad messianism because of its similarity to Christianity *see,* David Berger, *The Rebbe the Messiah, and the Scandal of Orthodox Indifference* [Hebrew] (Jerusalem, 2005).
42 *See,* Krauss, *The Seventh,* pp. 62, 65.
43 Joseph Weiss, *The Attraction of the Boundary, Studies in Bratslav Hasidism* [Hebrew] (Jerusalem 1975), pp. 96–108.
44 Ibid., 101.
45 Ibid.
46 *Chayei Moharan* (Jerusalem [5740] 1980), "His Travels and His Stay in Uman," 195 (11), 219.
47 Weiss, *Attraction,* 108. *See also,* on the "situation on the border" found in Rabbi Nachman's stories (ibid., p. 169).

48 Heilman and Friedman, *Rebbe*.
49 The general manager of the "Breslev Israel" internet site reported that twenty Indian women who had been exposed to Rabbi Nachman and his teachings online contacted him and formed a group for the study of Rabbi Nachman's writings. He says that, "At first, they were very self-conscious because they were gentiles, but they were made to feel comfortable and we told them that we accept them as they are." Adi David, "There is no Despair at all in India," Ynet Nov, 12, 2007.
50 Krauss, *The Seventh*.
51 On the spreading of "the inner Torah" among the Hasidic groups of Chabad and Breslav *see*, Garb, *The Chosen*, p. 66.
52 Dan, *Modern Jewish Messianism*, p. 196.
53 Yehuda Goodman, "Return to Orthodox Judaism and New Religious Identities in Israel at the Start of the 21st Century," in *Not to be Believed, a Different View of Religiosity and Secularism,* Aviad Kleinberg, ed. [Hebrew] (Tel Aviv 2004), pp. 177–198.
54 Jacob A. Szubin, "Why Lubavitch Wants Messiah Now: Religious Immigration as a Cause of Millenarism," in *Apocalyptic Time,* Albert L. Baumgarten, ed., pp. 215–240 (Leiden 2000); Zvi Mark, "The Messianic Revolution and the Echoes of the Scrolls among the Breslav Chasidism today," in *The Scroll*, pp. 247–254.
55 Goodman, "Return," pp. 144–148.
56 A list of Jewish homes in the spirit of Breslav is available on the internet site "New Spirit" [Ruakh Akheret]: http://212.199.163.143/~newspirit/. Recently, a Chabad emissary established "Israel House" [habayit hayisraeli] in Chicago (*Talk of Redemption* [siakh hage-ula] 758, July 31, 2009, p. 4), possibly as a response to the appearance of Breslav's "Jewish House" [habayit hayehudi].
57 Garb, *The Chosen*, pp. 130–131; Zvi Mark, "A Righteous Man Caught in the Jaws of the Sitra Akhra: The Holy Man and the Profane Site—the Pilgrimage to the Grave of Rabbi Nachman of Breslav in Uman on Rosh Hashana," *Reshit* [Hebrew] 2 (2010), pp. 112–146.
58 Garb, *The Chosen*, p. 121.
59 Garb, *The Chosen*, p. 114. For an argument against the proposition that the replacement of the holy site with the holy person is a process that characterizes the early twentieth century, and a claim that this process had already taken place in eighteenth- and nineteenth-century Hasidism *see*, Zvi Mark, "Kabbalah, Hasidism and New Age in the Twentieth Century: on The Chosen Will Become Herds: Studies in Twentieth-Century Kabbalah" (Review), *Kabbalah: Journal for the Study of Jewish Mystical Texts* 17 (2008), pp. 89–99.
60 "For the truly righteous one is more powerful than the High Priest who enters the inner sanctum," Rabbi Nathan of Nemirov, *Likutei Halakhot* (Jerusalem [5744] 1984) Laws of Bailment, law 5, "On the matter of the greatness of the Land of Israel and the Holy of Holies etc., but the 'four cubits' of our Rabbi is not found anywhere." Rabbi Shmuel Horowitz, *Zion Hametzuyenet*, (Jerusalem 5760 [2000]), p. 7.
61 Mark, *The Scroll*, p. 250.
62 Bonnie Morris, *Lubavitcher Women in America: Identity and Activism in the Postwar Era* (New York 1998).
63 Dahan, "A Dwelling Below," pp. 188–196; Eldad Weil, "The Start of the Era of Women: Women and Femininity in the Thought of the Lubavitcher Rebbe," *Akdamot* [Hebrew] 22 (2009), pp. 61–85.
64 Weil, "The Start," pp. 76–85.
65 Cf. Moshe Shokeid, *Children of Circumstances: Israeli Immigrants in New York* (Ithaca 1988), pp. 139–160.
66 This is not to argue that these expanded categories are homogeneous. The very openness encourages multiplicity and sectarianism. Returnees to orthodoxy are distinguishable within the absorbing communities. Apparently, even within Chabad and Breslav, the differences between the returnees and the Hasidim from Hasidic families are preserved (*see*, Goodman, "Return").

67 It should be mentioned that the idea for this article was originally conceived following a visit to the celebration [*hilula*] in memory of Rabbi Israel Abukhatzera (the Baba Sali) that took place in the city of Netivot on 2/3 Shevat 5769 (February 2009). We were surprised by the large presence of Chabad and Breslav Hasidim and by the fact that at the fair erected near the mausoleum, pictures of Rabbi Menachem Mendel Schneerson and books by Rabbi Nachman of Breslav outnumbered the portraits and works of Sephardic and Mizrahi sages. The comfortable presence that the representatives of these Ashkenazic Hasidic groups enjoy, along with the great interest ignited among the pilgrims, the majority of whom are of Mizrahi extraction, reinforced our sense that the future outlines of religious association and identity in Israel are undergoing significant change, at least in connection to Chabad and Breslav.
68 *Havakuk* = Chabad, Breslav, (Rabbi Abraham Isaac) Kook and (Rabbi Shlomo) Carlebach.
69 See, Krauss, *The Seventh*, pp. 65–66.
70 On Chabad, *see,* Shandler, *Jews, God, and Videotape*, pp. 230–274.
71 On distinguishing between technoscape and ideoscape, *see,* Arjun Appadurai, *Modernity at Large: Cultural Dimensions of Globalization* (Minneapolis 1996).
72 On the use of "The Holy Letters" as an oracle, *see,* Yoram Bilu, "With us more than ever: The presence of the Rebbe in the messianic branch of Chabad," In *Leadership and Authority in Haredi Society in Israel*, Kimmy Caplan and Nurit Stadler, eds., [Hebrew] (Jerusalem 2009), pp. 186–209.
73 *See,* Michal Kravel-Tovi and Yoram Bilu, "The Work of the Present: Constructing Messianic Temporality in the Wake of Failed Prophecy among Chabad Hasidim," *American Ethnologist* 35 (2008), pp. 1–17. On Hasidim testifying having experienced waking apparitions of the Rebbe, mostly at 770, *see, Lifko'ah et Ha-Einayim* (New York 2007).
74 Symbols in spatial or temporal proximity to the subject. The Rebbe's house, "770," his chair, water from the Rebbe's mikve, dollar bills that he distributed—are all examples of objects that are metonymically related to the Rebbe.
75 Maya Balakirsky Katz, *The Visual Culture of Chabad*, (New York 2010); Shandler, *Jews, God, and Videotape*.
76 On confession in Breslav *see,* Ada Rapoport Albert, "Confession in the Circle of Rabbi Nahman of Bratslav," *Bulletin for the Institute of Jewish Studies*, I (1973), pp. 65–96; on confession at the grave of Rabbi Nachman *see,* Rabbi Nachman of Tcherin, *The Desserts of Wisdom* [parperaot lekhokhma] (Jerusalem [5343] 1983) 4, p. 5b. Though it should be noted that the confession at the grave is made "before God, may He be blessed" and does not appear to be addressing Rabbi Nachman, from the context it becomes clear that the confession at the grave is a fulfillment of Rabbi Nachman's instruction to confess to a *tsaddiq*.
77 See, Breslev.co.il, Jan. 1, 2008.
78 On the epistemological revolution of photography *see,* Roland Barth, *Camera Lucida* [Hebrew] (Jerusalem 1988); Susan Sontag, *On Photography* [Hebrew] (Tel Aviv 1980).
79 *See,* Roee Horen, "The Belief in the Tzadik in Rabbi Nathan of Nemirov's Liqqutei Halakhot: Myth Ritual and Narrative," [Hebrew] Master's Thesis, Bar Ilan University 2008, pp. 68–70.
80 "The version commonly used among Breslav Hasidim today is 'With my prayer (or with another of the *mitzvot* one does), I hereby attach myself to all the true *tsaddiqim* in our generation, and to all the true *tsaddiqim* who dwell in the earth, holy ones that rest in the ground, and in particular to the *tsaddiq*, the foundation of the world, the flowing river, the source of wisdom, our rabbi, Nachman, son of Feige, may their merit protect us and all of Israel, amen.'" (Response of Rabbi Erez Moshe Doron on the Kipa internet site, 27 Iyar, 5766 (2006), http://www.kipa.co.il/ask/show/90092). This version was accepted by Breslav at the early part of the twentieth century, *see, Ayin Zokher* (Warsaw 1928 [5688]), p. 3. *See also, She-erit Yitzkhak,* (Jerusalem [5765] 2005), p. 76. Rabbi Levi Yitzchok Bender, the most outstanding of the Breslav leaders of the last generation, emphasized the totality

of connection: "Connecting to the *tsaddiq* is always very good, but it is especially good when there is [also] a connection before and afterward, not only during the time when I am connected to him—when I am communicating to him through the words before the prayer. One must see to it that one is always conscious of the *tsaddiq*, thinking of our rabbi, thinking of him, thinking of the greatness of the *tsaddiq*—how he invigorates me... and without him—without his holy advice—I could not even exist!...And therefore one must be always connected to him. Rabbi Levi Yitzchok Bender, *Noam Siakh, Discussions and Lessons from the Rabbi and Hasid Rabbi Levi Yitzchok Bender* (Jerusalem [5755] 1995) Part 2, p. 206.

81 Yakov Singer, "The Personality Cult" [pulmus hadiukan], *Besha'a Tova, no.* 297, [weekly portion] *Vayikra 5769* (2008), pp. 18–33, 43.
82 *See,* Gilles Deleuze and Felix Guattari, *A Thousand Plateaus: Capitalism and Schizophrenia*, translated by Brian Massumi (Minneapolis 1987).
83 *See,* Garb, *The Chosen*, p. 227.
84 Following is an example of a letter sent by Rabbi Yitzhak to Rabbi Nachman: "Blessed be God, Wednesday, [week of the Torah portion] *Nitzavim* 5690 (1930), Warsaw. To the honored soul of our rabbi, of blessed memory, I hereby send my confession by Breslav messengers of the city of Uman, as I do every year. I, Yitzhak, son of Esther Breindel, who for twenty years have followed their ways...I confess to you our holy and pure rabbi, that I am sunken deep into the lust for money, that I daily fall deeper and deeper into debt...therefore I beseech you to grant me holy strength so that I will merit, from now on, to live a good life in holiness and purity...*Rebbe*, I wish to merit coming to the Land of Israel soon and for this purpose I am collecting money...your student, Yitzhak, son of Esther Breindel, *She-erit Yitzkhak*, (Jerusalem 2005 [5765]), pp. 147–152.
85 *See,* Garb, *The Chosen*, p. 127.
86 Rabbi Nachman's teachings and that of his Hasidim emphasize that the vision of redemption will be achieved with ease—"without wars" and "without raising the voice" (Rabbi Levi Yitzchok Bender, *Noam Siakh* (Jerusalem 1995 [5755]) Part 2, p. 63.
87 Ravitzky, *Messianism*, pp. 249–276.
88 On a similar process of making God a close and intimate friend in the evangelical congregations in the United States *see,* Tanya M. Luhrmann, "Metakinesis: How God Becomes Intimate in Contemporary American Christianity," *American Anthropologist* 106 (2004), pp. 518–528; "The Absorption Hypothesis: Learning to Hear God in Evangelical Christianity," *American Anthropologist* 112 (2010), pp. 66–78.
89 Including, for example, "psycho-spiritual preparation for childbirth according to the teachings of Rabbi Nachman."
90 *See,* Krauss, *The Seventh*, p. 39.
91 *See,* Garb, *The Chosen*, p. 126.
92 Ibid., p. 127.
93 *See,* Wolfson, *Open Secret*. Indeed the Rebbe expected, in his words, "that through the revelation of the *yekhida* in the soul of each and every one of Israel—that is (part) of the messiah that is in each and every one of Israel... there will be a revelation of the general *yekhida*, our righteous messiah" (Dvar Malchus, (weekly portion) *Korakh*, 28 Sivan 5751 (1991), p. 19.
94 Alon Dahan, "'Long Live our Master, Teacher and Creator:' The Divine Man, Characteristics of Chabad Messianism and its Accompanying Polemic," *Reshit Iyunim Beyahadut* [Reshit: Studies in Judaism] [Hebrew] 2 (2010), pp. 147–182 (p. 172).
95 Ibid., p. 173.
96 According to Rabbi Shalom Duber Wolpe, "Rabbi Nachman of Breslav said that the messiah will be one of his descendants, as is written in *Chayei Moharan,* par. 274: 'What will become of me, I do not know, but through my prayers it was revealed to me from God, may He be blessed, that the righteous redeemer will be the issue of my loins.' Several Chabad and Breslav Hasidim called me and told me that it is known that Mr. Schneur Zalman,

of blessed memory (President Shazar), once asked this question of Our Holy Master and Teacher may He Live Long and Prosper [Rabbi Schneerson], the latter answering that he was indeed a descendant of Our Teacher and Rabbi, Rabbi Nachman, of blessed memory, but I did not succeed in investigating these things fully." (Shalom Duber Wolpe, *Mevaser Tov*, Kfar Chabad, 5754 (1994), p. 169. Quoted by Shmuel Krauss, *Nasi Vechasid*, Kfar Chabad 5759 (1999), p. 367, n.3).

97   Aharon Klieger, "A Mysterious Connection in Brooklyn," 3, Breslev.co.il; Manis Lavi, "Meetings with the Rebbe: Revealed: Two Hours a Month in the Rebbe's Room," *Kfar Chabad Weekly* 644 (5 Tevet 5755/Aug. 8, 1994) pp. 14–17.

98   We heard from Rabbi Zvi Telsner, rabbi of the Chabad congregation in Melbourne, that according to Rabbi Schneerson's secretary, Rabbi Leibel Groner, after the death of Rabbi Yitzchok Yosef (Schneerson), Rabbi Menachem Mendel (Schneerson) called in Rabbi Zvi Arieh Rosenfeld and asked him to bring him the "books of Breslav" that deal with prostration on the monument of the *Admor*. The family connection between the person who related the story and the secretary—Rabbi Telsner's son-in-law is Rabbi Groner's brother—strengthens the credibility of this information—and of the possibility that Rabbi Menachem Mendel indeed wanted to prepare the groundwork for the situation of a Hasidic sect without an acting Rebbe.

99   Ishai Rosen-Zvi, "The Imaginary Patient—The Justification of the Holocaust in the Teachings of Rabbi Zvi Yehuda Kook and his Circle," [hakholeh hamedumeh] *Democratic Culture* [Hebrew] 6 (2002), pp. 165–209; Elior, *Lubavitch Messianic Resurgence*; Friedman, *Habad as Messianic Fundamentalism*.

Bibliography

Ada Rapoport Albert, "Confession in the Circle of Rabbi Nahman of Bratslav," *Bulletin for the Institute of Jewish Studies*, I (1973), pp. 65–96.

Adi David, "There Is No Despair at All in India," Ynet Nov, 12 2007.

Aharon Klieger, "A Mysterious Connection in Brooklyn," 3, Breslev.co.il.

Alon Dahan, "'Long Live our Master, Teacher and Creator:' The Divine Man, Characteristics of Chabad Messianism and its Accompanying Polemic," *Reshit Iyunim Beyahadut* [Reshit: Studies in Judaism] [Hebrew] 2 (2010), pp. 147–182.

Alon Dahan, "A Dwelling Below: Menachem Mendel Schneerson's Messianic Doctrine," Doctoral Thesis [Hebrew] submitted to the Hebrew University in Jerusalem (2006).

Alon Dahan, "A Final Redeemer without Heirs: Did Rabbi Menachem Mendel Schneerson (The Lubavitcher Rebbe) Choose neither Heirs nor Successors for Messianic Reasons?" *Kabalah* [Hebrew] 17 (2008), pp. 289–309.

Arjun Appadurai, *Modernity at Large: Cultural Dimensions of Globalization* (Minneapolis 1996).

Aviezer Ravitzky, "The Contemporary Lubavitch Hasidic Movement: Between Conservatism and Messianism," in *Fundamentalism Observed*, Martin E. Marty and R. Scott Appleby, eds., pp. 303–327 (Chicago 1991).

Aviezer Ravitzky, *Freedom Inscribed: Diverse Voices of the Jewish Religious Thought* [Hebrew] (Tel Aviv 1999).

Aviezer Ravitzky, *Messianism, Zionism and Jewish Religious Radicalism* [Hebrew] (Tel Aviv 1993).

Ayin Zokher (Warsaw 1928 [5688]).

Benzion Dinur, *Historical Writings* [Hebrew], (Jerusalem 1955).

Bonnie Morris, *Lubavitcher Women in America: Identity and Activism in the Postwar Era* (New York 1998).

Chayei Moharan (Jerusalem [5740] 1980).

Chayei Moharan [The Life of our Teacher Rabbi Nachman] with restored omissions [Hebrew] (Jerusalem [5760] 2000).
David Assaf, "Happy Are the Persecuted: The Struggle against the Hasidim of Breslav," in *Caught in the Thicket, Crisis & Discontent in the History of Hasidism* [Hebrew] (Jerusalem 2006), pp 179–234.
David Berger, *The Rebbe the Messiah, and the Scandal of Orthodox Indifference* [Hebrew] (Jerusalem, 2005).
Don Handelman, "Framing," in *Theorizing Rituals: Issues, Topics, Approaches, Concepts*, Jens Kreinath, Jan Snoek & Michael Stausberg, eds., pp. 571–582 (Leiden, The Netherlands 2006).
Donald Weber, "From Limen to Border," *American Quarterly* 47 (1995), pp. 526–536.
Dov Schwartz, *Habad's Thought: From Beginning to End* [Hebrew] (Ramat Gan 2010).
Dvar Malchus [Words of the King], [weekly Torah portion] *Shemot* (22 Tevet 5752) [1992].
Dvar Malchus [Words of the King], [weekly Torah portion] *Vayera* (18 Mar-Chesvan 5752) [1992].
Dvar Malchus, (weekly portion) *Korakh*, 28 Sivan 5751 (1991).
Eldad Weil, "The Start of the Era of Women: Women and Femininity in the Thought of the Lubavitcher Rebbe," *Akdamot* [Hebrew] 22 (2009), pp. 61–85.
Elliot R. Wolfson, *Open Secret: Postmessianic Messianism and the Mystical Revision of Menahem Mendel Schneerson* (New York 2009).
Erving Goffman, *Frame Analysis* (New York 1974).
Eviatar Zerubavel, *The Fine Line: Making Distinctions in Everyday Life* (Chicago 1991).
Fredrik Barth, *Ethnic Groups and Boundaries* (Boston 1969).
Georg Simmel, "The Social Boundary," *Theory, Culture & Society* 24 (2007).
Gershom Scholem, *Elements of the Kabbalah and Its Symbolism* [Hebrew] (Jerusalem 1976).
Gershom Scholem, *Major Trends in Jewish Mysticism* (London 1955).
Gilles Deleuze and Felix Guattari, *A Thousand Plateaus: Capitalism and Schizophrenia*, translated by Brian Massumi (Minneapolis 1987).
Isaiah Tishby, "The Messianic Idea and Messianic Trends during the Flowering of Hasidism," [Hebrew] *Zion* 32 (1967) pp. 1–45.
Ishai Rosen-Zvi, "The Imaginary Patient—The Justification of the Holocaust in the Teachings of Rabbi Zvi Yehuda Kook and his Circle," [hakholeh hamedumeh] *Democratic Culture* [Hebrew] 6 (2002), pp. 165–209.
Israel Jacob Yuval, "Moses Redivivus: Maimonides as an Assistant of the King Messiah," *Zion* [Hebrew] 82 (2007), pp. 161–188.
Jacob A. Szubin, "Why Lubavitch Wants Messiah Now: Religious Immigration as a Cause of Millenarism," in *Apocalyptic Time*, Albert L. Baumgarten, ed., pp. 215–240 (Leiden, The Netherlands, 2000).
Jacob Gotlieb, *Rationalism in Hasidic Attire: Habad's Harmonistic Approach to Maimonides* [Hebrew] (Ramat Gan 2009).
Jeffrey Shandler, *Jews, God, and Videotape: Religion and Media in America* (New York 2009).
Jonathan Garb, *The Chosen Will Become Herds: Studies in Twentieth Century Kabbalah* [Hebrew] (Jerusalem 2005).
Joseph Dan, *Modern Jewish Messianism: From Safed to Brooklyn* [Hebrew] (Tel Aviv 1999).
Joseph Weiss, *The Attraction of the Boundary, Studies in Bratslav Hasidism* [Hebrew] (Jerusalem 1975).
Kimmy Caplan, *Internal popular Discourse in Israeli Haredi Society* [Hebrew] (Jerusalem 2007).
Lamont, Michele and Virag Mollnar, "The Study of Boundaries in the Social Sciences," *Annual Review of Sociology* 28 (2002), pp. 167–195.
Leon Festinger, Henry W. Riecken, and Stanley Schachter, *When Prophecy Fails* (Minneapolis 1956).
Lifko'ah et Ha-einayim (To Open the eyes) [Hebrew] (New York 2007).
Likutei Moharan: Collected Works of our Teacher Rabbi Nachman [Hebrew] (Jerusalem 1992).

Manis Lavi, "Meetings with the Rebbe: Revealed: Two Hours a Month in the Rebbe's Room," *Kfar Chabad Weekly* 644 (5 Tevet 5755/Aug. 8th, 1994) pp. 14–17.

Martin Buber, *The Hassidic "Garden of Knowledge" Studies in Hassidism* [Hebrew] (Tel Aviv 1945).

Martin Katchen, "Who Wants Moshiach Now? Pre-Millennialism and Post-Millennialism in Judaism," *Australian Journal of Jewish Studies* 5 (1991), pp. 59–76.

Mary Douglas, *Purity and Danger* (London 1966).

Maya Balakirsky Katz, *The Visual Culture of Chabad*, (New York 2010).

Menachem Friedman, "Habad as Messianic Fundamentalism: From Local Particularism to Universal Jewish Mission," in *Accounting for Fundamentalism: The Dynamic Character of Movements*, Marty E. Martin and R. Scott Appleby, eds., pp. 328–357 (Chicago 1994).

Menachem Friedman, "Messiah and Messianism in Chabad-Lubavitch Hassidism," in *The War of Gog and Magog: Messianism and Apocalypse in Judaism in the Past and Present*, David Ariel-Joel and others, eds. [Hebrew] (Tel Aviv 2001) pp. 174–229.

Michal Kravel-Tovi and Yoram Bilu, "The Work of the Present: Constructing Messianic Temporality in the Wake of Failed Prophecy among Chabad Hasidim," *American Ethnologist* 35 (2008), pp. 1–17.

Mor Altschuler, *The Messianic Secret of Hasidism* [Hebrew] (Haifa 2002).

Moshe Idel, "Sabbatai (Saturn) the Planet and Sabbatai Zvi: A new approach to Sabbateanism," *Mada-ei haYahadut* [Judaic Studies] [Hebrew] 37, (1997), pp. 161–184.

Moshe Idel, *Messianic Mystics* (New Haven, CT 1998).

Moshe Shokeid, *Children of Circumstances: Israeli Immigrants in New York* (Ithaca 1988).

Naftali Lowenthal, "Contemporary Habad and the Paradox of Redemption," in *Perspectives on Jewish Thought and Mysticism,* Alfred I. Ivry, Elliot R. Wolfson, and Allan Arkush, eds., pp. 381–402 (Sidney 1994).

Naftali Lowenthal, *Communicating the Infinite: The Emergence of the Habad School* (Chicago 1990).

Rabbi Levi Yitzchok Bender, *Noam Siakh, Discussions and Lessons from the Rabbi and Hasid Rabbi Levi Yitzchok Bender* (Jerusalem [5755] 1995) Part 2

Rabbi Nachman of Tcherin, *The Desserts of Wisdom* [parperaot lekhokhma] (Jerusalem [5343] 1983) 4.

Rabbi Nathan of Nemirov, *Likutei Halakhot* (Jerusalem [5744] 1984).

Rachel Elior, *Unity of Opposites: The Mystical Theosophy of Habad* [Hebrew] (Jerusalem 1992).

Rachel Elior, "Lubavitch Messianic Resurgence: The Historical and Mystical Background 1939–1996," in: *Toward the Millennium*, P. Schafer and M.R. Cohen, eds, pp. 383–408 (Leiden, The Netherlands 1999).

Reece Jones, "Categories, Borders and Boundaries," *Progress in Human Geography* 33 (2009), pp. 174–189.

Rivka Schatz Uffenheimer, *Hasidism as Mysticism: Quietistic Elements in Eighteenth-Century Hasidic Thought* [Hebrew] (Jerusalem 1968).

Roee Horen, "The Belief in the Tzadik in Rabbi Nathan of Nemirov's Liqqutei Halakhot: Myth Ritual and Narrative," [Hebrew] Master's Thesis, Bar Ilan University 2008.

Roland Barth, *Camera Lucida* [Hebrew] (Jerusalem 1988).

Samuel Heilman and Menachem Friedman, *The Rebbe: The Life and Afterlife of Menachem Mendel Schneerson*, (Princeton, NJ 2010).

Shalom Duber Wolpe, *Mevaser Tov*, Kfar Chabad, 5754 (1994).

She-erit Yitzkhak, (Jerusalem [5765] 2005).

Shmuel Horowitz, *Zion Hametzuyenet*, (Jerusalem 5760 [2000]).

Shmuel Krauss, *Nasi Vechasid*, Kfar Chabad 5759 (1999).

Simon Dein, "Moshiach Is Here Now: Just Open Your Eyes and You See Him," *Anthropology and Medicine* 9 (2002), pp. 25–36.

Simon Dein, "What Really Happens When Prophecy Fails?" *Sociology of Religion* 62 (2001), pp. 383–401.
Simon Deine and Lorne L. Dawson, "The Scandal of the Lubavitch Rebbe: Messianism as a Response to Failed Prophecy," *Journal of Contemporary Religion* 23 (2), pp. 163–180.
Simon Dubnow, *The History of Hasidism* (Tel Aviv 1960).
Sue Fishkoff, *The Rebbe's Army: Inside the World of Chabad Lubavitch*, (New York 2003).
Susan Sontag, *On Photography* [Hebrew] (Tel Aviv 1980).
Talk of Redemption [siakh hage-ula] 758, July 31, 2009, p. 4.
Tanya M. Luhrmann, "Metakinesis: How God Becomes Intimate in Contemporary American Christianity," *American Anthropologist* 106 (2004), pp. 518–528.
Tanya M. Luhrmann, "The Absorption Hypothesis: Learning to Hear God in Evangelical Christianity," *American Anthropologist* 112 (2010), pp. 66–78.
Victor Turner, *The Forest of Symbols* (Ithaca 1970).
Victor Turner, *The Ritual Process, Structure and anti-Structure* [Hebrew] (Tel Aviv 2004).
William Shaffir, "Interpreting Adversity: Dynamics of Commitment in a Messianic Redemption Campaign," *Jewish Journal of Sociology* 36 (1994), pp. 43–53.
William Shaffir, "Jewish Messianism—Lubavitch Style: An Interim Report," *Jewish Journal of Sociology* 35 (1993), pp. 115–128.
William Shaffir, "When Prophecy Is Not Validated: Explaining the Unexpected in a Messianic Campaign," *Jewish Journal of Sociology* 37 (1995), pp. 119–135.
Yakov Singer, "The Personality Cult" [pulmus hadiukan], *Besha'a Tova*, no. 297, [weekly portion] *Vayikra 5769* (2008), pp. 18–33, 43.
Yehuda Goodman, "Return to Orthodox Judaism and New Religious Identities in Israel at the Start of the 21st Century," in *Not to Be Believed, a Different View of Religiosity and Secularism*, Aviad Kleinberg, ed. [Hebrew] (Tel Aviv 2004), pp. 177–198.
Yehuda Liebes, "Brings Forth the Horn of Redemption [*Yeshuah*]," *Mekhqarei Yerushalayim be-Makhshevet Yisrael* [Jerusalem Studies in Jewish Thought] [Hebrew] 3 (1984) pp. 313–348.
Yitzchak Krauss, *The Seventh: Messianism in the Last Generation of Chabad* [Hebrew] (Tel Aviv 2007).
Yoram Bilu, "With Us More Than Ever: The Presence of the Rebbe in the Messianic Branch of Chabad," In *Leadership and Authority in Haredi Society in Israel*, Kimmy Caplan and Nurit Stadler, eds., [Hebrew] (Jerusalem 2009), pp. 186–209.
Yori Yanover and Nadav Ish-Shalom, *Dancing and Crying: the Truth about the Chabad Movement* [Hebrew] (Jerusalem 1994).
Zvi Mark, "Kabbalah, Hasidism and New Age in the Twentieth Century: On *The Chosen Will Become Herds: Studies in Twentieth-Century Kabbalah*" (Review), *Kabbalah: Journal for the Study of Jewish Mystical Texts* 17 (2008), pp. 89–99.
Zvi Mark, "A Righteous Man Caught in the Jaws of the Sitra Akhra: The Holy Man and the Profane Site—the Pilgrimage to the Grave of Rabbi Nachman of Breslav in Uman on Rosh Hashana," *Reshit* [Hebrew] 2 (2010), pp. 112–146.
Zvi Mark, *le-Akhar Matayim Shana—miTikkun Ishi leTikkun Olam, Hitgalut veTikkun* [Two Hundred Years Later—from Personal Rectification to Universal Rectification, Revelation and Rectification], [Hebrew] (Jerusalem 2011).
Zvi Mark, *Mysticism and Madness: The Religious Thought of Rabbi Nachman of Bratslav* (London 2009).
Zvi Mark, *The Scroll of Secrets: The Hidden Messianic Vision of R. Nachman of Breslav* (Brighton, MA 2010).
Zvi Sobel, *A Small Place in the Galilee: Religion and Social Conflict in an Israeli Village* (New York 1993).

Four

"The Besht Passed His Hand over His Face"

On the Besht's Influence on His Followers: Some Remarks

Moshe Idel

Very few individuals have been able to change the entire life course of so many Jews in modern times and contribute in so profound a manner to an intense spiritual life as Israel Ba'al Shem Tov, the master of the good name, known as the Besht (c. 1698–1760). A healer, an exorcist, a teacher—orally to be sure, since he left no written book—he became a leader of disciples, some of whom were remarkable personalities themselves. Through his activities and teachings, a new form of Judaism emerged toward the end of the 18th century. It grew from a modest movement to one that changed the spiritual physiognomy of much of Eastern European Jewry. The full-fledged movement diversified in the 19th century into numerous sects, each with its own founding figure but all recognizing the Besht as the primal source. Modern Judaism has been deeply affected by these movements, which witnessed, more than any other segment of Judaism, the annihilation of their members during the Shoah. Afterwards, the movement slowly recuperated from its terrible losses by building institutions, mostly in Israel and the USA, and disseminating its spiritual messages at large. Today it has again become one of the decisive forces in Jewish religious life, both in its traditional forms and in Neo-Hasidism. Without the special personality of the Besht, these vital developments would never have taken place.

Charisma?

The manner in which the Besht was able to attract disciples and convince them to become his followers is a key reason for the impact he had before his teachings were recorded and printed, thus allowing him to become known to larger audiences. His career as a healer, a magician and a spiritual guide was not accompanied by a written record, and his direct disciples were paramount in both the preservation and dissemination of his teachings. Scholars have often suggested the term *charisma*, which stems from a religious background, to explain the emergence of Hasidism, assuming that the Besht possessed a special gift to attract people. Gershom Scholem and many of his followers as well as other scholars[1] have noted the Besht's charisma though that word has been implicitly rejected by Martin Buber in his various descriptions of this figure. Like Scholem, Buber too, refuses to attribute too much weight to such phenomena as suggestion and auto-suggestion in efforts to understand the Besht's success.[2] No doubt the description of the Besht as a charismatic contains more than a grain of truth, as it attributed a special quality to his personality that attracted people to him personally, not only to his spiritual teachings. According to another leading scholar of early East European Hasidism, charisma is related to the prophetic claims of members of the group to which the Besht was connected at the beginning of his career, who should also be described as charismatics.[3]

However, the problems posed by this term, helpful as it is in some cases, are quite significant. First, although the term is commonly applied to large-scale movements, which attract many people in a short period of time, that was hardly true in the case of the Besht: He was indeed successful in attracting many students but certainly not enough to qualify as a mass movement. Hasidism in its earlier stages was quite a small group, only about some few dozen people.[4] If charisma is to be judged by numbers of people attracted to a certain person, it is hard to ascertain how much charisma the Besht had. It seems that the person who continued the propagandistic efforts of the Besht, the Great Maggid of Miedziresz, attracted many more students than his master did, perhaps a few hundred. Thus, though he was a founder of the spiritual basis of Hasidism, which did turn eventually into a mass movement, the Besht did not attract audiences large enough to be described as a movement. Another basic problem with this proposal is that it is too general, and in the theories of personality that may sustain it, we must include too many diverse figures and cultures, from King David,[5] to ancient seers in Greece,[6] and prophets in Israel, to a variety of Kabbalists including R. Isaac Luria Ashkenazi,[7] Sabbatai Tzevi, to Joseph Smith, or Martin Luther King, and to the Besht and his follower the Great Maggid of Miedziresz,[8] as all falling into the category of religious charismatics.

Last but not least, Max Weber's definition, which underlines the scholars' views of charisma in Hasidism, is useful, however, only insofar as it strives to explain how a traditionally religious society understood the charismatic person as acting under the influence of God. According to Weber, charisma should be understood as

> a certain quality of an individual personality, by virtue of which one is considered extraordinary and treated as endowed with supernatural, superhuman, or at least specifically exceptional powers or qualities. These as such are not accessible to the ordinary person, but are regarded as divine in origin or as exemplary, and on the basis of them the individual concerned is treated as a leader.[9]

If for a traditional society this explanation may make perfect sense, in a more critical approach, which is the approach that concerns us here, the assumption of a divine gift is much less an explanatory strategy than an attempt to avoid explanation by adopting a slightly secularized religious point of view. Indeed, as is well known, the term charisma has a clear religious background. I am certainly not the first to criticize Weber's definition,[10] but it seems that just reiterating an "explanation" based on charisma for the Besht's success analyzes little of the possible pertinent material.

Several years ago, in my book on Hasidism I proposed, quite succinctly, a possible explanation for the relationship between the righteous man, the *Tzaddiq,* and his followers. I described this affinity as a "quasi-hypnotic interaction between the magician and his audience" and proposed that "we should be aware of another interesting category of magic, influential in the Renaissance, that can help us understand the emergence of Hasidism."[11] I relied on two theories of magic developed by such scholars of Renaissance magic as Daniel P. Walker[12] and Ioan P. Couliano,[13] who used the terms "transitive magic" and "intersubjective magic," respectively. To my best knowledge, the extensive studies of Hasidism or the Besht and his activities published since 1995, when my book appeared, have overlooked my analysis, and I would like to point out here some of the reasons behind my remarks. I shall analyze and reflect on the implications of six short passages in the famous hagiography *Shive̲hei ha-Besht,* all of which deal with a special gesture the Besht has been reported to have used to alter the state of consciousness in other people and, in one case, his own consciousness.

Two Cases of Auto-Suggestion

Let me start with the manner in which the Besht recovered from a brief state of intoxication:

> Once the Besht was in the state of Walachia,[14] where they have grape wine, which is so strong that even when you mix two or three drops in a glass of wine it is too strong to drink. The householder offered the Besht a glass of this wine. When he tasted it the Besht said: "Your wine is delicious. Why is your glass so small?" The householder answered: "Because it is dangerous to drink a large portion." The Besht said: "I am not afraid of that." They gave him a large glass and he drank it all. All of them stared at him in fright as his face became red[15] and his hair stood up as though it were on fire. But the Besht passed his hand over his face and at once he returned to normal.

> All of them were very surprised but he said that our Rabbis, blessed their memory, said: "Wine is strong but fear works it off."[16] When he looked at the greatness of the Blessed One, he was struck by fear and trembling, and it completely undid the effects of the wine.[17]

There are two elements related to the Besht's recovery from the impact of the strong wine: one is the movement of the hand; the other is his becoming aware of the grandeur of God. One is corporeal, the manual movement; the other is spiritual. Though the latter can be attained without the former, both are mentioned in this passage. The spiritual explanation also corresponds to what the Besht says before drinking the wine, that he is not afraid of anything, a statement that is also made elsewhere in the hagiography.[18] However, this statement is qualified later on by the assumption that he does fear God's grandeur. It should be pointed out that the Besht was fond of wine according to another story in the hagiography.[19]

In another story, a much more mysterious one, the same gesture is mentioned again:

> Once the Besht went to the bathhouse with Rabbi David Forkes. As they were on their way a very handsome man came toward them. His curly locks were combed[20] and his clothes were well groomed. When the man came close to them the Besht jumped aside as far as he could. When he went by the Besht returned to the path, passed his hand over his eyes, and said: "Look who has passed us." He saw that it was "a brand plucked out of fire."[21] The fire glowed in his hair.[22]

I prefer not to speculate here about the possible meaning of this passage, which deals with some form of transmigration in the line of Lurianic Kabbalah, where the figure of this Great Priest is mentioned. The salient point for our discussion is that the Besht immediately recognized the "real" identity of the person he met, and this insight is related in one way or another to the hand gesture over his own face or eyes. In the hagiography this is part of his technique for changing his consciousness. This gesture recurs also in four other cases, in which it precedes the shift in someone else's consciousness. In any case, in the wine-drinking episode as well as the episode of perceiving the previous life of the man passed on the path, it is clear that charisma has no explanatory force.

Inducing Amnesia:
Three Other Cases of Instant Erasure of Memory

In one of the most complex stories in the hagiography, the first important follower of the Besht, R. Arieh Leib, a Rabbinic figure known as the Admonisher of Polonnoye, came to his master in order to learn the language of the animals and birds. When accompanying the master on his journey, he is told by the

Besht that this ability depends upon his recognition of the dependence of the lower creatures on the higher ones, found in the supernal chariot, the *Merkavah*.[23] In this context, the Besht is reported to have revealed to his disciple the secrets of *Pereq Shirah*[24] and of the two layers of the Zoharic literature, the *Zohar* and *Tiqqunei Zohar*.[25] While R. Arieh Leib was listening to the teachings of his master with one ear, "with the other ear he listened to the conversation of the birds, the animals and the beasts."[26] After he admitted that he understood all those secrets, the Besht performed the following action: "Then the Besht passed his hands over the Preacher's face, and he forgot all the secret details of this knowledge."[27] The Besht told his disciple that he had introduced him to that esoteric knowledge only because of his curiosity, but this sort of knowledge was not necessary for a true worship of God, which should be "wholehearted."[28] This indicates a sharp distinction between the Besht as the spiritual guide who was teaching people an exoteric lore and other spiritual topics and the Besht as the religious leader who was reported later on to have conceived of such lore as being unnecessary for religious behavior that would be eventually described as Hasidism. Thus, one assumes that the Besht possessed some form of knowledge he did not share fully, or permanently, with his disciples as he erased it even after he disclosed it. This situation is reminiscent of the claim the Besht made in the *Holy Epistle* that he possessed the teachings revealed to him by the Messiah, which are described as relatively simple, but he was not allowed to disclose them to anyone.[29]

Here the situation differs from that in the first story of drinking the strong wine: there the Besht is reminded of the grandeur of God after the hand gesture, while here the Admonisher must forget the sublime knowledge that the Besht taught him. It should be pointed out that this is exactly the same type of knowledge that the Besht taught his other important disciple, R. Dov Baer, known as the Great Maggid of Miedziresz, but in that case inducing forgetfulness is not mentioned. However, the Great Maggid never displays his acquaintance with this type of knowledge in any other context or nor do his other students attribute it to him.[30] Also in that case, the Besht was reported as introducing his disciple into secrets found in esoteric books like *Sefer Raziel ha-Malakh*.[31]

Let me turn to another similar example: During the Besht's stay in Istanbul, on his way to the land of Israel, he is described as temporarily curing a blind boy:

> At once they brought the sick boy to the Besht and he whispered something in his ear. Then he immediately ordered a Gemara to be brought to him and he told the boy to read. He read as everyone does. The family was joyous. Then the Rabbi passed his hand over the boy's eyes, and they reversed to their former condition.[32]

This deleterious reversal was performed, according to the Besht, because the family had denied earlier the powers of the holy names of God.[33] Here the hand gesture is repeated, but there is an additional similarity to the story of R. Arieh Leib: The Besht whispers something in the ear of the patient. In both cases we have a sudden acquisition of some form of knowledge and then its sudden evaporation. Thus we have two different cases in which whispering is combined with the gesture of passing the hand over the face or eyes.

A third example differs from the two earlier ones. The Besht exposes the malpractices of a *shohet* and of the cantor of a community, and then he revealed to the Rabbi of that community the result of the cantor's sin:

> The Besht passed his hands over the rabbi's face, and he saw several demons and ghosts sitting on the synagogue. The rabbi was amazed. The Besht explained that each time before his prayers the cantor had an accidental emission.[34,35]

Here we have again the acquisition of paranormal knowledge—this time a vision—but the gesture is not related to the removal of a certain type of vision, but on the contrary, to its induction. This time, there is no whispering.

The Besht's Hand Gesture as Undoing R. Joseph Ashkenazi's Vision of a Ghost

Closer to the last case but sharing some features with the other cases, the longest and most elaborated case deserves a detailed analysis. R. Joseph Ashkenazi, a remote relative of the Besht, was reading to the Besht out of *'Ein Ya'aqov*, a 16th-century popular compendium of Talmudic legends with commentaries, presumably one of the preferred sources of the founder of Hasidism. While listening, the Besht made comments on the content.[36] Here is the translation of most of the pertinent part of the legend:

> Once at the end of Sabbath, the Besht ordered his step-father/son-in-law Rabbi Joseph Ashkenazi,[37] to read him from *'Ein Ya'aqov* while he lay on the bed and listened.[38] At one place the Besht said Torah concerning a saying in the *'Ein Ya'aqov*. Then Rabbi Joseph continued to recite the *'Ein Ya'aqov*, and during the reading Rabbi Joseph envisioned a *maggid meisharim*,[39] whose name was also Rabbi Joseph,[40] who passed away about three-quarters of a year before that time. He saw him entering the house dressed in Sabbath clothes and wearing a hat, called hut, and he said aloud: "A good week to our rabbi." He carried a stick in his hand and he walked as if he were alive. When Rabbi Joseph saw him he became frightened and the book of *'Ein Ya'aqov* fell from his hand. The Besht passed his hand over R. Joseph's face, and Rabbi Joseph Ashkenazi saw the dead man no more.. . .Rabbi Joseph stepped aside, and the dead man remained with the Besht for about half an hour or more. Rabbi Joseph Ashkenazi saw the Besht talking with him. Then the Besht called to Rabbi Joseph Ashkenazi in these words: "Deutsch, come over here." He went over to him and recited more of the *'Ein Ya'aqov*. During their study, the Besht was angry with him and said: "Why were you frightened? Did Rabbi Joseph the *maggid* slaughter a *deutscher* like you while he was alive so that you were afraid of him after his death?" Rabbi Joseph

asked him: "Why was I privileged to see him?" The Besht said to him: "because you recited [aloud] to me, and I recited before you, and my words purified you. We were united as one, and because of that, you were able to see him. If your mind had been stronger, you would have heard what he said to me, and you, too would have been able to ask him whatever your heart wished. Moreover, you would have been made known to him, you would be able to envision him at any time." Rabbi Joseph grieved about this matter very much because seeing the soul of a righteous man is at the level of prophecy[41] as it is said in the book *Sha'arei Qedushah* of Rabbi Hayyim Vital.[42] Rabbi Joseph asked the Besht why he had come and what his needs were, and the Besht told him that he came because it was necessary for him [the Maggid] to come.[43]

This is a very rich and compact passage, which if it is accepted from the historical point of view, may add some information about the Besht—how the Besht studied, what he studied, and how he and his immediate entourage imagined interaction with the other worlds. We are, however, concerned here only with a small part of this passage. The Besht resorted again to the hand gesture in order to remove a vision, that is, to cause a shift in the state of consciousness of his amanuensis. Here too we have some form of linguistic contact preceding the experience, a fact that is emphasized by the Besht himself. Though not a whisper, some form of causality is connected to verbal activity as suggested by the Besht to explain the emergence of the vision. Rabbi Joseph has seen the ghost because he and the Besht were linked previously as an effect of their shared linguistic activity with the same book: the one recited it and the other expounded upon it. The verb used to convey the concept of connectivity is *hitqashsher,* and via this linkage the two persons are described "as one." This verb has a long history in the Beshtian teachings and in those of his students, which we cannot explore at length here. In most of the cases it stands for the linkage of the *tzaddiq* to others in order to elevate them during his prayer or to produce a connection to all the levels of reality in order to raise sparks from them.[44] Here, however, the concept is different though the verb is the same: not the soul or the spark is linked but the mind. This union, is the explanation explicitly offered in the text for a shared experience, which, however, is not completely shared because the mind of R. Joseph was not strong enough to see anything more than the soul of the dead. He could not hear the conversation of the Besht and the dead man.

Most probably this episode took place during the Besht's stay in Miedzibusz, sometime within the years 1740 to 1760. The other cases discussed here took place, if we accept the hagiography, in Istanbul, Walachia, Sharigorod or Nemirov.

Synergesis and Concomitance

Let me turn now to the claim that R. Joseph's vision is the result of his soul or his mind being purified by the words of the Besht, who was then connected to him, allowing the two to become one. The Besht was reported to have said that this was caused by the exchange of words that took place beforehand: R. Joseph Ashkenazi read to the Besht, and the latter discussed an issue from that reading. The assumption is that during the recitation of sections from *'Ein Ya'aqov*, the minds of the two persons were connected to each other, and therefore, according to the hagiography what the Besht could see and hear could, in theory, be seen and heard also by his companion, but the latter's weaker mind allowed him only to see but not to hear the conversation between R. Joseph, the dead preacher, and the Besht. This mental linkage as the result of a prior linguistic exchange seems to me quite evident in the passage and is not an imposition of a modern reading, an issue to which we shall return below. Connectivity was the source of the vision, and the Besht terminated it by his specific hand gesture.

Let me turn now to another episode with the same two persons, in which the gesture does not occur but connectivity is invoked again. R. Joseph, described now as the cantor of the Besht, had a complex dream in which a Hasid asked him to intervene to prevent an unfavorable match of the man's son. In this dream he also sees an ascent of the souls of the dead. In the morning, he went to the Besht and told him about the dream. The Besht then said to him: "Do you think it was a dream that you had? Not at all. It was a vision that you saw. I saw it as well and it became a reality before my eyes."[45] Apparently the Besht distinguishes between the personal aspect of the account, which has to do with the Hasid's son, and the part related to the celestial world, which he insists that it is not a dream but a vision. He has seen this vision too, the Besht claims, and he is able to decode its details for R. Joseph. Here, the assumption is that both have seen an event taking place in heaven that has been materialized and witnessed by the two men at the same time. The Besht insinuates that the vision, which materialized before his eyes, has been seen also by R. Joseph, who believed that it was a dream, perhaps some form of telepathy.[46]

This materialization may explain also the appearance of the apparition in the first passage about R. Joseph Ashkenazi. There, the apparition of the "soul" of the dead righteous, is depicted in anthropomorphic terms, including his hat and stick. In accordance to the worldview expressed in the hagiography, there is no contradiction between the dead "soul" and the appearance of the living man. We learn this from another instance in the same book, when a spark of a wicked dead man came to demand redemption from the Besht and was afterwards described as walking like an ordinary person.[47] That the Besht was visited by righteous as well as wicked persons is evident from the hagiography, where the visits of Elijah, Ahijah the Shilonite, Sabbatai Tzevi,[48] and an unnamed wicked person are mentioned. They too appear in some form of visible body, and they spoke with the Besht, though others in his presence could not see or hear them.

Some Implications for Shivehei ha-Besht

The existence of six examples in which the Besht has been reported as performing the hand gesture in one rather short book, is, in my opinion, much more than an accident. Nevertheless it might be explained in more than one way. Someone may claim that the gesture is a topos used by the editors of the hagiography in the early 18th century, and thus it has nothing to do with the actual activity of the Besht himself. To the best of my knowledge, in the teachings reported in the name of the Besht, this gesture is not mentioned.

Nevertheless, this attribution of the gesture to a later period (after the Besht's death) is problematic: first, there is, to my best knowledge, not one single example in which this gesture occurs in contexts similar to what we have seen above. The most similar example would be a passage attributed to R. Isaac Luria, in the late 18th century Hasidic master R. Israel ben Sabbatai of Kuznitz, in which it is reported that after Luria listed all the sins a person had committed, then that person confessed that he indeed committed all those sins with the exception of one. Then, Luria "passed his hand over his face and he put the very sin in front of him."[49] Even if this passage, which I could not locate in the printed versions of Lurianic books, is authentic, the situation does not change. What is missing here is the resort to the gesture in order to change one's state of consciousness. It seems that Luria took the sin that was believed to have been inscribed on the sinner's face, reified it, and rendered the invisible visible. Or, to use the concept discussed in the context of the Besht, the sin was materialized by Luria's gesture. Thus, even the most similar description does not approximate the Hasidic stories, and therefore it seems that there is no model for any of the six cases related to the Besht in the available Jewish traditions before the publication of the hagiography. Thus, the Besht was not portrayed by his later admirers in a manner that would fit a paradigm in Jewish culture. Was it possible that the editors doctored the legends in a systematic manner by introducing the gesture, which had not been used by the Hasidic elites after the death of the Besht in 1760, until 1814? On the basis of what we know, I see no reason to presume that redactors would insert the available material for no noticeable purpose.[50] I would not say that the legends discussed here belong to a certain cluster, a hypothesis that is correct in other cases, as suggested by Elhanan Reiner,[51] nor do they belong to a certain specific period of his life, since several different locales, in fact several different countries, are mentioned.[52]

The Great Maggid's "Rebirth"

Let me turn now to another story, related to the Great Maggid of Miedziresz, concerning the manner in which the Besht examined him and exemplified to him. When called in the middle of the night to the Besht, the Great Maggid was reported to have said:

> I found the Besht sitting with a small pillow on his head, and he was dressed in a coat of wolf fur turned inside out, and he asked me whether I have studied Kabbalah. I answered that I had. A book was lying in front of him on the table and he commanded me to recite to him from this book. And the book was written in short paragraphs, each of which began: "Rabbi Ishmael said: Metatron, the Prince of Presence, told me." I recited a page or half page to him. The Besht told me: "It is not so. I will recite it to you." He began to recite, and while he read he trembled.[53] He rose and said: "We are dealing with *Ma'aseh Merkavah* and I am sitting down?"[54] He stood up and continued to read. During the utterances he lay me down[55] in the shape of a circle[56] on the bed. I was not able to see him any more. I only heard voices and saw awesome flashes and torches. This continued for about two hours. I was extremely afraid and that fear caused me to feel faint."[57]

This story contains a mixture of themes related to the Sinaitic revelation, and the manner in which the study of the early Jewish esoteric literature related to the divine chariot, or Heikhalot literature, has been employed. However, this is no doubt also some form of initiation, which includes an element reminiscent of that of R. Joseph Ashkenazi reciting before the Besht and that of R. Tzevi reading the *Zohar* to the Besht. In both cases, the Besht repeated the recited text or commented on the text that was recited by his companion. Also here, as in cases studied above, the Besht introduces his disciple to an esoteric text by recitation, which assumes some conjuration, which brings about the paranormal phenomenon and the experience. In the last case, however, the Great Maggid has also a paranormal experience, similar to the Sinaitic one. Also he, like R. Joseph Ashkenazi, was frightened by the experience. What is quintessential for understanding the above passage is the centrality of vocal performance, which is not just a statement but also an assumption that the text possesses some incantational dimension, and it depends on the psychological mood of the person who recites it, what I have called a psychological-experiential reading.[58] As pointed out in many of my studies, performance is part and parcel of Judaism, and it shaped the different types of mysticism that emerged within it.[59]

The manner in which the Great Maggid has been allegedly positioned in the bed is interesting: it points to some form of uroboros or to the position of a fetus. Is this pointing to a form of regeneration or spiritual rebirth that is accompanied by the transmission of some form of higher knowledge? In a way it is reminiscent of what is called the posture of Elijah—head between the knees⁶⁰— mentioned in another context in the hagiography in the dream of R. Joseph Ashkenazi mentioned above, but that is in a sitting position, while here the Great Maggid is lying down.

Another Hebrew version of the initiation/new birth experience of the Great Maggid (which I see as derivative⁶¹) was already in print in 1794/5, and its very existence shows that before 1794 there existed a legend dealing with the manner in which the Besht initiated his future disciple. Therefore the legend has an earlier source. Even more interesting in this context is the Yiddisch version, which differs from the two Hebrew versions on several points, one of which is worth highlighting. The Besht expressly declares that he wanted to make the Great Maggid "a new creature," an interpretation that fits the manner in which I interpreted the initiation story as part of the cycle starting with his unsuccessful healing.⁶² It is probable that the existence of this interpretation points to an earlier Hebrew version, different from the versions extant today, which has been translated into Yiddisch.

This legend should be compared to the other one found in the hagiography dealing with the descent of the Prince of the Torah which, like the texts mentioned in this passage, is a practice belonging to the so-called Heikhalot literature of late antiquity. It seems that in both cases the Besht produces some form of descent.⁶³

The comment that follows this passage is extremely interesting:

> I, the writer,⁶⁴ say that it seems to me that that was the way his Torah was revealed to him. I heard several times from the mouth of the Hasid, the Rabbi of the holy community of Polonnoye that he received from the Baal Shem Tov the Torah that belongs [specifically] to the root of his soul, amidst thunder and lightning.. . .But I heard from the rabbi⁶⁵ this statement⁶⁶: "Just as all [the people of] Israel had received the Torah as a whole, the Besht has received it as an individual."⁶⁷,⁶⁸

The Hasid mentioned here is, most probably, R. Arieh Leib, the Admonisher of Polonnoye, mentioned above as one of the first followers of the Besht.⁶⁹ If the writer is reliable, that is, if indeed he received such a tradition from R. Arieh Leib, the Besht may have resorted to some form of initiation when introducing his students to some form of advanced knowledge, designated in the last quote as the Torah that belongs in a primordial manner to the disciple's soul, constituting its root. This last passage also assumes that the Great Maggid received his Torah as it was received at Sinai. In both cases, the legends capitalize upon the Kabbalistic view that each person interprets the Torah in his own way, which had been revealed at Sinai, and each is obliged to flesh out his unique interpretation and commit it to writing.⁷⁰ The Besht was considered, at least implicitly, as someone who had received all the details of the Sinaitic revelation, and this is why he was able to transmit to each person the Torah, that special understanding that belongs to each individual.

It should be pointed out that in the continuation of the last passage, when the Besht is told about an interpretation offered by the Great Maggid to a statement in the *Zohar*, he then said, "Do you think that he learned the Torah by himself?"[71] The insinuation is that the Great Maggid's knowledge emanates ultimately from the Besht. The word *Torah* means here just a "teaching," in the manner that the Hasidim are dealing with their innovations delivered as sermons on biblical themes.[72]

Let me turn to the manner in which the above scene of the initiation has been depicted. The Besht was uttering the passages from the Heikhalot literature when he initiated the Great Maggid. The Hebrew term for the utterances is *dibburim*. It occurs again in the description of how the Besht tried to heal the ailing R. Dov Baer:

> He wanted to cure him with speeches [*dibburim*]. I heard from Rabbi Gershon of the community of Pavlych that the Besht visited him daily for about two weeks and sat opposite him and recited Psalms. After that the Besht said to him, "I wanted to cure you with speeches [*dibburim*] since this is an enduring remedy, [*refu'ah qayyemet*] but now I have to cure you with medication."[73]

Again, speech was the main form of activity supposed to have a religious impact on the other person. In the two cases related to the Great Maggid, the Besht recites some religious texts over the body of someone who is supposed to acquire thereby some kind of higher state—healing, a more advanced type of knowledge, or some form of experience. It is as if his very pronunciation is transmitting either vitality or an insight that does not depend upon a merely semantic approach to the written text that is not recited "properly" according to the Besht. Let me point out that the initiation passage may be better understood as part of the process of healing after the unsuccessful attempts to cure him first by speech alone and then by medication—using a powdered diamond.[74] It is perhaps an attempt to cure the Great Maggid's soul, or the root of his soul, by delivering to him "his" Torah.

Let me turn to another connection between speech and engendering. The Besht's grandson reports that he heard the Besht make a rather enigmatic statement, to the effect that "his father took him without speech, as Moses, our master, may he rest in peace, [did] but would his father take him by [means of] speech, he would fill the spaces of the entire world by his teaching, and would exterminate all the shells and bring the Messiah."[75] My reading of the passage is based on the assumption that speech or utterance may be the instrument of a higher form of engendering and is corroborated to a certain extent by another remark concerning the birth of the Besht. In the hagiographical collection of stories *In Praise of the Baal Shem Tov*, there is an observation which may be pertinent to a better understanding of the above passage: "The Besht said that it had been impossible for his father to draw his soul [from heaven] until he had lost [first] his sexual desire."[76] The Besht claimed that his own son was born by word or speech.[77]

Thus, it seems that we may discern another pattern used by the Besht that is related to some form of transmission of knowledge, which has nothing to do with the induction of oblivion by the hand gesture as it was the case of R. Arieh Leib, in the first incident here. The Besht considered himself to be the source of the religious knowledge imparted to his disciples, someone who had easy access to the largest reservoir of religious knowledge. He was able to impart this knowledge to his students, some of whom then had individual "Sinaitic" experiences.[78] In any case, in all the versions of the initiation of the Great Maggid, there is no trace of amnesia or the gestures supposed to induce it.

Acquisition, Transmission and Control of Religious Knowledge

Let me put some of the preceding discussions in a more general context. The hagiography about the Besht is permeated with questions related to the acquisition of extraordinary knowledge, its transmission and its control. The very beginning of the hagiography deals with the childhood and youth of the Besht, and the story of the transmission of the secret books of Kabbalah from the legendary R. Adam to the Besht is provided to explain what the source of his religious knowledge was.[79] For this purpose the authors of the hagiography adopted and adapted stories found in Yiddisch literature as has been pointed out so convincingly by Chone Shmeruk.[80] In the same cycle of legends dealing with the earlier phases of his life, which are the less reliable parts of the hagiography, the Besht is described as twice causing the descent of the Prince of the Torah, an angelic figure that was imagined to be capable of disclosing secrets by means of conjurations.[81] Though the topic was raised in several discussions throughout the Middle Ages, the Besht is the first historical personality who was attributed such abilities, though in quite a fantastic part of the hagiography.[82] These descents are accompanied by fiery phenomena reminiscent of what the Great Maggid reported as part of his experience. Then, the Besht is also reported as having access to other supernal sources of knowledge, especially that of his angelic mentor, Ahijah the Shilonite, Elijah, seeing the soul of a righteous, and the Messiah himself.[83] Moreover, in one well-known case, as reported by his grandson, R. Moshe Hayyim Efrayyim of Sudylkov, the Besht told him: "I swear to you that there is a person in the world that hears the Torah from the mouth of the Holy One, blessed be He, and His *Shekhinah*, not from the mouth of an angel and not from the mouth [of a seraph], etc."[84]

There can be little doubt that the Besht was speaking here about himself as someone who studies the Torah with God. This is a rather uncommon type of boasting in the history of Jewish mysticism, whereby someone attributes to himself a similar experience to that of Moses. It should be pointed out that at the beginning of the hagiography the Besht's soul is described as being in the likeness of Moses, and other affinities are found further on.[85] Moses is described in one of the Besht's teaching in a way that reminiscent of the Besht himself:

> This is the issue of the rank of Moses, blessed be his memory, that he elevated and amended his speech, at the beginning they were the flock, which he was shepherding, and afterwards they became his disciples and he gave them the Torah, and studied with them, etc., and the words of the sage are gracious.[86]

The Besht is described in the hagiography as amending his speech,[87] and the assumption that Moses had disciples and gave them Torah is also reminiscent of the founder of Hasidism, as seen above. Elsewhere in the hagiography, the Besht is reported as meeting the angel Hadarniel, the angel met by Moses when he ascended to receive the Torah according to some traditions, especially the *Zohar*.[88]

From this point of view, the sources of his alleged extraordinary knowledge are quite heterogeneous, but the material extant in the hagiography presents a more coherent picture than does the legacy as preserved in the writings of his immediate disciples. However, some other forms of extraordinary knowledge are related to the Besht's gazing on the written (and perhaps also spoken) letters of the Torah or in the *Zohar*.[89] This is a type of information obtained *ad hoc* and intended to answer practical questions by resorting to mantic techniques, and it is related much more to the Besht qua magician than to the Besht as spiritual guide. However, let me point out that in most of the cases, these revelations are hardly sources of what were reported to be the teachings of the Besht that subsequently became Hasidism.

Also the process of transmission differs from the conventional forms in both Rabbinic and Kabbalistic sources, where the common study, basically a vocal activity, is done in groups, rather than *tete-à-tete*. In a way, the resort to the extraordinary types of initiation and his alleged studies with the legendary son of the equally legendary R. Adam, is a great departure from the discursive nature of the more traditional forms of knowledge acquisition in Rabbinic Judaism. The events described above require the presence of an additional person and an extraordinary event: dead souls, supernal fires, sudden understanding of the languages of animals and birds, sudden recovery from blindness, etc. This is part of a fantastic religious *imaginaire,* which explains another quandary—why learned figures, like R. Dov Baer of Miedziresz, R.

Arieh Leib of Polonnoye, and R. Jacob Joseph of Polonnoye, were attracted so deeply to the teachings of the Besht. The answer offered by the hagiography is, that at least two of them had received from the Besht a special learning that belonged solely to them, and for those figures, there was an extraordinary experience that impacted their initiation. Unfortunately, neither the Great Maggid nor R. Arieh Leib of Polonnoye left any direct report of the moment of their initiation, their entering the circle of the Besht's followers, nor the specific reasons for such an association with him. All we have are the much later reports preserved in the hagiography, some of which have been discussed above. However, the attraction of some elite figures to the Besht was not based upon the legends, which were less the patrimony of his immediate disciples than of later and more popular circles.

However, even if the legendary portrayals and explanations I have discussed here are unacceptable for a critical understanding of the historical Besht, the question that prompted these legends still remains: Why did all those distinguished figures became disciples of the Besht and admire him so much years after his death? I would say, without generalizing as to all the followers of the Besht, that a common denominator for some of them would be necessary in order to better account for the unusual impact his personality had, and the term charisma, as used by many scholars, the evasive common denominator. To be sure, this does not exclude the impact of his teachings, which over the short and long term shaped Hasidism.

Hypnoid States of Consciousness and the Besht's Acquaintances

I believe that some insight into the nature of the processes that attracted some people to the Besht may be extracted from the manner in which he controlled his followers, not only by imparting to them his knowledge in extraordinary circumstances but also by the manner in which he could control that knowledge by undoing it. I assume that we may discern a recurrent sequence of events, a pattern that consists basically of a conversation-recitation or a resort to some vocal activity, followed then by a sharp change of consciousness in the patient, and then a return from it at the hand gesture of the Besht. This sequence is reminiscent of the hypnotic situation as described by Amir Raz and Theodore Shapiro: "Historically, hypnosis was defined as an altered state of consciousness, characterized by heightened compliance with suggestion and extreme focused attention."[90] To be sure, even if I assume the role played by the hypnoid moments in the relations of some of the followers to the Besht, I cannot be sure whether the Besht was aware of the mechanism of the hypnotic state or only understood that he could awaken them by his gesture. The nature of those mechanisms is still actively debated in modern scholarship on hypnosis.

Let me address now the transition from one state of consciousness to another. In a number of cases as analyzed above, the shift has been caused by the movement of the hand over the face, which generated an immediate change in the other person. Here the main concern is not admiration of the Besht as a religious leader, veneration of his personality, or a deep evaluation of the depth of his teachings. It is an immediate response to a hypnotic voice and to a hand gesture, and these responses are hardly conscious ones. This is especially obvious in the story about R. Joseph Ashkenazi, where the tone of the Besht is quite commanding. The gesture provokes, if one believes the story in the hagiography, an instant reversal from a hypnoid state of consciousness that in some instances was triggered by vocal activity by the Besht. In these instances the routine explanation of the impact of the Besht—the concept of a charismatic personality alone—is quite a vague and, thus, problematic diagnosis. From this point of view, Haviva Pedaya's analysis of the Besht's personality and experiences without bringing up the subject of charisma is indeed a very laudable effort.[91]

The Besht's self-perception of his role in terms reminiscent of Moses's receiving and imparting the Torah, recurrent in the hagiography, is no doubt part of his strongly assertive presence in many parts of the hagiography. This presence would have been a necessary condition for inducing a hypnotic state in some of his followers, who probably were what scholars dealing with hypnosis would call *sub assertive*. This hypothesis would explain how some form of suggestions passed from the Besht, orally or mentally, to his followers, and would also explain some of the miraculous aspects of his deeds.

In addition to the more nebulous claims as to the charismatic personality of the Besht being able to impress some larger—though still small—audiences, we may assume that he was able to produce some form of hypnoid impact by means of his voice on some of his immediate entourage in one-to-one encounters. Consciously or not, he probably induced some form of a hypnotic state of consciousness, became a hypnotic operator while speaking with others, and then had to awaken them by means of the manual gesture or trigger what scholars call a posthypnotic amnesia.[92] Whether these are cases of unconsciously induced hypnoid states of consciousness would be quite difficult to prove.[93] In any case, the affinities between mystical experiences and hypnotic states are an issue that increasingly began to preoccupy scholars.[94] However, the existence of a certain pattern in the behavior of the Besht reported in several places in the hagiography seems too obvious to be ignored.

Whether the pattern has to do with modes of behavior of the Besht himself, whether it was part of the very early history of Hasidism, or whether it was invented later by the copyists or the editors of the hagiography is difficult to decide conclusively with the available data. A perusal of the hagiography shows that it has been edited rather carelessly and it is hardly plausible that the editors inserted the hand gesture in six different places in the book. This is the reason why I am inclined to accept the authenticity of the gestural pattern in the historical Besht, and I assume that in one way or another he impacted the minds or the imagination of his subjects. It should be mentioned that the idea that it is possible to have such an impact is reminiscent of the theories of the famous Franz Anton Mesmer, active in the last decades of the 18th century in Central and Western Europe, regarding human magnetism. However, after examining the details of the mesmerian theories and practices, in my opinion, it is implausible that they could have influenced the details of the Hasidic hagiography, because the quasi-hypnotic transmission in mesmerism was related to healing of several people as a group, who were linked to each other in a frame (a *banquet*) by the touching of the patients' limbs by the hands of the healer or by transmitting a vital cosmic fluid.[95] Also the concept of induced amnesia is missing in the material related to mesmerism. Moreover, would this impact on Hasidic authors start only at the beginning of the 19th century, or would it be plausible to find other instances of influence in the vast Hasidic literature in addition to the hagiography? The absence of such an influence in the 19th century shows that this was a Beshtian practice that disappeared in Hasidism with his death. How he learned this practice or from whom is unclear.

Concluding Remarks

Last but not least, I assume that the voice of the Besht played an important role in his activities in general, either magical or spiritual, and in his hypothetical quasi-hypnotic effects in particular. Indeed, in many of his teachings, voice and pronunciation played a paramount role in the ritual more than in any other Jewish mystic.[96] Of interest in this context is the fact that when he lost his voice, Satan tried to hurt him,[97] and according to another passage, his death was preceded by a loss of his voice.[98] This apotheosis of the voice, which played indubitably a major role in both the emergence and the phenomenological structure of Hasidism, might have also played a certain role in fascinating some of the first followers of the Besht. Thus, the six miraculous stories discussed above differ quite significantly from the equally legendary stories of Luria because of the centrality of the hand gesture, the induction of amnesia, and the importance of the voice. This does not mean that Lurianic and other Kabbalistic influences are not operating on the Besht's activities or on the way his image has been shaped by others.[99]

However, the occult powers attributed to the Besht should be understood also in a broader structure in Jewish elites: that of Ashkenazi occultists, which left a strong impression on a variety of elite figures: R. Abraham Axelrod of Cologne, active also in Spain in the mid-13th century,[100] R. Lapidot Ashkenazi[101] and R. Isaac Luria Ashkenazi in mid-16th-century Safed,[102] and last but not least, the Besht. They differed in the breadth of their knowledge, the depth of their writings, or in their personality. I do not assume that there was anything like a secret tradition among the Ashkenazi elites has been transmitted orally since the end of the 13th century. However, we may assume a greater openness toward the unknown, which was more visible in the Ashkenazi culture than in other forms of Jewish communities that allowed the emergence of these types of personalities. The astonishment of even accomplished Kabbalists when encountering the Ashkenazi occultists is evident in some of the cases concerning those figures.[103] The exceptional powers attributed to the last Rabbi of Lubavitch are only one of the most remarkable examples in this line of Ashkenazi occultists.

Notes

1 *Major Trends in Jewish Mysticism* (Schocken Books, New York, 1995), p. 334, and his important article, "The Historical Image of the Besht," reprinted in *ha-Shalav ha-'Aḥaron*, eds. D. Assaf and E. Liebes ('Am 'Oved and the Magnes Press, Jerusalem, 2009), pp. 113, 124–125, 128–129, 138, 215 n. 77 (Hebrew), and see also in more general terms, ibidem, pp. 186–187. See also Louis Jacobs, *Hasidic Prayer* (Schocken Books, New York, 1978), p. 9; Ada Rapoport-Albert, "God and the Zaddik as the Two Focal Points of Hasidic Worship," in ed. G.D. Hundert, *Essential Papers on Hasidism* (New York University Press, New York, 1991), p. 313, Shmuel Ettinger, "The Hasidic Movement-Reality and Ideals," ibidem, pp. 237–238; Arthur Green, "The *Zaddiq* as *Axis Mundi* in Later Judaism," in ed. L. Fine, *Essential Papers on Kabbalah* (New York University Press, New York, London, 1995), p. 303; Stephen Sharot, *Messianism, Mysticism and Magic* (University of North Carolina Press, Chapel Hill, 1982), pp. 138, 158–164; Joseph Dan, *The Hasidic Story* (in Hebrew), (Keter, Jerusalem, 1975), pp. 88–90 (Hebrew); S. Daniel Breslauer, "Charisma and Leadership: Images of Hasidism," *Hebrew Studies*, vol. 20–21(1979–1980), pp. 88–97; and Rachel Elior, *The Mystical Origins of Hasidism*, (The Littman Library, Oxford and Portland, OR, 2006), pp. 72, 184. More recently, see the intense resort to charisma in the context of Hasidism in Philip Wexler, *Mystical Interactions, Sociology, Jewish Mysticism and Education* (Cherub Press, Los Angeles, 2007), pp. 27–33, 68, 170. See also Moshe Idel, *Ben: Sonship and Jewish Mysticism* (Continuum, London, New York, 2008), pp. 531–534.
2 See Gershom Scholem, *ha-Shalav ha-'Aharon*, p. 113, who asserts that those widespread terms do not reveal the entire truth, and Martin Buber, *Tales of Hasidim, Early Masters*, tr. Olga Marx, (Schocken Books, New York, 1964), p. 12, who rejects the assumption of "suggestive powers" attributed to the Besht.
3 See Joseph Weiss, *Studies in Eastern European Jewish Mysticism*, ed. D. Goldstein, (The Littman Library, Oxford, 1985), pp. 4, 6. This statement is less clear to me, and it refers probably to the pneumatic nature of some of the persons in this circle.
4 See, especially, Ada Rapoport-Albert, "The Hasidic Movement after 1772, Structural Continuity and Change," Ada Rapoport-Albert, ed., *Hasidism Reappraised* (The Littman Li-

brary of Jewish Civilization, London, Portland, OR, 1996), pp. 76–140, and Imanuel Etkes, "The Zaddik: The Interrelationship between Religious Doctrine and Social Organization," ibidem, p. 160; idem, *The Besht: Magician, Mystic, and Leader* (Brandeis University Press/University Press of New England, Waltham, MA/Hanover, NH, 2004), tr. Saadya Sternberg, p. 249.

5 See Max Weber, *Ancient Judaism*, tr. H.H. Gerth and D. Martindale (The Free Press, New York, 1952), p. 260.
6 See Michael Attiyah Flower, *The Seer in Ancient Greece* (University of California Press, Berkeley, 2008), pp. 5, 29–30, 42, 49, 51, 58–59.
7 See Ivan G. Marcus, "Judah the Pietist and Eleazar of Worms: From Charismatic to Conventional Leadership," *Jewish Mystical Leaders and Leadership in the Thirteenth Century*, eds. M. Idel and M. Ostow (Jason Aronson, New York, 1998), pp. 97–126; Lawrence Fine, "The Art of Metoposcopy: A study in Isaac Luria's Charismatic Knowledge," in ed. L. Fine, *Essential Papers on Kabbalah* (New York University Press, New York, London, 1995), pp. 315–317, and Jonathan Garb, "The Cult of the Saints in Lurianic Kabbalah," *JQR*, vol. 98 (2008), pp. 203–229.
8 See Etkes, *The Besht*, p. 258.
9 Max Weber, *Economy and Society: An Outline of Interpretative Sociology*, eds, by G. Roth and C. Wittich (University of California Press, Berkeley and London, 1978), vol. I, p. 241.
10 Clifford Geertz, "Centers, Kings, and Charisma," *Local Knowledge: Further Readings in Interpretive Anthropology*, ed. C. Geertz (New York, 1983), pp. 121–146, and Charles Lindholm, *Charisma*, (Blackwell, London, 1993).
11 See my *Hasidism: Between Ecstasy and Magic* (SUNY Press, Albany, 1995), p. 207.
12 D.P. Walker, *Spiritual and Demonic Magic: From Ficino to Campanella* (London, The Warburg Institute, 1958), pp. 82–83.
13 Ioan P. Couliano, *Eros and Magic in the Renaissance* (University of Chicago Press, Chicago, London, 1987), pp. 108–109. Couliano resorts in this context to the concept of hypnosis.
14 The north-eastern region of modern Romania, Bukovina or Northern Moldavia, was designated in the Besht's time as Wallachia. On this issue see M. Idel, "R. Israel Ba'al Shem Tov 'In the State of Walachia': Widening the Besht's Cultural Panorama," in *Holy Dissent: Jewish and Christian Mystics in Eastern Europe*, ed. Glenn Dynner (Wayne State University Press, Detroit, 2011), pp. 69–103.
15 His face became inflamed or radiant. This is a leitmotif related to the Besht's change of countenance. See, e.g., *In Praise of the Baal Shem Tov*, pp. 28, 136. See also ibidem, p. 30, 45–46. See also the description of Sabbatai Tzevi, in Gershom Scholem, *Sabbatai Sevi, The Mystical Messiah 1626–1676*, tr. R. J. Zwi Werblowsky, (Princeton University Press, Princeton, NJ, 1973), p. 132. In both cases, it seems that the fiery appearance of the face is related to a status close to that of Moses. On the affinity between Besht and the biblical Moses see below.
16 This is an inversion of a statement found in *BT, Babba Batra*, fol. 10a.
17 *In Praise of the Baal Shem Tov, [Shivhei ha-Besht]*, trs. and eds., Dan Ben-Amos & Jerome R. Mintz (Schocken Books, New York, 1984), p. 250, no. 242; *Shivhei ha-besht*, ed. A. Rubinstein (Reuven Mass, Jerusalem, 1991), p. 206:

"פעם אחת היה הבעש"ט במדינת וואלחיא ושם היה אצלם יין קרוש שנוטף מן הענבים, וכשמערבין בכוס שתים או שלוש טיפין קטנים אי אפשר לשתות מפני חזקו. וכיבד בעל הבית את הבעש"ט בכוס קטן מיין. וכשטעמו אמר הבעש"ט: הלא יינך טוב, למה כוסך קטן. השיב בעל הבית כי סכנה הוא לשתות כוס גדול. ויאמר הבעש"ט: אין אני מתיירא מזה. ונתנו לו כוס גדול ושתה את כולו. והסתכלו כולם בו שנעשו פניו אדומים, וכל שערותיו עמדו כמו שב ממש, ונתבהלו כולם. אבל הבעש"ט העביר ידיו על פניו והפיג יינו כרגע. ותמהו מאוד על זה. ואמר כי ידוע שיין קשה פחד מפיגו, וכאשר התבונן בגדולתו יתברך, נפל עליו פחד ורעדה מגדולתו ית' והפיג את היין מכל וכל."

18 See ibidem, p. 11 and the suggestion of Dov Noy, "The Besht in the Carpathian Mountains," *Mahanayyim*, vol. 46 (1960), pp. 66–73 (Hebrew), that this statement reflects a possible impact of the Hutzul group, which was active in the Northern Carpathians.
19 See *In Praise of the Baal Shem Tov*, p. 124.
20 Cf. *Sifrei* Naso, 22. See also R. Jacob ibn Haviv, *'Ein Ya'aqov*, Nazir I.
21 Zakhariah 3:4. According to some legends it is Joshua ben Yehotzadaq, a Great Priest in the first temple. See *Midrash Tanhuma'* on Leviticus 6, and R. Bahya ben Asher, on Leviticus 4:2 and Louis Ginzberg, *Legends of the Jews* (Jewish Publication Society, Philadelphia, 1968), vol. IV, pp. 336–367, vol. VI, pp. 426–427, n. 108. However, it is important for our understanding of the Besht to note that this tradition occurs also in *'Ein Ya'aqov*, in the Palestinian Talmud, in *Ta'anit*, ch. 30. This book was known to the Besht as we shall see. See also Weiss, p. 100.
22 *In Praise of the Baal Shem Tov*, p. 220, cf. ed. Rubinstein, p. 279:
פעם אחת הלך הבעש״ט עם הרב מ׳ דוד פרקעס למרחץ ובהליכתם בא כנגדם איש יפה תואר קווצותיו סדורות לו תלתלים ולבוש בגדים נאים וכשבא האיש קרוב אליהם קפץ הבעש״ט לצדדין הרחק מאוד. כשעבר מלפנים חזר הבעש״ט העביר ידיו על עיניו ואמר ראה מי הוא מי שעבר לפנינו וראה שהוא אוד מוצל מאש בכל בקצותיו אכלה האש.
23 This part of the story will be discussed separately in another study. See also below, the story about the initiation of the Great Maggid.
24 On this treatise, see Malakhi Beit-Arié, *Perek Shira, Introductions and Critical Edition* (Ph.D. Thesis, Hebrew University, Jerusalem, 1966), 2 volumes (Hebrew). According to Beit-Arié, this composition belongs to the earliest phase of the *Ma'aseh Merkavah* literature.
25 *In Praise of the Baal Shem Tov*, pp. 243–244.
26 Ibidem, p. 244.
27 Ibidem, p. 244, ed. Rubinstein, no. 201, p. 299.
28 Ibidem, pp. 244–245.
29 See Idel, *Hasidism*, pp. 79–80.
30 See the Introduction of R. Shelomo of Lutzk to *Maggid Devarav le-Ya'aqov* (The Magnes Press, Jerusalem, 1976), pp. 2–3, and Haviva Pedaya, "The Besht, R. Jacob Joseph of Polonoy, and the Maggid of Mezeritch: Basic Lines for a Religious-Typological Approach," *Daat*, vol. 45 (2000), p. 39 (Hebrew).
31 Introduction, ibidem.
32 *In Praise of the Baal Shem Tov*, p. 238, ed. Rubinstein, p. 239.
33 Ibidem, pp. 237–238.
34 See also ibidem, p. 210. On this question see Shilo Pachter, *Shemirat ha-Berit, The History of the Prohibition of Wasting Seed* (Ph.D. thesis, Hebrew University, Jerusalem, 2006) (Hebrew).
35 *In Praise of the Baal Shem Tov*, p. 255.
36 *In Praise of the Baal Shem Tov*, pp. 124–125.
37 See also ibidem, p. 53, where he is described as the cantor of the Besht.
38 Compare also to the description of how R. Tzevi Sofer was reading the book of the *Zohar* to the Besht, and the description of his position, ibidem, p. 79.
39 That is, the preacher.
40 This is a historical figure that was active in Miedzibusz in the Besht's lifetime. See *In Praise of the Baal Shem Tov*, pp. 206–207.
41 This is an interesting reference as to a view that being in the immediate ambiance of the Besht gave one the powers of a prophet. This passage should be added to the material I adduced in my "The Besht as Prophet and as Talismanic Magician," in eds. Avidov Lipsker and Rella Kushelevsky, *Studies in Jewish Narrative: Ma'aseh Sippur, Presented to Yoav Elstein* (Bar Ilan University Press, Ramat Gan, 2006), pp. 122–133 (Hebrew), and "On Prophecy and Early Hasidism," in ed. Moshe Sharon, *Studies in Modern Religions, Reli-*

gious Movements, and the Babi-Baha'i Faiths (Brill, Leiden, The Netherlands, 2004), pp. 65–70. See also below the similarities between the Besht and Moses.

42 See ed. A. Gross (Tel Aviv, 2005), 3:7, p. 126; 4:1, p. 129.

43 *In Praise of the Baal Shem Tov*, pp. 124–125, ed. Rubenstein, pp. 169–171:

פ"[עם]א[חת] במוצאי־שבת ציווה הבעש"ט לחתן חורגו רבי יוסף אשכנזי שיאמר לפניו עין יעקב. והוא שכב על המטה ושמע מפיו העין יעקב. ובמקום א' אמר הבעש"ט תורה על מאמר א' מעין יעקב, וחזר ואמר לפניו עין יעקב. ובתוך האמירה ראה רבי יוסף הנ"ל את המגיד מישרים ושמו רבי יוסף שנפטר ערך ג' רבע שנה מקודם זה, וראה אותו שנכנס לבית לבוש בגדי שבת וכובע על ראשו שקורין "הוט", ואמר בקול רם: שבוע טובה לרבינו, והולך כמו בחיים ומטה בידו. וכשראה אותו, חרד מאוד ונפל העין יעקב מידו, והעביר הבעל־שם־טוב את ידו על פניו ושוב לא ראה אותו... ושהה עמו כחצי שעה או יותר, ושמע שהבעל־שם־טוב מדבר עמו. ואחר־כך קרא הבעל־שם־טוב לרבי יוסף ואמר בזה"ל: דאייטש בוא אלי! ובא, ואמר לפניו עוד עין יעקב. ובתוך הלמוד התחיל הבעל־שם־טוב להתרעם עליו ואמר לו: למה פחדת? האם שחט רבי יוסף המגיד דייטש כמוך בחייו שפחדת ממנו לאחר מותו. שאל אותו: מחמת איזה זכות ראיתי אותו? אמר לו: מפני שאמרת לפני ואני אמרתי לפניך והייתי מזכך אותך בדיבורי ונתקשרנו שנינו והיינו לאחד, ומחמת זה ראית אותי, ואילו היית מתחזק בשכלך היית שומע מה שדיבר עמי, וגם אתה היית שואל אותו כל מה שליבך חפץ והיה משיב לך, ולא עוד אלא שהיה לך עמו היכרות והיית רואה אותו בתמידות. והיה רבי יוסף מצטער מאוד על זה הדבר, כי היא מדרגת נבואה כשרואין נשמת צדיק, כאמור בספר שערי קדושה של רבי חיים וויטאל. ושאל: למה בא ומה הצטרכותו? ואמר: בשביל הצטרכות שלו בא.

On this legend, see Haviva Pedaya, "The Besht, R. Jacob Joseph of Polonnoye, and the Maggid of Mezeritch," p. 36, n. 36.

44 See my "'Your Word Stands Firm in Heaven'—An Inquiry into the Early Traditions of R. Israel Baal Shem Tov and Their Reverberations in Hasidism," *Kabbalah*, vol. 20 (2009), pp. 250–252 (Hebrew).

45 *In Praise of the Baal Shem Tov*, p. 54:

אמר לו: כסבור אתה שחלמת חלום, לא כן, ראית חזון. גם אני ראיתי ובעיני נתגשם.

See also Pedaya, "The Besht, R. Jacob Joseph of Polonnoye, and the Maggid of Mezeritch," pp. 53–54. In this context also another passage from the hagiography should be mentioned, ibidem, p. 182, where the Besht instructed a preacher how to see a demon and then how to remove such a vision.

46 See other instances of telepathy discussed in Jonathan Garb, *Shamanic Trance in Modern Kabbalah*, (University of Chicago Press, Chicago, 2011), pp. 108–112.

47 *In Praise of the Baal Shem Tov*, p. 256.

48 On the details of the report of this meeting, in fact more than one, see M. Idel, "R. Israel Ba'al Shem Tov's Two "Encounters" with Sabbatai Tzevi," *The Beauty of Japheth in the Tents of Shem, Studies in Honour of Mordechai Omer*, eds. H. Taragan and N. Gal, [= *Assaph, Studies in Art History*, vol. 23–24] (Tel Aviv, 2010), pp. 471–491.

49 'Avodat Yisrael, Commentary on Pirqei 'Avot, ch. 5:8 (Warsaw, 1875), fol. 89b:

והעביר האר"י ז"ל ידו על פניו והציב לפניו העבירה עצמה :

On the technique of Luria to discern one's sins on the face of the sinner, see Lawrence Fine, *Physician of the Soul, Healer of the Cosmos, Isaac Luria and His Kabbalistic Fellowship* (Stanford University Press, Stanford, CA, 2003), pp. 150–167.

50 For the assumption that the printed versions of the legend have been doctored in order to serve the argument of the son of the founder of Habad Hasidism, R. Dov Baer, in his polemic with a competitor about the succession of the leadership of this Hasidic movement, see Moshe Rosman, *The Founder of Hasidism, A Quest for the Historical Ba'al Shem Tov* (University of California Press, Berkeley, Los Angeles, London, 1996), pp. 187–211.

51 See his "*Shivḥei ha-Besht: Mesirah, 'Arikhah, Hadpasah*," *Proceedings of the 11th World Congress of Jewish Studies* (Jerusalem, 1994), vol. C2, pp. 145–152 (Hebrew).

52 On this issue, see especially Rosman, *The Founder of Hasidism*, pp. 143–170, Etkes, *The Besht: Magician, Mystic, and Leader*, pp. 3–4, 203–248, Israel Bartal, "Aliyyat Rabbi Eleazar Roqeaḥ, me-'Amsterdam le-'Eretz Yisrael" (in Hebrew) *Meḥqarim 'al Toledot*

Yahadut Holland, ed. Y. Michman (Magnes Press, Jerusalem, 1985), vol. 4, pp. 7–25, and my study "R. Israel Baʻal Shem Tov 'In the State of Walachia': Widening the Besht's Cultural Panorama," (n. 14 above). A positive attitude toward the content of at least parts of the hagiography is the ground for Joseph Weiss's reconstruction of early Hasidism, as it is predicated on some passages dealing with the circle of the pneumatics related to the Besht. See especially his *Studies*, pp. 27–42.

53 This is a recurring feature related to the Besht's prayer. See in the earlier passage quoted above and *In Praise of the Baal Shem Tov,* pp. 50–52.
54 See *BT., Hagigah*, fol. 14b.
55 In the early manuscript it is written סבב which may be understood as laying him down in a circle form, namely in a fetal position.
56 In the early manuscript it is written עיגל, which may mean a lamb, while all the other versions have here עגול, that is, circle.
57 *In Praise of the Baal Shem Tov*, p. 83. I changed slightly the English translation, at times following the Hebrew text as printed in Yehoshua Monshine, ed., *Shivhei Ha-Baal Shem Tov* (Jerusalem 1972), pp. 170–171:

ובאתי ומצאתי אותו יושב וכר קטן על ראשו ומלובש בעור של זאבים מהופך. ושאל אותי אם למדתי חכמת הקבלה, ואמרתי: הן! והי" ספר א' מונח לפניו על השולחן, וצווה אותי לאמור לפניו בספר זה. ובספר היה כתוב במאמרים קטנים, וכל מאמר היה התחלה: אמר ר"י סח לי מט"ט שר הפנים. ואמרתי לפניו עמוד או חצי עמוד, ואמר הבעל-שם-טוב: לא כן הוא, אני אומר לפניך. ואמר לפני. ובתוך כך נזדעזע וקם ואמר: אנחנו עוסקים במעשה מרכבה ואני יושב. ואמר בעמידה. ובתוך הדבורים סבב אותי במטה כמו עיג[ו]ל. ושוב לא ראיתי אותו רק שמעתי קולות, וראיתי ברקים ולפידים נוראים. והיה כך ערך שני שעות, ונתפחדתי מאוד, ומזה הפחד התחלתי להתעלף.

See the notes of the English translators ibidem, pp. 322–323 and to additional bibliography on this story, see Idel, *Hasidism*, p. 353 n. 3. See also Martin Buber, *Origin and Meaning of Hasidism*, ed. and tr. M. Friedman (Horizon Press, New York, 1966), p. 37 and Naftali Loewenthal, *Communicating the Infinite: The Emergence of the Habad School* (University of Chicago Press, Chicago, 1990), pp. 18–19, who offers another English translation, and Garb, *Shamanic Trance in Modern Kabbalah*, pp. 44–45.
58 See what I wrote on this passage in Idel, *Hasidism*, pp. 171–173, and p. 353, n. 5. Compare, however, Pedaya, "The Besht, R. Jacob Joseph of Polonnoye, and the Maggid of Mezeritch," p. 31, who gives the impression that she, not I, emphasized the importance of performance. Compare what she wrote ibidem, p. 41, n. 66. Interestingly enough, she refers only to one part of my analysis of the passage on p. 172 and ignores both the opening and the continuation of my discussion of this passage on pp. 171, 173 and 353, n. 5. This fragmentary and selective reference creates an artificial contradiction by the gist of her two discussions and what she wrongly attributes to me, which is quite close to her "innovative" claims. A superficial reading of my book on *Hasidism*, as well as many of my other studies, will easily show that the importance of performance was central to my entire academic project. See, e.g., my discussion of the category of the pneumatic interpreter in *Kabbalah: New Perspectives* (Yale University Press, New Haven, CT, 1988), pp. 241–243, and *Absorbing Perfection: Kabbalah and Interpretation* (Yale University Press, New Haven, CT, 2002), pp. 181–185. See also the next footnote.
59 For the dominance of the oral performance in Jewish mysticism see, in addition to the book on Hasidism, also, e.g., my "Reification of Language in Jewish Mysticism," in ed. Steven Katz, *Mysticism and Language* (Oxford University Press, New York, 1992), pp. 61–63, and for the many references to my earlier discussions of performance, see M. Idel, "Performance, Intensification and Experience in Jewish Mysticism," *Archaeus,* vol. XIII (2009), pp. 93–134. For more on this issue, see my "Modes of Cleaving to the Letters of the Alphabet in the tradition of Israel Baʻal Shem Tov—A Sample Analysis," forthcoming in *Jewish History* (2012).

60 On this posture see M. Idel, *Kabbalah: New Perspectives*, pp. 78–79, 82–83, and *Hasidism*, p. 353 n. 4; Paul Fenton, "La "tête entre les genoux": contribution à l'étude d'une posture méditative dans la mystique juive et islamique," *Revue d'Histoire et de Philosophie Religieuses,* vol. LXXII (1992), pp. 413–426, and Pedaya, "The Besht, R. Jacob Joseph of Polonnoye, and the Maggid of Mezeritch: Basic Lines for a Religious-Typological Approach," pp. 53–54.
61 In this other version of the Great Maggid's initiation story, many of the details found in the translated version are missing. I consider it derivative. It has been preserved in R. Aharon Kohen Perlov of Apta in his compilation printed in 1794/1795, *Keter Shem Tov*, cf. ed. J.E. Shohet, *Keter Shem Tov ha-Shalem*, (Kehot, Brooklyn, 2004), p. 264, n. 424.
62 See Avraham Ya'ari, "Two Basic Versions of 'Shiv<u>h</u>ei ha-Besht,'" *Qiriat Sefer*, vol. 39 (1964), pp. 403–407 (Hebrew) and the different approach of Monshine, *Shive<u>h</u>ei ha-Besht,* p. 278.
63 Such a vision is consonant with statements concerning his causing the descent of supernal light or power by a variety of activities, as found in the writings of his disciples. See my "'Your Word Stands Firm in Heaven,'" pp. 272–273, and "Modes of Cleaving to 'Letters' and Their Effects," n. 86, 133. Compare, however, to Pedaya, "The Besht, R. Jacob Joseph of Polonnoye, and the Maggid of Mezeritch: Basic Lines for a Religious-Typological Approach," pp. 25–73, a study based upon the assumption (incorrect as pointed out in my articles cited in this footnote) that the Besht was solely an "elevating" and ascending figure, not someone who caused the descent of supernal entities. See, especially pp. 36, 70, where dealing with the impact of the Heikhalot literature, she does not refer to the legend about the Besht's causing the descent of the Prince of the Torah as found in the hagiography.
64 The meaning is that the copyist reacted to a text found before him, which indicates that it may predate the edition and certainly the printing. See *In Praise of the Baal Shem Tov*, p. 32.
65 From R. Arieh Leib.
66 Literally, *language*.
67 See also below the passage adduced from the book of the Besht's grandson.
68 *In Praise of the Baal Shem Tov*, pp. 83–84, *Shive<u>h</u>ei ha-Besht,* ed. Monshine, p. 171:
ואומר אני הכותב: כמדומה לי שזה הי׳ קבלת התורה, שכן שמעתי כמה פעמים מפי הרב החסיד דקהילת קודש פולנאה, שקיבל מהבעש״ט תורתו השייך לשורש נשמתו בקולות וברקים...שמעתי מהרב זה הלשון כמו שקבלו ישראל את התורה בכלל כן קבל הבעש״ט בפרט
69 For the possibility that this is R. Jacob Joseph, see Loewenthal, *Communicating the Infinite*, p. 19.
70 On this view, see Scholem, *On the Kabbalah and Its Symbolism*, tr. Ralph Manheim (Schocken, New York, 1996), pp. 64–65, and Idel, *Absorbing Perfections*, pp. 96–99, and the pertinent footnotes. This is a common theme, and it has been adopted also by R. Arieh Leib. See his *Qol 'Arieh*, (Koretz, 1793), fols. 38d, 40b.
71 *In Praise of the Baal Shem Tov*, p. 84. Compare to Pedaya, "The Besht, R. Jacob Joseph of Polonnoye, and the Maggid of Mezeritch," p. 32, n. 24.
72 See Idel, *Absorbing Perfections*, pp. 470–481.
73 *In Praise of the Baal Shem Tov*, p. 82. The Hebrew text, ed. A. Rubinstein, *Shivhei ha-Besht,* (Reuven Mass, Jerusalem, 1991), p. 127:
ורצה לרפאות אותו בדיבורים. ושמעתי מרבי גרשון דקהילת קודש פובליץ שהבעל-שם-טוב היה הולך אליו כמו שני שבועות וישב כנגדו ואמר תהלים, ואחר-כך אמר הבעל-שם-טוב אליו: הייתי רוצה לרפאת אותך בדיבורים כי היא רפואה קימת, ועכשו אני צריך לעסוק עמך ברפואות.
In regard to the assumption that mystics acquire some extraordinary powers as part of their experiences, see, e.g., Jess Byron Hollenback, *Mysticism, Experience, Response, and Empowerment* (Penn State University Press, University Park, PA, 1996). For healing with words in modern Hasidism, see the material cited by by Don Seeman, "Ritual Efficacy, Hasidic Mysticism and 'Useless Suffering in the Warsaw Ghetto," *HTR*, vol. 101, 3–4 (2008), p. 478, n. 54.

74 *In Praise of the Baal Shem Tov*, p. 83.
75 *Degel Maḥaneh 'Efrayyim*, p. 257:

עוד שמעתי ממנו שאביו שלו לקחו בלא דיבור כמו משה רבינו ע"ה ואם היה לוקחו בדיבור היה ממלא בתורתו כל חללי דעלמא וביער כל הקליפות והיה מביא משיח

Compare this statement with the position that has been expressed in the *Holy Epistle*, where the dissemination of religious knowledge is accompanied by extermination of shells, as a prelude to the advent of the Messiah. See also Isaiah Tishby, *Studies in Kabbalah and Its Branches* (The Magnes Press, Jerusalem, 1993), vol. 2, pp. 507–508 (Hebrew).

76 *In Praise of the Baal Shem Tov*, p. 11.
77 Ibidem, p. 258.
78 See also the story of R. Barukh of Miedzibusz, who told his brother, R. Efrayyim of Sudylkov, that because of his visit to the tomb of the Besht, he received the Torah as Moses did in Sinai. See *Butzina' di-Nehora'* (Lemberg,1884), no pagination. Thus, it seems that a family tradition preceded the composition of the hagiography as to the relation between the Besht and the Sinaitic experiences that others experienced because of some form of contact with him. R. Efrayyim died in 1800.
79 *In Praise of the Baal Shem Tov*, pp. 13–18.
80 Chone Shmeruk, *Yiddish Literature in Poland, Historical Studies and Perspectives* (The Magnes Press, Jerusalem, 1981), pp. 119–146 (Hebrew).
81 *In Praise of the Baal Shem Tov*, pp. 17–18.
82 See Idel, *Absorbing Perfections*, pp. 140–142, 145–146, 173–178.
83 See the famous passage in the *Holy Epistle*.
84 *Degel Maḥaneh 'Efrayyim* (Jerusalem, 1995), p. 257:

דא שווער איך אייך שיש איש בעולם ששומע תורה מפי קודשא בריך הוא ושכינתיה לא מפי מלאך ולא מפי וכו'

85 *In Praise of the Baal Shem Tov*, p. 6. See also similar comparisons to Moses, adduced in the name of the Besht in ibidem, pp. 28, 198, 204. In modern times, the Besht has been compared to Moses by Abraham Y. Heschel. See M. Idel, *Old Worlds, New Mirrors: On Jewish Mysticism and Twentieth-Century Thought* (University of Pennsylvania Press, Philadelphia, 2010), p. 222.
86 See *Ben Porat Yosef*, (Koretz, 1781), fol. 99bc:

מעלת משה רבינו עליו השלום שהעלה ותיקן דיבורו, ותחלה היו צאן שהיה רועה אותן, ואחר כך בגלגול נעשו תלמידיו, שנתן להם התורה, ולמד עמהן וכו' ודפח"ח

87 *In Praise of the Baal Shem Tov*, p. 129.
88 See *Shivehei ha-Besht*, ed. Monshine, p. 218.
89 See my "Modes of Cleaving to the Letters."
90 Amir Raz and Theodore Shapiro, "Hypnosis and Neuroscience, A Cross Talk Between Clinical and Cognitive Research," *Arch Gen Psychiatry*, vol. 59 (Jan 2002), p. 85.
91 "The Besht, R. Jacob Joseph of Polonnoye, and the Maggid of Mezeritch."
92 See Ernest R. Hilgard, "A Neodissociation Interpretation of Hypnosis," in *Theories of Hypnosis: Current Models and Perspectives*, eds. S.J. Lynn and J. W. Rhue (The Guilford Press, New York, London, 1991), pp. 84–85.
93 For an attempt to deal with the relationship between auto-hypnosis and some aspects of Jewish mysticism see M. Bowers and S. Glasner, "Autohypnotic Aspects of the Kabbalistic Concept of Kavanah," *Journal of Clinical and Experimental Hypnosis*, vol. 6 (1958), pp. 3–23, and see the reservations about this explanation found in M. Idel, *The Mystical Experience in Abraham Abulafia* (SUNY Press, Albany, 1987), pp. 40–41. For the resort to hypnosis as a partial explanation of some other aspects of Jewish mysticism, see Yoram Bilu, "A Psychologist Looks at 'The Angels of Oil': The Nexus between Divination and Hypnosis in a Jewish Perspective," *Megamot*, vol. 27, 3 (1982), pp. 251–261 (Hebrew), and Garb's more comprehensive thesis related to the place of hypnosis in his *Shamanic Trance in Modern Kabbalah*, pp. 1, 8–11, 22.

94 See Jerome Kroll and Bernard Bachrach, *The Mystic Mind: The Psychology of Medieval Mystics and Ascetics,* (Routledge, New York, London, 2005), pp. 40–46; Jess B. Hollenback, *Mysticism, Experience, Response and Empowerment,* pp. 182–183, 185, or Robert W. Marks, *The Story of Hypnotism,* (Prentice-Hall, New York, 1947), pp. 149–169.
95 See Robert Darnton, *Mesmerism and the End of the Enlightenment in France,* (Harvard University Press, Cambridge, MA., 1968), p. 8. Though the theory of the cosmic fluid is reminiscent of the Hasidic theory of *hiyyut,* vitality, the sources of the Hasidic views are found in Cordoverian Kabbalah. It is plausible that the affinity between the Hasidic widespread resort to the concept of *hiyyut* and Mesmer's theory of cosmic fluid, are connected to a common astrological theory widespread in the Middle Ages, a point interesting in itself but it does not concern us here.
96 See Idel, "Modes of Cleaving to Letters."
97 See *In Praise of the Baal Shem Tov,* pp. 187–188.
98 See ibidem, p. 136.
99 See Idel, "The Tzaddiq and His Sparks, From Kabbalah to Hasidism," forthcoming in *JQR,* vol. 103.1 (2013).
100 M. Idel, "Ashkenazi Esotericism and Kabbalah in Barcelona," *Hispania Judaica Bulletin,* vol. 5 (2007), pp. 86–100.
101 See M. Idel, "R. Yehudah Hallewah and His Composition *Zafenat Pa'aneah*," *Shalem,* vol. 4 (1984), pp. 146–148 (Hebrew).
102 See Fine, *Physician of the Soul.*
103 See in the previous three footnotes.

Bibliography

Aharon Kohen Perlov of Apta, *Keter Shem Tov,* ed. J.E. Shohet, *Keter Shem Tov ha-Shalem* (Kehot, Brooklyn, 2004) (Hebrew).

Arieh Leib of Polonnoye, *Qol 'Arieh* (Koretz, 1793) (Hebrew).

Attiyah Flower, Michael, *The Seer in Ancient Greece,* (University of California Press, Berkeley, 2008).

Bartal, Israel, "Aliyyat Rabbi Eleazar Roqeah, me-'Amsterdam le-'Eretz Yisrael," *Mehqarim 'al Toledot Yahadut Holland,* ed. Y. Michman (Magnes Press, Jerusalem, 1985), vol. 4, pp. 7–25 (Hebrew).

Barukh of Miedzibusz, *Butzina' di-Nehora'* (Lemberg, 1884), (Hebrew).

Beit-Arié, Malakhi, *Perek Shira, Introductions and Critical Edition* (Ph.D. thesis, Hebrew University, Jerusalem, 1966), 2 volumes (Hebrew).

Bilu, Yoram, "A Psychologist Looks at 'The Angels of Oil': The Nexus between Divination and Hypnosis in a Jewish Perspective," *Megamot,* vol. 27, 3 (1982), pp. 251–261 (Hebrew).

Bowers, M. and Glasner, S. "Autohypnotic Aspects of the Kabbalistic Concept of Kavanah," *Journal of Clinical and Experimental Hypnosis,* vol. 6 (1958), pp. 3–23.

Breslauer, S. Daniel, "Charisma and Leadership: Images of Hasidism," *Hebrew Studies,* vol. 20–21 (1979–1980), pp. 88–97.

Buber, Martin, *Tales of Hasidim, Early Masters,* tr. Olga Marx (Schocken Books, New York, 1964).

———. *Origin and Meaning of Hasidism,* ed. and tr. M. Friedman (Horizon Press, New York, 1966).

Couliano, Ioan P., *Eros and Magic in the Renaissance* (University of Chicago Press, Chicago, London, 1987).

Dan, Joseph, *The Hasidic Story* (Keter, Jerusalem, 1975) (Hebrew).

Darnton, Robert, *Mesmerism and the End of the Enlightenment in France* (Harvard University Press, Cambridge, MA., 1968).

Elior, Rachel, *The Mystical Origins of Hasidism* (The Littman Library, Oxford and Portland, OR, 2006).
Etkes, Imanuel, "The Zaddik: The Interrelationship between Religious Doctrine and Social Organization," in Ada Rapoport-Albert, ed., *Hasidism Reappraised* (The Littman Library, London, Portland, OR, 1996), pp. 159–167.
———. *The Besht: Magician, Mystic, and Leader* (Waltham, MA/Hanover, NH: Brandeis University Press/University Press of New England, 2004), tr. Saadya Sternberg.
Ettinger, Shmuel, "The Hasidic Movement—Reality and Ideals," in ed. G.D. Hundert, *Essential Papers on Hasidism* (New York University Press, New York, 1991), pp. 251–166.
Fenton, Paul, "La "tête entre les genoux": contribution à l'étude d'une posture méditative dans la mystique juive et islamique," *Revue d'Histoire et de Philosophie Religieuses*, vol. LXXII (1992), pp. 413–426.
Fine, Lawrence, "The Art of Metoposcopy: A Study in Isaac Luria's Charismatic Knowledge," in ed. L. Fine, *Essential Papers on Kabbalah* (New York University Press, New York, London, 1995), pp. 79–101.
———. *Physician of the Soul, Healer of the Cosmos, Isaac Luria and His Kabbalistic Fellowship* (Stanford University Press, Stanford, CA, 2003).
Garb, Jonathan, "The Cult of the Saints in Lurianic Kabbalah," *JQR*, vol. 98 (2008), pp. 203–229.
———. *Shamanic Trance in Modern Kabbalah* (University of Chicago Press, Chicago, 2011).
Geertz, Clifford, "Centers, Kings, and Charisma," *Local Knowledge: Further Essays in Interpretive Anthropology*, ed. C. Geertz (Basic Books, New York, 1983).
Ginzberg, Louis, *Legends of the Jews* (Jewish Publication Society, Philadelphia, 1968).
Green, Arthur, "The *Zaddiq* as *Axis Mundi* in Later Judaism," ed. L. Fine, *Essential Papers on Kabbalah* (New York University Press, New York, London, 1995), pp. 327–347.
Hilgard, Ernest R., "A Neodissociation Interpretation of Hypnosis," eds. S.J. Lynn and J.W. Rhue, *Theories of Hypnosis, Current Models and Perspectives* (The Guilford Press, New York, London, 1991), pp. 83–104.
Hollenback, Jess B., *Mysticism, Experience, Response and Empowerment* (Pennsylvania State University Press, University Park, PA, 1996).
Idel, Moshe, "R. Yehudah Hallewah and His Composition *Zafenat Pa'aneaḥ*," *Shalem*, vol. 4 (1984), 119–148. (Hebrew).
———. *The Mystical Experience in Abraham Abulafia* (SUNY Press, Albany, 1987).
———. *Kabbalah: New Perspectives* (Yale University Press, New Haven, CT, 1988).
———. "Reification of Language in Jewish Mysticism," ed. Steven Katz, *Mysticism and Language* (Oxford University Press, New York, 1992), pp. 42–79.
———. *Hasidism: Between Ecstasy and Magic* (SUNY Press, Albany, 1995).
———. *Ben: Sonship and Jewish Mysticism* (Continuum, London, New York, 2008)
———. "Performance, Intensification and Experience in Jewish Mysticism," *Archaeus*, vol. XIII (2009), pp. 93–134.
———. "'Your Word Stands Firm in Heaven'—An Inquiry into the Early Traditions of R. Israel Baal Shem Tov and Their Reverberations in Hasidism," *Kabbalah*, vol. 20 (2009), pp. 219–286 (Hebrew).
———. *Old Worlds, New Mirrors: On Jewish Mysticism and Twentieth-Century Thought* (University of Pennsylvania Press, Philadelphia, 2010).
———. "R. Israel Ba'al Shem Tov's Two 'Encounters' with Sabbatai Tzevi." Eds. H. Taragan and N. Gal, *The Beauty of Japheth in the Tents of Shem, Studies in Honour of Mordechai Omer* [= *Assaph, Studies in Art History*, vol. 23–24] (Tel Aviv, 2010), pp. 69–103.
———. "R. Israel Ba'al Shem Tov 'In the State of Walachia': Widening the Besht's Cultural Panorama," ed. Glenn Dynner, *Holy Dissent: Jewish and Christian Mystics in Eastern Europe* (Wayne State University Press, Detroit, 2011), pp. 69–103.
———. "Modes of Cleaving to the Letters of the Alphabet in the tradition of Israel Ba'al Shem Tov—A Sample Analysis," forthcoming in *Jewish History* (2012).

———."The Tzaddiq and His Sparks, from Kabbalah to Hasidism," forthcoming in *JQR*, vol. 103.1 (2013).
In Praise of the Baal Shem Tov, [Shivhei ha-Besht], trs. and eds. Dan Ben-Amos and Jerome R. Mintz, (Schocken Books, New York, 1984).
Israel of Kuznitz, *'Avodat Yisrael, Commentary on Pirqei 'Avot* (Warsaw, 1875).
Jacob Joseph of Polonnoye, *Ben Porat Yosef* (Koretz, 1781) (Hebrew).
Jacobs, Louis, *Hasidic Prayer* (Schocken Books, New York, 1978).
Kroll, Jerome and Bachrach, Bernard, *The Mystic Mind: The Psychology of Medieval Mystics and Ascetics* (Routledge, New York, London, 2005).
Lindholm, Charles, *Charisma* (Blackwell, London, 1993).
Loewenthal, Naftali, *Communicating the Infinite: The Emergence of the Habad School* (University of Chicago Press, Chicago, 1990).
Ivan G. Marcus, "Judah the Pietist and Eleazar of Worms: From Charismatic to Conventional Leadership," eds. M. Idel and M. Ostow, *Jewish Mystical Leaders and Leadership in the Thirteenth Century* (Jason Aronson, New York, 1998), pp. 97–126.
Marks, Robert W., *The Story of Hypnotism* (Prentice-Hall, New York, 1947).
Monshine, Yehoshua, ed., *Shivhei Ha-Baal Shem Tov* (Jerusalem 1972) (Hebrew).
Moshe Hayyim Efrayyim of Sudylkov, *Degel Mahaneh 'Efrayyim* (Jerusalem, 1995) (Hebrew).
Noy, Dov, "The Besht in the Carpathian Mountains," *Mahanayyim*, vol. 46 (1960), pp. 66–73 (Hebrew).
Pachter, Shilo, *Shemirat ha-Berit, The History of the Prohibition of Wasting Seed* (Ph.D. thesis, Hebrew University, Jerusalem, 2006) (Hebrew).
Pedaya, Haviva, "The Besht, R. Jacob Joseph of Polonoy, and the Maggid of Mezeritch: Basic Lines for a Religious-Typological Approach," *Daat* vol. 45 (2000), pp. 25–73 (Hebrew).
Rapoport-Albert, Ada, "God and the Zaddik as the Two Focal Points of Hasidic Worship," in ed. G.D. Hundert, *Essential Papers on Hasidism* (New York University Press, New York, 1991), pp. 296–325.
———. "The Hasidic Movement after 1772, Structural Continuity and Change," ed. Ada Rapoport-Albert, *Hasidism Reappraised*, (The Littman Library, London, Portland, 1996), pp. 76–140.
Raz, Amir, and Shapiro, Theodore, "Hypnosis and Neuroscience, A Cross Talk Between Clinical and Cognitive Research," *Arch Gen Psychiatry*, vol. 59, (Jan. 2002), pp. 85–90.
Reiner, Elhanan, "*Shivhei ha-Besht: Mesirah, 'Arikhah, Hadpasah,*" *Proceedings of the 11th World Congress of Jewish Studies* (Jerusalem, 1994), vol. C2 (Hebrew).
Rosman, Moshe, *The Founder of Hasidism: A Quest for the Historical Ba'al Shem Tov* (University of California Press, Berkeley, Los Angeles, London, 1996), pp. 145–152.
Rubinstein, Avraham, ed. *Shivhei ha-Besht* (Reuven Mass, Jerusalem, 1991) (Hebrew).
Scholem, Gershom, *Major Trends in Jewish Mysticism* (Schocken Books, New York, 1995).
———. *On the Kabbalah and Its Symbolism*, tr. Ralph Manheim (Schocken Books, New York, 1996).
———. *Sabbatai Sevi, The Mystical Messiah 1626–1676*, tr. R. J. Zwi Werblowsky (Princeton University Press, Princeton, NJ, 1973).
———. "The Historical Image of the Besht," Reprinted in *ha-Shalav ha-'Aharon*, eds., D. Assaf and E. Liebes, ('Am 'Oved and the Magnes Press, Jerusalem, 2009) (Hebrew), pp. 106–138.
Seeman, Don, "Ritual Efficacy, Hasidic Mysticism and 'Useless Suffering' in the Warsaw Ghetto," *HTR*, vol. 101, 3–4 (2008), pp. 465–505.
Sharot, Steven, *Messianism, Mysticism and Magic*, (University of North Carolina Press, Chapel Hill, 1982).
Shelomo of Lutzk, Introduction to *Maggid Devarav le-Ya'aqov* (The Magnes Press, Jerusalem, 1976) (Hebrew).
Shmeruk, Chone, *Yiddish Literature in Poland: Historical Studies and Perspectives* (The Magnes Press, Jerusalem, 1981) (Hebrew).

Tishby, Isaiah, *Studies in Kabbalah and Its Branches*, (The Magnes Press, Jerusalem, 1993) (Hebrew).
Vital, Hayyim, *Sha'arei Qedushah,* ed. A. Gross (Tel Aviv, 2005) (Hebrew).
Walker, D.P., *Spiritual and Demonic Magic: From Ficino to Campanella* (London, The Warburg Institute, 1958).
Weber, Max, *Ancient Judaism*, trs. H.H. Gerth and D. Martindale (The Free Press, New York, 1952).
———. *Economy and Society: An Outline of Interpretative Sociology,* eds. G. Roth and C. Wittich (University of California Press, Berkeley and London, 1978), vol. I.
Weiss, Joseph, ed. D. Goldstein, *Studies in Eastern European Jewish Mysticism* (The Littman Library, Oxford, 1985).
Wexler, Philip, *Mystical Interactions, Sociology, Jewish Mysticism and Education* (Cherub Press, Los Angeles, 2007).
Ya'ari, Avraham, "Two Basic Versions of 'Shivḥei ha-Besht,'" *Qiriat Sefer*, vol. 39 (1964), pp. 272–249; 394–407; 552–562 (Hebrew).

FIVE

Society and Mysticism

Philip Wexler

Sociologists have had remarkably little to say about mysticism. Why this should be so, from a sociologist's of knowledge point of view, may have to do with the long historical wave of secularity in society, but it also derives from the continuing influence of so-called classical sociology, the reflexive voice of modernity. Durkheim, who defined the central focus of the field as social integration and its paradigmatic methodology as multivariate social statistics, cared—analytically—deeply about religion, but as cultic performance and collective belief. Magic is intentionally excluded because it is not institutional. ("There is no church of magic," in his oft-cited turn of phrase), and mysticism is only an adjectival modifier to the social energies created by collective, ritual assemblies.

It was Weber who addressed mysticism directly, from his interest in the question of meaning. And it was Weber who, in the words of his influential colleague, Ernst Troeltsch, assigns to it a "secondary" importance. Unlike Troeltsch, and Gershom Scholem—who follows him closely, in this regard—for whom mysticism is secondary to tradition, Weber degrades the social importance of mysticism because it is not the religious foundation of the dominant culture of modernity—rationalization and its apparatus of experts and specialists. It is worth, first quoting Troeltsch (1911/31) on the meaning of mysticism and its place in religion (pp.730–31):

> In the wider sense of the word, mysticism is simply the insistence upon a direct inward and present religious experience. It takes for granted the objective forms of religious life in worship, ritual, myth, and dogma; and it is either a reaction against these objective practices, which it tries to draw back into the living process, or it is the supplementing of traditional forms of worship by means of a personal and living stimulus. Mysticism is thus always something *secondary* (italics added). . .

Gershom Scholem, the founding and canonical scholar of Jewish mysticism, quotes Troeltsch approvingly (1967, p. 2):

> In conformance with Troeltsch's use of the term, I shall use 'mysticism' here as meaning the striving for immediacy, inwardness and presence of religious experience, as an awareness of the living experience of the Divine, vouchsafed to individuals living in institutional and traditional forms of religion. I agree with those who see in mysticism a *secondary* (italics added) state of religious development which evolves in visible tension to the traditional forms of religion, in ritual as well as in theology.

For Weber, mysticism is not secondary to institutions or to ideas. Rather, it is, on the roads to salvation," in the words of the American poet, Robert Frost, the "road less traveled by." Soteriology, the salvific, redemptive way, splits, between the ascetic and mystic paths, between action and contemplation. As we well know from Weber, the ascetic path, in its inner-worldly branch, provided the religious foundation for the culture of instrumental rationality which is the driving force not only of capitalism, but of modern, European civilization. The contemplative path is clearly the minor, religious-cultural theme, since its central tendency is toward flight *from* the world, otherworldliness. Even when it remains within the world, it is either quietistic, having no social impact, or represented by the minority cases of acosmic, universal brotherly love which leads to communities, which, however, are of only passing impact in the rationalizing world, where asceticism has both lost its initial religious meaning and, triumphed.

Why it triumphed over mysticism is worth considering for a moment, because it reveals the core causal elements of Weber's theory of religion and points to the historical reasons that make Weber's theory at once so generally valuable, but particularly, increasingly, causally inappropriate to a changing historical reality.

"Sanctification" is the meaning of the social action of salvation religions. And, as Weber explains: "*Self-deification was the prevalent goal of sanctification,* from the beginnings of the soma cult of intoxication in ancient Vedic times up through the development of sublime methods of intellectualist ecstasy and the elaboration of erotic orgies. . . (emphasis added)." This primordial goal of religious action, as the focus of sacred practice, namely, self-deification, becomes displaced, both by the need for a more permanent state of sacred grace than is afforded by ephemeral orgiastic ecstasy—which is to say, the elementary, microcosmic form of the routinization of charisma, or rationalization—and secondly, the changing conception of divinity. It is again worth quoting Weber, in a condensed statement of what is a more general dynamic of the core elements of his sociological theory of religion (1978, p. 536):

"As the process of rationalization went forward, the goal of methodically planned religious sanctification increasingly transformed the acute intoxication induced by orgy into a milder but more permanent *habitus*, and moreover one that was consciously possessed. This transformation was strongly influenced by, among other things, the particular concept of the divine that was entertained. *The ultimate purpose to be served by the planned procedure of sanctification remained everywhere the same purpose which was served in an acute way by the orgy, namely the incarnation within man of a supernatural being and therefore of a god. Stated differently, the goal was self-deification. Only now this incarnation had to become a continuous personality pattern, so far as possible...*

"But wherever there is a belief in a transcendental god, all-powerful in contrast to his creatures, the goal of methodical sanctification can no longer be self-deification... Hence the goal of sanctification becomes oriented to the world beyond and to ethics. The aim is no longer to possess god, for this cannot be done, but either to become his instrument or to be spiritually suffused by him. Spiritual diffusion is obviously closer to self deification than is instrumentality... (emphasis added)"

Recognizing Mysticism

Mysticism is less and less now a "secondary" aspect of religion. A variety of empirical survey research (Heelas, 2008, p. 233–35) shows how the inwardness and direct experience elements of mysticism have become more socially prevalent. Wuthnow's (1998) social transition from a religion of dwelling to a spirituality of seeking, Forman's "grassroots spirituality (2000) "Parsons" (1999) "unchurched mysticism" and Heelas' (2008, p. 19) "inner-life spirituality," which present empirical evidence of the shift from 'traditional' 'institutional' aspects of religion, all reflect what Troeltsch early on described (1911 p. 31):

> The active energies in mysticism of this kind can become independent in principle, contrasted with concrete religion; they then break away from it and set up a theory of their own which takes the place of the concrete religion and its *mythos* or doctrine...mysticism realizes that it is an independent religious principle; it sees itself as the real universal heart of all religion, of which the various myth-forms are merely the outer garment. It regards itself as the means of restoring an immediate union with God; it feels independent of all institutional religion and possesses an entire inward certainty, which makes it indifferent towards every kind of religious fellowship. This

is its fundamental attitude; it does not vary whether the mystic adheres externally to the religious community or not. Henceforward union with God, deification, self-annihilation, become the real and only subject of religion.

"Mysticism" is beginning to be recognized as a significant topic of study by sociologists, under the rubric, however, of "spirituality." The term-shifting reflects, on the one hand, that inner-worldly mysticism may not be a historically consistent minor aspect of religion; on the contrary, the evidence suggests that the opposite of Weber's view is now the case. Yet, in the separation of the terms, along with the recognition of mysticism, is its forgetting of long traditions, not of institutional religion, but of mysticism itself. Heelas (2008) makes an effort to see in the contemporary "expressivist humanism" of "inner-life spiritualities" a cultural continuity; but it is with British and German Romanticism. He fails to take the further step, shown by M.H. Abrams (1971) and, more recently, Suzanne Kirchner (1996), who argue for not only the Romantic, but the religious origins of aspects of contemporary culture from poetry to psychoanalysis. Late post-modern "spirituality" de-sacralizes religion, though, I suggest that it extracts and re-contextualizes from mystical traditions, basic social processes that have become increasingly necessary as mechanisms of constituting society, more generally.

It is not enough to castigate the spiritual and New Age appropriations of mysticism as simply cheap deformations, though it is certainly tempting for scholars of mystical traditions. White (2003 xiii-xiv) cannot resist:" New Age Tantra is to medieval Tantra what finger painting is to fine art . . . This colonialization and commodification of another people's religious belief system and the appropriation and distortion of its very use of the term 'Tantra, is not only deceptive. . . New Age 'Tantric sex' is a Western fabrication. . ."

Collins (2008) is more sanguine about contemporary continuities in mysticism. Indeed, he prefers that term, and follows the Weberian typology in a search for current examples of innerworldly mysticism. Following Tilly (2004), Collins takes a political view of social movements and argues that innerwordly asceticism is all-too evident in authoritarian religion/political movements. There is, in his view, an alternative, in liberalizing and humanitarian innerworldy mystical political movements:

> . . . losing the ascetic edge. . . a parallel but alternative source of political mobilization that is much more human than the ascetic moralistic reformers. This is mysticism in-the-world. . . We can see the difference between ascetics-in-the-world and mystics-in the-world both in their worldviews and practices. ..Mystics-in-the-world see the world permeated by holiness . . . they could take another step, and instead of withdrawing from politics, enter the world of politics with their pantheistic vision. . ..I suggest that this step was taken by Christian mystics, who created a form of activist politics that is radically humanitarian rather than harsh and moralistic. . . The Franciscans were radical democrats. . .we go from the example of the Franciscans to the Quakers, to the

abolitionists, to the gentle altruistic movements of today. . ... To explain the conditions for these movements are problems on the agenda for sociologists of the future.

On the other hand, Troeltsch (1911/31, pp.797, 817, 818), who analyzed the radical "spiritual reformers" and sects in what he referred to as the "sociological results of modern spiritual idealism," was much less sanguine. "In this respect, Christian Socialism certainly has a mission, although it will scarcely be able to build up the new social order." Like Weber, for Troeltsch, modernity has cast its lot with the other "road to salvation:" "On the other hand, the social influence of Ascetic Protestantism upon the history of civilization has been penetrating and comprehensive." While he observes: "'Spiritual religion' or mysticism is not a product of particular social conditions. It proceeds from other causes. . ."

Yet, he and Weber both suggest that a social class dynamic is at work in mysticism. Troeltsch goes on to note: ". . . its extension depends upon the existence of classes which live apart from the crude struggle for existence, and can seek spiritual refinement for their own sake. . ."

Similarly, Weber wrote (1946): "And, in the midst of a culture that is rationally organized for a vocational workaday life, there is hardly any room for the cultivation of acosmic brotherliness, unless it is among strata who are economically carefree."

The contemporary relation of society and mysticism is that mysticism becomes a central constitutive process of society. The importance of mysticism, I want to suggest, lies less in the de-mysticized continuities with a commercialized culture of spirituality, or even the possibility of altruistic inner-worldly mystical social movements. On the contrary, it is not brotherly love, but the mechanism of sanctification through self-deification which again becomes relevant, if indeed, the concept of the divine, which is the causal 'primo motore' for Weber, has again shifted—away from a theistic transcendental divide between the human and the divine. If, on the contrary, there has been a re-cosmologization of everyday life and a diminution of transcendental conceptions of the divine (Toulmin, 1982; Loy, 2009), then, it is self-deifying, incarnating, immanent divinization, and a mysticism of suffusion, which becomes a primary, and not a 'secondary,' aspect of religion.

Further, this process of self-deification, as a social/cosmic process, offers neither a traditionalization, nor revolution of society, but its reconstitution, as a social mechanism; one that replaces the historic integrative methodology of "socialization." It is indeed "politics," but of a different sort than described by Collins, that has returned to mysticism, along with the cosmos itself, which now begins to surpass de-sacralized spirituality. It is both these dynamics of a "new mysticism" of society that I want to explore: the contemporary meaning of self-deifying practices of sanctification and the replacement of socialization as the link between individual and society, by a new/old set of methodologies of cosmic, social interaction, as its constitutive principle.

New Mysticism

The "new mysticism" is beyond "spirituality." First, it must be said, however, that if sociologists have had little to say about mysticism, scholars of mysticism have had little to say about society. The founder of the academic study of Jewish mysticism, Gershom Scholem (1966 pp.1–3) begins a rare discussion of mysticism and society, in this way:

"If we wish to discuss mysticism and society in their mutual relationship there is one astonishing fact which should be pointed out from the outset. In the infinite welter of literature on mysticism which, especially during the last two generations, has taken on quite extraordinary proportions, the *problem of mysticism and society has received but scanty attention.*" (italics added). After indicating some main areas of work in mysticism, Scholem continues: "Even the history of such developments in different systems and religions has aroused the interest of the historian. The social context of mysticism and its implications, however, have, as far as I am aware, a marginal place in these discussions. On the contrary, we easily discern a tendency to take the phenomena of religious mysticism out of their social context, to isolate them and to stress their alleged basic difference from historical and social phenomena." After briefly discussing the experiential "life of inwardness," he observes: "It is this aspect of mysticism which is so intensely stressed in the theoretical literature of the mystics, and, in its wake, in the contemporary discussions of mysticism where psychology rules supreme." Scholem tries to get beyond what he refers to (1967, p. 6) as ". . .one of the central weaknesses of the many purely psychological explanations of mysticism," which is the failure to account of the mystic's communication, the "consequences of his rapture (p.7)," and particularly, "the interrelation between the mystic and his social group."

Still, following Troeltsch, he describes the social meaning of mysticism as, in the first instance, a renewal of traditions—we might say today, following Wallace (1956), a revitalization movement—which "tend to become stale and worn out." Though he acknowledges a revolutionary possibility, his main example of the relation between mysticism and society is eighteenth-century Hasidism, which though it is transformative, and though it has a "radical branch" (p. 20), is a movement of "basically conservative reformers. . . who thought of it as a nucleus for a renewal of Jewish society in its wider meaning. (pp. 20–21)." The "revolutionary propensities of mysticism" "come to the fore mainly in mystical sects. . .these sects were of particularly social impact when mysticism combined with Messianism." Here, using Weber's term for charismatic movements, he cites Sabbatian movements as a Jewish example, and directly following Troeltsch (p. 23–24: "The many facets of Anabaptism and its later ramifications present the student with instructive examples of the revolutionary turn of mystical teachings. Social forces which at the outset had nothing to do with mysticism used slogans borrowed from mystical teaching, as in the case of Thomas Munzer, and decidedly mystical inspiration entered the social sphere in Quakerism."

The "new mysticism" that I want to indicate is not a marginal, sectarian phenomenon, coded messianically or not, that Troeltsch described in terms of the Protestant spiritual reformers and radical sects, that Scholem adapted to Hasidism and Sabbatainism, and which Weber relegated to a past, culturally emptied by rationalization, and whose prophetic, future re-appearance—as a mass phenomenon—is clearly deferred. Rather, in a historically changed context, the re-enchantment of the world is socially less potent in radical, messianic sects, although they exist, than in an alteration of the religious foundations of the mainstream, secularized culture. That is what Heelas (1996; 2005; 2008) is trying to describe and to explain in terms of what he now refers to as "spiritualities of life" (2008). This self, inner-spirituality, which is manifested in a variety of mainstream institutional domains, including health, business and education, defines the emergent culture. This culture is a contemporary version of Durkheim's "religion of humanity," in which, according to Heelas' analysis of the data, (2008, p. 126), ". . . the ethic of humanity is widely abroad within New Age spirituality of life circles." ". . .the ethic can be experienced as functioning as an inner-directed, that is expressivist, form of the Durkheimian sacred." Spirituality is new age Romanticism, and its causes are to be found in processes of cultural continuity and diffusion.

I tried to explain the socially salient emphasis on inner experience and "boundless being," not as a continuity with Romantic culture, or even as a renewal of traditional mystical cultures, but as a broad, decentralized social movement which develops in response to contemporary, social structural conditions. In "Mystical Society" (Wexler, 2000), I took a Marxist approach, following Manuel Castells and David Harvey, and extended their analysis (particularly, against Castells' emphasis on "fundamentalism" as social re-anchoring), understanding the social structural de-bounding of institutions which is homologously reflected in the de-bounding of the experiential self, to be an effect of changes in forces of production. Informational technology induces a mystical informationalism, that may be seen as a revitalization movement, since it draws on mystical traditions from within the classical religions, but which, more deeply, alters the basic terms of the culture: a technologization of Sorokin's sensate, materialist premise that has reached its limit.

"Spirituality" does not go far enough to capture the incipient phenomenon—which is neither the marginal sectarian renewal of traditional religious movements, nor the de-transcendentalized, individualist expressivism of religious yearning. Rather, the meaning of "the social" itself is changing; not simply cultural belief or institutional boundaries or personal attitudes, but the nature of social relationality. This change was heralded, in my view, by the founder of American psychology, William James, and more recently, by the philosopher Stephen Toulmin.

As I argued in the recent paper on "Micro-sociology and Mysticism," James is increasingly acknowledged as a founder also of modern social science, particularly through his influence on Dewey and Mead. At the same time, James's social psychology and micro-sociology were de-spiritualized and de-mysticized. I am referring not only to the denial of James's "spiritual self" or the incontrovertible importance which he attached to psychic phenomena, and of the marginal as being only ephemerally subliminal and always potentially central (1910, p. 92). "We shall not understand these alterations of consciousness either in this generation or the next," he wrote in his 1910 paper, "A Suggestion about Mysticism." Rather, I am referring to James's late interest in the inter-personal and the social. Against the de-mystification of James in American social science—while lauding his contribution—he, himself, was swimming against the tide of his own earlier materialist assumptions and drawing the implications of such a reversal for theory and practice.

James wanted to define the social cosmically. "From a pragmatic point of view," he wrote (2007, p. 14) in his last book, "A Pluralistic Universe," "the difference between living against a background of foreignness and one of intimacy means the difference between a general habit of wariness and one of trust. One might call it a social difference, for after all the common *socius* of us all is the great universe whose children we are. If materialistic, we must be suspicious of this socius, cautious, tense, on guard. If spiritualistic, we may give way, embrace and keep no ultimate fear."

In a parallel vein, though now well into the twentieth century (1982, p.12), the eminent philosopher of science, Stephen Toulmin, aims to describe and understand what he calls a "return to cosmology." He writes:

"Thirty years ago, the separateness of different intellectual disciplines was an unquestioned axiom of intellectual procedure, and the obstacles to thinking of the natural world in other than strict, disciplinary terms was still very substantial." He goes on to discuss (p.13) the rise of an interdisciplinary organization of knowledge and its contextual meaning: ". . . at least it made it possible to reopen, in a serious spirit, questions about the cosmological significance of the world picture. . . So the disciplinary specialization of the natural sciences can no longer intimidate us into setting religious cosmology asides as 'unscientific.'" Toulmin sees the "task of constructing a conception of the "overall scheme of things" as part of the development of a "new cosmology (p.17)." In his discussion of "green "and "white" philosophies (pp. 262–269), Toulmin draws comparsions between classical antiquity and contemporary intellectual movements, emphasizing the internal, inner-looking search for psychological meaning and transformation, and the outer, ecological orientation.

Implied, but undeveloped in James and Toulmin, is a redefinition of the meaning of social relationality, of social interaction, to include a wider, "universal" screen, reaching inward and outward, beyond the meaning that symbolic interactionism in sociology has given to the symbolic. There, what is symbolic, what is "other," are the embodiments and ethical standards of a "community," the "generalized other," which is taken as an advance on individualist psychology. Likewise, in Durkheimian, functionalist sociology, society is constituted by an integrative process which Dennis Wrong described in his famous phrase critical of the model that links the individual and the collective through the internalization of shared norms and values, as the "oversocialized conception of man in modern sociology (1961)."

Instead of either of these tacks—symbolic interactionism and functionalism—as the theoretical subject and, instead of either Durheimian inner-life culture or Marxist technological de-boundarying as the object of understanding—I want to take the cosmological perspectives of James and Toulmin not only seriously, but historically, as social facts and as the basis of social explanation. Contemporary social interactional life, as Emerson (1940/50) put it already in the middle of the nineteenth century, always has, beyond the evident dyadic interactants, a "third party." Symbolic interaction needs to be understood as "cosmic interaction."

If we return to the sociology of knowledge vantage-point with which we began, contemporary academic religious studies and mass-cultural interest in dynamic models of cosmic interaction both explain and represent historical changes in the meaning of social life and in the methods of societal re-integration or, constitution. The threshholds, screens and filters on consciousness which James saw as marginal, but reducible and permeable, have been lowered, its walls breached in theory and practice.

This hypothesized shift in the nature of social life occurs in a historical context. I want to suggest that the move toward a cosmic type of interactionism occurs simultaneously with the revision of the social, toward a new model of politics, and a re-sexualization of academic social understanding and everyday mass practice—which demonstrates that an alternative to Marcuse's (1955) "repressive de-sublimation" of eros is now part of the social imaginary.

What has brought politics, sex, and the cosmos back to social life is, I think, not only the technologically instigated triumph of flow over form, to use Scott Lash' (2005) re-staging of Simmel. Indeed, Simmel's (1918/1997) understanding of "The Conflict of Modern Culture, "is between "life" and form, but especially as enacted in the religious yearning of mysticism (1997, pp. 20–21)" Mysticism appears to be the last refuge for religious individuals who cannot free themselves from all transcendental forms, but only, as it were temporarily, from those which are determined and fixed in content" (p. 23). "I wonder," he wrote, "whether the fundamental will of religious life does not inevitably require an object... (p. 23) we are moving toward a typical cultural change, the creation of new forms adapted to contemporary forces..."

While Weber's religious typologies, including that of mysticism, are best known in the corpus of his sociology of religion, Weber was primarily a historical sociologist. It is in this historical sociology of religion that he offers an important clue, which takes us beyond the cultural and the technological, beyond the alternation of flow and form, to see mysticism politically.

Politics, Sex and the Cosmos

Historically, the quest for religious salvation is a political quest, undertaken as a *compensation* for a political loss. Religious creativity is induced by the loss of power (1968, pp.503–504):

"The development of a strong salvation religion by socially privileged groups normally has the best chance when demilitarization has set in for these groups and when they have lost either the possibility of political activity or the interest in it. Consequently, salvation religions usually emerge when the ruling strata, noble or middle class, have lost their political power to a bureaucratic-militaristic state. The withdrawal of the ruling strata from politics, for whatever reason, also favors the development of a salvation religion;..."

"The Near Eastern salvation religions, whether of a mystagogic or prophetic type as well as the oriental and Hellenistic salvation doctrines, whether of a more religious or philosophical type of which lay intellectuals are the protagonists, were insofar as they included the socially privileged strata at all, virtually without exception, the consequence of the educated strata's enforced or voluntary loss of political influence and participation."

Weber observes further that "such modes of thought (religious salvation) tend to lead a kind of underground existence, normally becoming dominant only when the intellectuals have undergone de-politicization."

My suggestion, is that a "new mysticism" arises at the conjuncture of this de-politicization, the continuing intensification of the "cult of the individual," and a reduction in the transcendental system of theistic belief in favor of inner-life spirituality. When, as Weber explained in the forking of paths between asceticism and mysticism, there is a transcendental gap between the divine and the human, the earlier social technology of sanctification as self-sanctification, or more specifically, self-deification or divinization, become less possible. But, under conditions that combine loss of power, a changing conception of divinity that de-transcendentalizes divinity and makes power both personal and inward, and where individualism has no limits, so that divinization appears on an endless horizon of acquisition, then pre-modern mysticism returns, albeit in de-traditionalized and de-contextualized forms. This de-contextualization and de-textualization in the new mysticism is what rouses the ire of scholars of medieval Hinduism like David White (2003) and Gavin Flood (2006). Yet, simultaneously, it is the demand for this social technology which revises traditional forms of mysticism and raises the level of interest in earlier, medieval models of empowerment.

Hollenback's (1996) redefinition of mysticism makes empowerment into one of its central aspects (p. 26):

> My third objective—and this is one of the most unusual aspect of this study—is to draw attention to the importance of *enthymesis*, or what I have I termed "empowerment" of thought, will, and imagination as a significant process that shapes visionary landscapes, ensures that a mystic's experiences will seem to confirm empirically the truths that his religious tradition proclaims in its myths or scriptures, and transforms the imagination and will into 'organs' of supernormal perception.

Individualistic empowerment and de-centered divinity are made even more salient with the "return to cosmology." In this return, the earlier models of divinization are re-activated, along with a renewal of the imaginal and envisioning senses.

Of course, one may argue that current scholarly interests are entirely removed from historical, social, contextual concerns. Yet, the search for models of reconstituting the destroyed sociality of modern commodification and rationalization, also leads to the renaissance of an academic "new mysticism." Among those models, it is Kabbalah and Tantra which garner the widest audiences. They present a cosmological order of a much wider domain of symbolic interaction that induces empowerment and vitality. In Boaz Huss' (2007) analysis of the "new age of Kabbalah," there is an efflorescence of a new mysticism which fuses ancient traditions and contemporary preoccupations: (2007, p. 109):

"During the 1970s and 1980s, and especially from 1990 onward, traditional kabbalistic *yeshivot* and Hasidic movements became more active and new Kabbalah and Neo-hasidic institutes, synagogues and study groups were established, mostly in Israel and in the United States. In the last three decades, thousand of people have been studying and practicing various forms of Kabbalah, hundreds of books about Kabbalah have been published and numerous Kabbalah related webpages can be found on the Internet."

Jonathan Garb (2009, p. 38) does contextualize, in a way reminiscent of Weber's more general thesis, suggesting the importance of empowerment in social history, where he concentrates on the relation between Kabbalah and Jewish history:

"On a broader level, the focus on power in twentieth century Kabbalah should be examined in the context of the transition from classical to modern Jewish thought. In Jewish diasporic experience, a schism evolved between the belief in an omnipotent God who bestowed some of his power upon his Chosen People and the political and military reality of inferiority and impotence. This disparity between faith in an absolute power and a historical reality of powerlessness generated a 'compensatory discourse,' in which hidden forms of power of a magical or theurgical nature could be activated through Jewish ritual or through the Hebrew language. This discourse helped redress the Jewish people's sense of powerlessness through focusing on its privileged access to supernatural power. The kabbalistic doctrine played a key role in this process. . ." Garb goes on to assert (p. 39): "Religious Zionism saw the empowerment of the Jewish people as an affirmation—not a negation—of divine power. Analyzing the circle of the Rav Kook, Garb cites R. David Kohen (p. 43):

> I am magnificent, a divine power sweeps through me .A power of courage and strength, a power of salvation of His right hand. Just by remembering this I ascend to sublime heights. . .The power of God is within me.

Even self-abnegation becomes a "passive model" of empowerment in the Kabbalah of the Rav Ashlag. Along with the personal psychologization of modern Kabbalah, Garb argues that the textual tradition itself changes (p.105): ". . .there has been a significant transition form a curriculum based on the study of Halakha to one based on the study of mystical texts. . . Kabbalah and Hasidism, one could say, have usurped the place not only of the study of Mussar, but also of the analytical study of Talmud as foci of spiritual enlightenment."

In his forthcoming book on 'Shamanic Trance in Modern Kabbalah,' Garb opens the field of practices of deification from internalized identification with God to an "imaginal geography (Henri Corbin)," and an architectural model, and, following Wolfson (2005, pp. 12–122, p. 101 in Garb) to a "process of spiritual entities assuming corporeal form within the imagination." Quoting Wolfson and citing Idel (p. 113 in Garb) ". . .on the shared 'as-if' mode of imaginary ascent, in which the practitioner visualized himself as present in the supernal worlds." (Wolfson, p. 194; Idel, 2005). As Garb puts it (p. 66) "the route to revitalization is the recovery of a more archaic consciousness, which is closely related to the elements, such as air and fire."

From our point of view, medieval cosmologies become the map of a re-cosmicized set of social interactions. The deep ascents and descents across worlds described by Moshe Idel (2005) are the expanded field of cosmic social interaction in an emergent new mysticism. New age "culture" is supplanted by more conscious borrowings from medieval cosmology and the social order is now an imaginal order, a symbolic interaction with "others" who are both supernal figures and potencies, but certainly, something different and more variegated than the symbolic community other of sociology, or the internalization of shared values that derive from transcendental, ethical commands. The "imaginal geography," becomes channeling, angelology and an incredible "corporealization of spiritual entities that appear in television series, and Hollywood movies for the masses, to say nothing of literary, "fictional "cosmologies.

In his critique of Scholem (2005, p. 19), Moshe Idel moves away from the ideational to the performative, so that the imagined universes are not theological constructs, but methods of energic performative practices. He writes of ". . . what may be described as the theologization of Kabbalah in Scholem's writings and in those of his followers.

"Unlike this propensity to understand Kabbalah as theology, I will try to emphasize in the following chapters some other, and more experiential, aspects of this mystical lore." While he makes a general assertion (p. 37) "The processes of interiorization of mythical modes of thought resorting to the new forms of spirituality are part and parcel of many developments in religion," he offers as a more particular observation (p. 53):

> Rabbi Vital combines this language with a certain theory of imagination that is not, however, entirely Aristotelian.. Due to the influence of some forms of Sufism, the role of the imaginary faculty is highlighted. Events are described as taking place in the imagination and in a place described as 'the world of images.

Idel goes on to describe various modes of ascension and angelization and, significantly, also descents. Against Weber's view of mysticism as divided between other-worldly and inner-worldly, in the Kabbalah of Idel, Wolfson, Garb and Abrams (2004), mysticism is neither. It is between worlds, dynamic, relational and empowering. This Kabbalistic imagination de-centers the Divine into a divine process, in which the righteous elite, and then, broader social constituencies, are emplaced, in an interaction that is transformative, even while it is symbolic. The renewed interest in such interactional models may have its scholarly roots, but it represents a change also in the everyday episteme, of at first those "economically carefree" classes who practice, again, the sanctification of the self, to "become as Gods."

Along with the reverse theurgic empowerment of Kabbalistic ascents, which are at once in the world and across its boundaries, as Wolfson has argued for almost twenty years (1994, p. 2005), and as Idel has more recently asserted (2005) and as Abrams emphatically describes, in an embodied reading of sexuality and the "Divine Feminine," sexualization as well as empowerment characterizes the cosmic interactional field of contemporary Kabbalistic interpretation. We have already noted White's complaint about the fabricating Westernization and distortion of Hindu Tantra, and the same may become increasingly true of sexualized readings of Kabbalah. Yet, within Kabbalah scholarship, Charles Mopsik makes explicit the connection between divine sexual dynamics and the emplacement of this-worldly relations, which are not only sexual, but more broadly social, within the ambit of divine dynamics. He writes (2005, p. 20): "The relationship within the couple is taken as the ideal type of social relationship." He describes: (p. 34) "The bisexual model of the world of emanation, the divine structure is reflected on the human level. As he specifies it (p.64):

"These two sefirot (Tiferet, the son and Malkhut, the daughter) thus form two gendered poles whose phases of union or disunion set the pace for the internal dynamics of the emanative structure, then spread to the angelic cosmos and from there to the world of man." And, more directly (p.124): "The divine world and the world of man is organized along fundamentally identical principles."

In medieval Hindu Tantra too, these cosmologies of divine coupling are about the much wider dynamics of cosmic forces and their constitutive power for human beings. White (2003, p. 97) cites a medieval text:

"Desire (kama) is the root of the universe. From desire all beings are born. . . Without Siva and Sakti creation would be nothing but imagination. Without the action of kama there would be no birth or death. The king represents a template (p. 125) ". . . the prime channel of communication between the upper and lower worlds—between the human, the divine, and the demonic— which he keeps 'open' through the mediation of the religious specialists. "He is "a pivot between heaven and earth,, the microcosmic godhead incarnate."

Gavin Flood (2006) reasserts the essential contextualization of Tantra within traditional scripture and ritual, arguing for the "entextualization" of the body in Hindu Tantra (here reminiscent of the role of the letters and the body in Hebrew Kabbalah). Here too, (p. 53) "The Tantras are dialogues between the main deity of the tradition and his/her spouse or sage. Tantras focused on Siva are presented as dialogues between him and his Goddess or Sakti." There is an imaginative, cosmic, symbolic interaction (p. 120): "Inhaling the image, it pervades the adepts's body from the thighs to the knees and is dissolved into its mantra, then into the energy of taste which he emits through the exhaled breath" (p. 113): It is perhaps in the divinization process that we see the particularity of the contextualiation of the variable indexicality that constitutes subjectivity in these traditions. . . (p. 145) Further; "Of particular importance are the purification and divinization of the body, in which we see the textual representation of the cosmos mapped onto the body and cosmological temporality of vast periods of the manifestation and contraction of the cosmos enacted in the microtemporality of daily ritual time." (p. 6). "This corporeal understanding shows itself in the great emphasis on transformative practices in the tantric traditions, ritual inseparable from vision, the body becoming alive in the universe within it, and vibrant with futurity in the anticipation of the goal of the tantric path."

Reconstituting Society

In both empowerment and sexualization, in the academic and popular domains, we can see the fulfillment and specification of James's and Toulmin's expansion of horizons and its implication for a much wider definition of the meaning of sociality. However, not only can the social be understood as interaction with imagined and corporealized supernal figures, and the inclusion of the physical elements of the universe, along with the spiritual/mystical, in the interactive process, but what is revealed is also a different social "mechanism." I think we can begin to see how Wrong's (1961) critique of "socialization" as the key mediating process between individual and society is being replaced by this wider, "cosmic interactionism." The internalization model of socialization is, I suggest, a secularized version of "imitation dei." An authority figure represents moral values that are acquired by identification with the external force of power. Weber argued that the sacred version was no longer possible, not only because the nature of transcendental conceptions of the divine created an unbridgeable gap between the human and divine, but also because societal rationalization had made the divinized figures less accessible (1946, p. 357)):

> Under the technical and social conditions of rational culture, an imitation of the life of Buddha, Jesus, or Francis seems condemned to failure for purely external reasons.

Both centralized, sacred imitatio Dei and secularized socialization became less socially effective with the long wave of modern destruction—the chronicling of which is the other side of classical, modern sociology. Not individualism, but anomie. Not material progress, but alienation, commodification and exploitation. Not efficient rationality, but de-magification and depersonalization.

We can see how the new/old social relations of cosmicization can lead to the reconstitution of subjectivities and to a broader field of micro social interactions. What is less clear is the implication of such changes for the character of the macro-structure of society. I agree with Simmel (1997), that mysticism signals a social transition and "religiosity" rather than "religion," ("spirituality," rather than mysticism) means that new social forms—I would say social structures—have not yet crystallized. In terms of Alberoni's theory of social movements (1984), we are in a "nascent state," with regard to the formation of institutions (1984, p. 20):

"It is, therefore, a transitional state, and it appears when there is a failure of those forces which constitute social solidarity. In such a case, solidarity is reconstructed beginning from certain points in the social system having quite specific properties. Broadly speaking, the nascent state is a proposal for reconstruction made by one part of the social system." Further on, he explains (pp. 20–21): "The nascent state is an exploration of the limits of the possible within a given type of social system, in order to maximize that portion of experience and solidarity which is realizable for oneself and for others at a specific historical moment."

I understand "spirituality" as aim-inhibited mysticism, analytically and, historically, as a precursor, though still continuing parallel, to the appearance of a "new mysticism." The new mysticism revives the ancient models and is more radical because it not only asserts an alternative set of moral principles or norms, but because it embodies and enacts a different practice of sociality. Indeed, my hypothesis is that the supercession of spirituality by mysticism indicates a different socially constitutive dynamic, both in theory and practice.

The sociological theory of spirituality, as most consistently articulated by Paul Heelas, is a cultural theory, abstracted from the historical dynamics of production, class, politics and sexuality. Moreover, it operates within the framework of the present cultural imaginary, the taken-for-granted of materialist individualism—though it very much registers the Romantic protest, and reaches out, from its core of sociocultural continuity, to an alternative way of being in the world. Yet, in its reinforcement not only of Durkheim's "religion of humanity," but also of his "cult of the individual," it occludes the possibility of recognizing not only changes in the content of culture, but a deeper alteration in the constitutive social mechanism.

If sociologies of spirituality are too constricted, so also are traditional and renewed theories of mysticism. For, while Scholem's call for a study of the social "context" of mysticism is surely an improvement against the continuing academic, scholasticism of the cult of textualization (beneath the shield of philological scholarship), it repeats the very psychologization of mystical experience which it decries. For it accepts the duality of individual and society, where mystical "experience"—no matter whether theologized or ritualized—belongs to the individual, who may be influenced and in turn, also influence, his "social group," "radiating" to the wider "social context."

This duality enables us to deny both that mysticism is a social relation, and that what is changing, socially are not simply cultural values, but the very constitutive principles of contemporary, historical society. To put it simply and boldly, both individualism and culturalism, as explanations, are historically inappropriate to an emergent world in which the meaning of society itself is changing. Against the "end of the social views," which argues the triumph, albeit dissentingly, of informationalization, or the supercessation of persons by the objectivization of social relations, the view presented here is that the social is being transformed in cosmicization. Within such a wider, transformed social field, mysticism comes to the fore as a societally central social relation. The character of mysticism, as described in classical Kabbalah and Tantra—their interactive dynamics of emanations and divine corporealizations, embodied entextualizations of classical mystical beliefs and practices—reveals itself to be—now, more evidently, because of the expansion of the meaning of the social horizon—a fully social relation.

Society becomes more mystical and the modern, individualist, psychological ideology of mysticism fades in the face of its evident social character. The "inwardness" of mysticism represents the "coagulation" of a moveable social field of transworldly social relations. Mysticism is a social process, which is temporally and spatially differentially and variously located, included both the inwardness, which, from Troeltsch forward had been seen as its defining attribute, and its sometimes existence in a relational, interactive, dynamic social field that represents its "external" positioning.

Even further, this social relation, which is more characterized by the surfacing of states of being that modernity called "altered" or, in James's time, "psychic," which is characterized by the entextualization of mystical myths, dogmas and theories and their trans-worldly interaction represents the new socially constitutive principle, at least in its nascent state, of societal integration, or "solidarity." Mysticism becomes, in the language of Functionalist sociology, a "functional pre-requisite" of the social system.

Its systemic value as a socially integrative principle is also entailed by its internal, generative logic, which Mopsik (2005), playing on the priority which he assigns to gender and sexual difference in his reading of Kabbalah, calls "engenderment." That is, it is a dynamic, interactive process which is continually pro-creative. Its creativity is lodged in the organic, living character of sexuality itself, as we see in the work of Wolfson (2005) and Abrams (2004) and not only in the combinations and permutations of gendered differentiated emanations, or "sefirot."

The "new vitalism" which Lash (2005) finds in adding "reflexivity" to flow, Marxizing Simmel, as it were, and returning Critical Theory to the information society, is a materialist vitalism. So too, is the "molecular vitalism" of theories of nanotechnology as a new view of self-organizing systems (Bensaude-Vincent, 2009). Instead, the transitional nascence of cosmicization stands against "socialization" and its more temperate versions in theories of social identity and symbolic interaction as the central constitutive principle for that organized aggregation and crystallization of movement which we still call "society." Unlike charisma, which is an evanescent antidote to the triumphant petrification of asceticism's rationalizing, prolific heir, mysticism carries a deeper, longer-run promise of installing a living, organic vitality of continuous creativity as the emergent social principle. Yet, in this historically familiar struggle, between materialism and spiritualism, sociological gnosticism cannot forget the power of even a cosmicized world to—in Weber's phrase—turn everything into stone. Still, it keeps open the possibility of an organic, social supernaturalism, as a "revolutionary force in history."

Bibliography

Abrams, Daniel. 2004. The Female Body of God in Kabbalistic Literature. Jerusalem. The Hebrew University Magnes Press (in Hebrew).
Alberoni, Francesco. 1984. Movement and Institution, Translated by Patricia C. Arden Delmoro. New York. Columbia University Press.
Bensaude-Vincent, Bernadette. 2009. "Self-Assembly, Self-Organization: Nanotechnology and Vitalism," Nanoethics (2009)3:31–42.
Collins, Randall. 2008. The Four M's of Religion: Magic, Membership, Morality and Mysticism. 2007 H. Paul Douglass Lecture. Review of Religious Research, vol. 50, number 1 (September, 2008) pp. 5–15.
Emerson, Ralph Waldo. 1940/50. The Complete Essays and Other Writings of Ralph Waldo Emerson, Edited with a Biographical Introduction, by Brooks Atkinson, Foreward by Tremaine McDowell. New York. The Modern Library.
Flood, Gavin, D. 1983. Body and Cosmology in Kashmir Saivism. San Francisco. Mellen Research University Press.
Flood, Gavin. 2006. The Tantric Body: The Secret Tradition of Hindu Religion. London and New York. I.B. Tauris.
Garb, Jonathan. 2009. The Chosen Will Become Herds: Studies in Twentieth-Century Kabbalah. New Haven, CT and London Yale University Press.
Garb, Jonathan. (2011). Shamanic Trance in Modern Kabbalah.
Heelas, Paul. 2008. Spiritualities of Life: New Age Romanticism and Consumptive Capitalism. Oxford. Blackwell Publishing.
Hollenback, Jess Byron. 1996. Mysticism: Experience, Response, and Empowerment. Unversity Park, PA. The Pennsylvania State University Press.
Huss, Boaz. 2007. "The New Age of Kabbalah: Contemporary Kabbalah, the New Age and Postmodern Spirituality," Journal of Modern Jewish Studies, vol 6, No. 2 July, 2007, pp:107–125.
Idel, Moshe. 2005. Ascensions on High in Jewish Mysticism: Pillars, Lines, Ladders. Budapest and New York. Central European University Press.
James, William.1977. The Writings of William James: A Comprehensive Edition, Edited with an Introduction and New Preface by John J. McDermott. Chicago and London.The University of Chicago Press.
James, William. 2007. A Pluralistic Universe. Chennai. Tutis Digital Publishing.

Mopsik,Charles.2005. Sex of the Soul: The Vicissitudes of Sexual Difference in Kabbalah. Los Angeles.Cherub Press.
Scholem, Gershom. 1967. "Mysticism and Society," Diogenes, vol. LVIII (Summer, 1967), pp.1–24.
Simmel, Georg. 1997. Essays on Religion. Edited and Translated by Horst Jurgen Helle in collaboration with Ludwig Nieder. Foreward by Phillip E. Hammond. New Haven, CT and London.Yale University Press.
Tilly, Charles. 2004. Social Movements, 1768–2004. Boulder and London. Paradigm Publishers.
Toulmin, Stephen. 1982. The Return to Cosmology: Postmodern Scioence and the Theology of Nature. Berkeley, Los Angles and London. University of California Press.
Troeltsch, Ernst. 1911/1931/1960. The Social Teachings of the Christian Churches. Two volumes. Translated by Olive Wyon. New York. Harper Torchbooks, Harper and Brothers.
Weber, Max. 1946. From Max Weber: Essays in Sociology. Translated, Edited and with an Introduction by H.H. Gerth and C. Wright Mills. New York. Oxford University Press.
Weber, Max. 1922/1956/1964/1991. The Sociology of Religion. Introduction by Talcott Parsons. With a new Foreword by Ann Swidler. Boston. Beacon Press.
Weber, Max. 1968/1978. Economy and Society: An Outline of Interpretive Sociology. Two vols. Edited by Guenther Roth and Claus Wittich. Berkeley, Los Angeles and London. University of California Press.
Wexler, Philip. 2000. Mystical Society: An Emerging Social Vision. Boulder, CO Westview.
White, David Gordon.2003. Kiss of the Yogini:'Tantric Sex' In Its South Asian Contexts. Chicago and London. The University of Chicago Press.
Wolfson, Elliot R. 2005. Language, Eros, Being: Kabbalistic Hermeneutics and Poetic Imagination. New York. Fordham University Press.
Wrong, Dennis.1961. "The Oversocialized Conception of Man in Modern Sociology," American Sociological Review. Vol. 26, No. 2 (April, 1961) pp. 183–193.

Part Two

Traditions East and West

SIX

Initiation and Communities of Secrecy in Papau New Guinea, Tantric Buddhism, and Contemporary Serial Drama

Louise Child

One of the most basic problems confronting the student of mysticism is a tension between the idea that mystical or visionary experience may entail a transcendent overcoming of the individual self and the social structures that govern the everyday world on the one hand, and the fact that this relinquishing inevitably takes place in the context of social and religious structures that wield power over individual selves in various ways on the other. One strand in the debate that this situation entails is a degree of scholarly caution with regard to notions of the sacred as outlined by scholars such as Eliade (1959) and Otto (1923), partly because it can be argued that the universalism implied in their work is rooted in an evolutionary paradigm wherein monotheism predominates in a hierarchy of religions. A related question, as Wolfson suggests, is the degree to which there can be any universal human experience that takes place prior to the language and cultural context in which it is transmitted. He argues that,

> that which is experienced by the mystic is mediated by meanings that accrue from a perception and reception of the world informed by the religious and cultural affiliation of the particular mystic. Indeed, as a variety of scholars have recognized, mysticism is always part of a larger whole, which is the concrete religion of a given mystic. It follows that the mystic's religious tradition provides an interpretive framework that is a constitutive factor of the mystical experience itself (Wolfson, 1994: 52–53).

While on one level this refers to the ways in which visionary phenomena become translated into the symbolic discourse of a given tradition or culture, on another there is also the issue of social structures within which mystical communities are engendered. This is because, even when the emphasis may be upon the experience of a solitary meditator, this experience usually has some kind of relational context. For example, although tantric Buddhism emphasizes the importance of solitary retreat as a context for more advanced visualization practices, such practices are preceded by complex secret training and initiatory rites wherein the disciple's mental and spiritual life are bound up with a relationship with a guru. This combination, of the creation of 'mystical communities' that may have spontaneous realizations and relationships, but which are also mediated by strict and bounded social structures in some form, is a feature of many societies, and although the precise detail of those structures and the practices that maintain them varies to a great degree, they have in common a certain ambivalence, particularly from the perspective of the scholarly observer. This is because the creation and channelling of collective emotions inevitably implies the creation of mechanisms for social control, wherein initiation and secrecy play an important role in the construction and maintenance of hierarchies and social boundaries, including those between men and women and between elders and young men. Similar suspicions are often expressed in the study, and especially psychoanalytic studies, of religious movements that are characterised by charismatic leadership, to the extent that it can be argued that many academics regard guru/disciple relationships as not simply potentially dangerous, but as a fundamentally dysfunctional dynamic. For example, Lindholm's analysis suggests that 'Freud accepted as well the crowd psychologists' image of the charismatic figure as a ruthless and overweening egoist, who by his very vainglory attracts the admiration of the herd' (Lindholm, 1993: 52). In this chapter, however, I aim to suggest ways in which the highly ambiguous phenomena of initiation and secrecy may also lie at the heart of intimate communications between persons, because secrecy both forms boundaries and is an important means of transcending them. In order to do so I begin with Herdt's anthropological study of the Sambia, suggesting that his exploration the complex nature of secrecy and its consequences for both social and intimate relationships in this society has important implications for scholarly understandings of broader debates concerning the ways in which secrecy and initiation both create social divisions between different groupings (such as age sets) and bind certain individuals together within those groups.

Men, Secrecy and Social Boundaries

Herdt, drawing from his fieldwork experiences with the Sambia people of Papua New Guinea, presents an analysis of ritual secrecy that has broader implications for the anthropology of religion. He suggests that scholarly engagements with ritual secrecy have been hampered by a number of factors, many of which are related to the fact that secrecy often contributes to the maintenance of separate ritual spheres and thus hierarchical relationships between men and women and between men in different age sets.

While acknowledging the ethical dilemma that this presents to academic enquiries, he nonetheless argues that anthropologists appear to be particularly squeamish about secrecy, tending to regard it as largely a hoax: a lie perpetrated by indigenous men in a bid for absolute power. While cultural relativism appears to have gained a strong voice in a number of other anthropological debates, he suggests that the romanticism with which Papua New Guinea was regarded in other contexts turned to cynicism when ethnographers were confronted with ritual secrecy (Herdt, 2003: xvi).

Herdt suggests that suspicions about secrecy are deep rooted in the political and social climate of Western societies, especially America, and that he himself subscribes to 'the ideology that transparency of intent through social action is the most preferable means of creating a positive social climate and promoting the ideals of democracy' (Herdt, 2003: xiii). At the same time, however, he is cautious about projecting those same values into a very different ethnographic context and suggests that many problems have been caused by a failure to distinguish the causes and consequences of ritual, collective secrecy, from the private versus public domains of Western societies and the political implications of hidden actions on the part of government organizations and conglomerate corporations.

Herdt does not deny the violence of many ritual initiations in Papua New Guinea. On the contrary, he maintains that boys are not only subjected to their elders in the men's house, they 'stand-in' for women as objects of intense ambivalence and desires, desires that are acted upon, in the case of the Sambia, through ritual insemination during which the youngest initiates perform fellatio upon the bachelors in the age set above them (Herdt, 2003: 45). Nevertheless, initiation into the men's house performs two vital services for Sambia society. It perpetuates a cultural construction of masculinity that prepares each generation anew for the almost continuous, and often bloody, warfare that is frequently endemic in Papua New Guinea (Herdt, 2003: 35). In addition, ritual secrecy erects a barrier that surrounds adult males, creating a social and cultural space within which bonds of *homosociality* can be fostered (Herdt, 2003: 77).

This concept of homosociality is, I think, a useful one. It may incorporate homosexual practices, but it does not necessarily entail sexual expression. On the contrary, Herdt suggests a rather broader base for the pleasures of male companionship and solidarity. The men's house and its secret rituals provide 'social regulation through the creation of hierarchy and a code of honour. . .a special trust, loyalty and belongingness' (Herdt, 2003: 39). I would therefore argue that detailed explorations of homosociality could be informed by, and contribute to, more broad-based studies of the nature of social solidarity.

Two theorists, Simmel and Durkheim, spring to mind as a starting point for this study. Herdt mentions both, but hesitates to dig deeper. In the case of Simmel this hesitation is related to Simmel's orientation towards a Western context, something which Herdt feels leads Simmel to emphasize more individualistic notions of privacy and remain ambivalent about collective or ritual secrecy (Herdt, 2003: 33 & 37). Herdt is also wary of essentializing tendencies in Durkheim's work, partly because Durkheim's analysis of ritual stresses ways in which it generates and expresses emotions and forms of consciousness rooted in society as a whole (Herdt, 2003: 47). Rather than viewing masculinity as problematic, Durkheim tends to speak from a masculine viewpoint. From this perspective, not only is masculine society regarded *as* society, but divisions between males tend to be played down. For Herdt, while ritual secrecy does promote social solidarity between males, it also, paradoxically, fosters individuality, hierarchy, and competition (Herdt, 1990: 361).

A second related point is Herdt's rejection of the idea that male supremacy in societies is a natural, or even a structured socially given base. Rather, he argues that ritual secrecy negotiates a paradox between the homogenous and public face of masculinity in Papua New Guinea and its tenuous and ever-threatened foundations (Herdt, 2003: 34). Nonetheless, bodily dimensions of initiation ensure that this negotiation is not simply a lie. The social bonds between men that secrecy helps to maintain extend well beyond the guarding of ritual, symbolic or mythical 'facts.' They permeate male personhood, desire and self-understanding.

Herdt's example of homosociality in Papua New Guinea is therefore not only an interesting study in its own right, but it has important implications for the study of initiation and secrecy in other social contexts. In particular, his exploration of the tension between the erection and permeation of social and bodily boundaries within the context of ritual secrecy is an important feature of tantric traditions that I explore in more detail later in this paper. Tantra's hierarchical structures and the binding of individuals to the person of the guru, for example, is further complicated by initiation and ritual secrecy being also features of consort relationships, some of which are described as happening between gurus and disciples. This hagiographical material therefore raises questions about the ways in which tantric Buddhism might frame or re-enforce hierarchical sexual relations, but it also leads one to consider more generally the ways in which power and secrecy operate at the micro (the dynamics that occur between individual persons in relations, including sexual relations) in addition to the macro level. In terms of its examination using the lens of social theory, therefore, I suggest that Simmel's work on the secret is useful in this context, because of the attention that he pays to secrecy in personal relationships in addition to its broader social significance.

Secrecy and the Sacred: Simmel and Durkheim

Simmel's analysis of the secret begins by suggesting that all human interaction is based on a certain amount of presumed mutual knowledge, knowledge that is, nonetheless, limited. The sheer volume of thoughts, emotions, and images that occur to a person at any given moment makes knowing another's thought completely impossible, and any attempt to communicate therefore entails a degree of selection and structuring on the part of the speaker, a process that is further complicated by the impression that a given communicator wishes to convey (Simmel, 1950 [1908]: 307–312).

Simmel suggests, however, that the lie can be distinguished by a deliberate intent to deceive and that lies perpetrated by powerful minorities are aimed at the subordination of society's weaker members (Simmel, 1950:312–314). He therefore does argue that democracy and truthfulness are ideally related. Nevertheless, he also points out that, 'the ethically negative value of the lie must not blind us to its sociologically quite positive significance' (Simmel, 1950: 315). Simmel explores this significance through the idea that forces of conflict are as essential to society's well-being as the energies of solidarity. He states that:

> concord, harmony, co-efficiency, which are unquestionably held to be socializing forces must nevertheless be interspersed with distance, competition, repulsion...the solid, organizational forms which seem to constitute or create society, must constantly be disturbed, disbalanced, and gnawed-at by individualistic, irregular forces, in order to gain their vital reaction through submission and resistance (Simmel, 1950: 315).

Simmel does not confuse the lie with the secret, but he does suggest that the two are related, because hiding information creates social barriers. Moreover, distances, intermissions and reserves are often as essential to intimate personal relationships as they are to society as a whole. Despite the prevalent notions in Western societies that 'true love' is based upon mutual absorption of the total personality, Simmel suggests that to reveal oneself, in one moment and without reserve, can lead to disappointments. This is because intimacy is not simply based on the amount of knowledge that we possess with regard to one another, it is, more precisely, related to the pleasures of revelation. Such pleasures require counter-measures of reciprocal discretion so that the couple remain fascinated by the veiled promises of future treasures to be discovered (Simmel, 1950: 328–329).

This observation indicates a complexity in Simmel's attitude to secrecy. While on the one hand he states that 'evil has an immediate connection with secrecy,' on the other the secret is 'one of man's greatest achievements' (Simmel, 1950: 331 & 330). In either case, the secret, regardless of its actual content, creates a bond between those who share it, excluding outsiders. This bond emanates power, and secrecy, thereby, fascinates (Simmel, 1950: 332). The attractions of secrecy are illustrated through a discussion of its opposite—betrayal:

> the secret contains a tension that is dissolved in the moment of its revelation. This moment constitutes the acme in the development of the secret; all of its charms are once more gathered in it and brought to a climax—just as the moment of dissipation lets one enjoy with extreme intensity the value of the object (Simmel, 1950: 333).

He therefore proposes that while secrecy places barriers between individuals or groups, the power thus concentrated within it threatens those boundaries, and that therefore both human interaction and society itself are permeated with the ebb and flow of concealing and revealing.

Despite differences in theoretical orientation, Simmel's discussion of secrecy contains ideas and themes that are also present in Durkheim's work, particularly Durkheim's conception of the sacred. For Durkheim, the category of the sacred is, paradoxically, both central to unifying forces within society, and, at the same time, a creator of social barriers par excellence. Drawing from an analysis of aboriginal Australian totemism, Durkheim argues that all religions are characterized by a division of the world into sacred and profane phenomena (Durkheim, 1995 [1912]: 19). Moreover, he suggests that the barrier between sacred and profane is 'absolute. In the history of human thought, there is no other example of two categories of things as profoundly differentiated or as radically opposed to one another' (Durkheim, 1995: 36). This division is, however, not simply cognitive. Rather, the sacred is rooted in the generation of powerful emotions, aroused by the nature of social life in general and religious rituals in particular. Durkheim suggests that the intense collective activity of religious rituals produces a corresponding series of emotions that both express and perpetuate the ties that bind people to one another in social life. In other words, the vitality aroused by ritual is not only related to collective behaviour, it is also the source of what Durkheim terms *collective consciousness*.

In addition, the energies of *collective effervescence* can alight upon, and permeate, certain objects and persons so that these objects, by association, also become designated as sacred. One example that Durkheim refers to is the *churinga*, a piece of wood or stone that has totemic designs or symbols engraved or painted upon it. Moreover, the aboriginal Australian term *churinga* is used for sacred things more generally. It therefore, counts among the most pre-eminently sacred things. Nothing has surpassed it in religious dignity...the profane; therefore—women and young men not yet initiated into religious life—may not touch or see the churingas; they are only permitted to look from afar and even then only rarely...the churingas are piously kept in a special...deserted place. The entrance is carefully closed with rocks placed so skilfully that a passing stranger never suspects that the religious treasury of the clan is nearby. Such is the churingas sacredness that it is passed on to the place where they are deposited; women and the unitiated may not come near it (Durkheim, 1995: 118).

The separation of sacred things therefore also enshrouds them in secrecy, creating a barrier that protects and contains collective energies that are both intensely powerful and dangerous. To inappropriately speak about or touch the sacred things such as blood shed for ritual purposes is thought to bring about sickness or death, because these energies have thereby been given a channel through which to escape into, and contaminate, unprepared profane spheres (Durkheim, 1995: 137). In a ritual context, therefore, initiation is primarily a matter of preparing young men for entrance into the world of sacred things. Without that preparation, contact with sacred forces may induce a 'shock' that Durkheim compares with an electrical charge (Durkheim, 1995: 37 & 192). This idea can, however, also contribute to our understanding of an ambivalence surrounding visionary or mystical phenomena that may or may not be preceded by ritual initiation in a direct fashion. Wolfson's exploration of tensions in Jewish mystical texts between accounts of visionary encounters with God, on the one hand, and the assertion that such encounters are impossible, on the other is a case in point, because of attempts within the tradition to reconcile these two positions with the assertion that seeing God is impossible, not because he has no visible forms, but because these forms radiate such intense power that most human beings would simply be destroyed by them (Wolfson, 1994: 92–96)

From this, one may derive a nonlinear model of religious secrecy in which initiations are imagined as a series of concentric circles, through which the initiate passes, travelling from a profane circumference into a sacred centre, and thereby gaining gradual exposure to the power of the sacred and the source from which springs the renewal of the energies of collective life. This image may be especially useful in the context of tantric Buddhism, a religious tradition saturated with secrecy.

Tantric Buddhism

On one level, tantric Buddhism differs from Judaism in its orientation to an engagement with vision and visualization as prescribed, rather than, proscribed spheres of religious activity. This is not to suggest, however, that the visual realization of oneself as a deity is unproblematic, but that its inherent dangers are recognized and negotiated through a number of progressively more secret ritual initiations that bring disciples into ever-more closely bounded relationships with persons who are thought to personally incarnate the sacred in their personhood.

References to secrecy in tantric Buddhist ritual and biographical material are, therefore, numerous and diverse, including references to communications between human beings in their enlightened forms using twilight, intentional or secret language (Shaw, 1994: 43) and visionary experiences that are thought to transcend language altogether, and can therefore only be vaguely articulated, even by the most indiscreet practitioner. Ritual secrecy thereby permeates structures that constitute tantric Buddhism, structures that focus on guru-disciple relationships which in turn form lineages. It is asserted that one cannot gain access to the more potent forms of ritual knowledge without having pledged oneself to a guru and undertaken a series of complex initiations that often entail periods of seclusion.

The centrality of ritual secrecy in tantric Buddhism raises a number of methodological problems for the inquisitive student, ranging from ethical and practical issues raised by reading texts only intended for initiates, to the power dynamic operating between the tradition's enclosed system of relational transmission and the penetrating gaze of the academic. Moreover, questions concerning the nature of power relations within tantra itself are opened up. Ritual secrecy protects and preserves hierarchies between initiates and the guru, wherein the disciple is expected, after an initial period of cool examination, to abandon judgements of the guru based on mundane appearances. Disciples are encouraged to foster a 'pure vision' of him or her and trust that the enlightened being, veiled beneath the guru as an ordinary person, will reveal itself, together with the initiate's *own* enlightened identity. This practice is problematic, particularly for those raised within a Western context, partly because of the potential danger of unscrupulous gurus, but also because it challenges the initiate to negotiate an intense relationship which Klein describes as,

> without projections from within. . .one is asked to interact with this person without being deluded by the kinds of sensory and conceptual experiences that usually delude mind and senses, namely substantial reality, or anything other than the free manifestation of enlightened energy itself. Pure vision is not for the reality challenged (Klein, 1999: 301).

One of the intriguing features of guru yoga in tantric Buddhism is that it synthesizes tantra's devotional and ritual practices together with philosophical orientations drawn from the broader corpus of Buddhist traditions. On one level, there lies the idea that contact with the guru brings the initiate into a sphere of secret power. On another, initiates learn to command powers of revelation, beginning, in good Buddhist fashion, with the exposing of, and moving beyond, the veil of their own mistaken perceptions. This aspect of the guru-disciple relationship is particularly problematic in the context of ritual and sexual relations between consorts, where one partner (most often the man) is also a guru to the other. Campbell explores such problems with particular reference to the Western contemporary context in which the 'awesome regard' for lamas or believing any human being to be divine is unusual and may lead to women making judgements about invitations to be consorts on that basis, suspending their usual frames of reference and reserve, 'and this is especially so if the lama invokes the use of sexual relations with a student as a means of either furthering his own practice or alleging spiritual benefit for the woman concerned' (Campbell, 1996: 9). Moreover, she suggests that the upbringing and social development for the males concerned is also an issue, particularly when young boys are taken from a family environment and placed in monastic care at an early age (Campbell, 1996: 82), a point which resonates with anthropological studies of societies in which initiation into the world of men entails seclusion from females. However, while such problems are worthy of note and regard, scholars such as Gross are wary of placing too much emphasis on the issue of the potential abuses of the consort relationship in a Western context, arguing instead for a broader revisioning of hierarchy and authority in Buddhism that would create a greater gender balance with regard to positions of power in the system (Gross, 1998: 66, 71–73).

In addition to contemporary material, it is also important to consider hagiographical references to consort relationships, not least because these stories question ways in which all personal relationships negotiate a tension between desires for transcendent forms of communication and the desire to control, or be controlled by, others. Gross, for example, in her exploration of the hagiographical material related to the eighth-century Tibetan female Yeshe Tsogyel, suggests that although these texts are not sufficient in themselves to suggest that female practitioners were as numerous or as powerful as male ones in this society, they nonetheless provoke challenging and interesting questions about models for relationships that are worthy of consideration (Gross, 1987: 31). She argues that the *dharmic* relationships portrayed in these texts are, 'not based on neurotic or unenlightened passions, they are neither mutually exploitative nor exploitative of one or the other of the partners. Regardless of who is the leading or more developed partner, the relationship serves to develop both partners more fully. . .the neurotically compulsive insanity that so often plagues relationships is not part of Tsogyel's relationships with her *dharmic* consorts and friends' (Gross, 1987: 23–24). She points, for example, to their unconventional and non-possessive conduct as suggested by the fact that although Yeshe is Padmasambhava's consort, she is able to devote significant amounts of time to other consorts or solitary practice. Moreover, she has important *dharmic* friendships with two of Padmasambvara's other consorts, Sakya Dema and Mandarava (Gross, 1987: 23–24).

If it is the case that consort relationships in tantric Buddhism have the potential to resist immersion in more egoistic patterns of behaviour, I would suggest that an important element in that potential is the recognition, and respect for, shared participation in experiences or states of consciousness that transcend individual concerns, language, and thought processes. Ray, for example, explores this idea in relation to the rite of *abhisheka,* an initiation into tantric deity practice that occurs after a series of preliminary practices known as *ngondro,* and which he describes as a 'meeting of two minds' between the disciple and the guru that is akin to a marriage (Ray, 2001: 195–196 & 204). Prior to this meeting the disciples commit themselves to *samaya,* a number of vows, including ones that forbid the disparaging of one's guru or women (Ray, 2001: 206). He argues that although this process may appear to reinforce uncomfortable hierarchies within the tradition, its purpose 'is not something extrinsic or external to the ritual itself. It is rather a natural outcome of the process of the *abhisheka*. It is like when two people experience a moment of truth or reality together. Once something real or genuine has been experienced, as human beings we naturally feel the need to honour that experience as having occurred. It is only and always the sharing of reality that truly binds two people together. After such a shared experience, to pretend that it never occurred, to deny it, to try to revert to previous conventional ways of behaving, is inherently painful, undermining, and dehumanizing' (Ray, 2001: 203).

From Ritual Drama to Melodrama: *Communitas* in *Skins*

Explorations of initiation in Papua New Guinea and tantric Buddhism are subject to difficulties that are encountered in the study of initiation more broadly, because while initiation rituals perpetuate social structures which often entail the enforcement of hierarchical relationships, they may also be the wellspring of mystical communities. The study of initiation is complicated by the variety of initiation practices worldwide combined with the fact that some of these involve the inflicting of pain on initiates, an issue where anthropologists negotiate opposing scholarly aims of understanding of, and respect for indigenous traditions, on the one hand, and the moral questions raised by the nature of the operations, on the other. Whitehouse, for example, argues that, 'terror is an integral component of the religious experience in many of the societies of Papua New Guinea' (Whitehouse, 1996: 703) and cites as examples of terrifying rites penis-bleeding among the Ilahita Arapesh (Tuzin, 1975: 56) and the piercing of the nasal septa and the burning of forearms in Bimin-Kuskusmin initiation (Poole, 1982: 144). While acknowledging the role of 'rites of terror' in producing effective subjugation in initiates, particularly when these rites are alternated with expressions of affection (Tuzin,1980: 77–78), he suggests that this paradigm does not fully investigate transformations in consciousness of the initiates or 'the complex imagery of the male cult' (Whitehouse, 1996: 709). Instead, Whitehouse suggests a deeper investigation into Chinnery and Beaver's (1915: 77) hypothesis that rites of terror produce in novices a 'receptive...frame of mind...an important quality of flashbulb memories is that they are unforgettable, vivid and haunting' (Whitehouse, 1996: 710 & 712).

Further to this, he investigates the notion of flashbulb memories as 'vivid recollections of inspirational, calamitous, or otherwise emotionally arousing events' arguing that 'an advantage of this theory is that it fits with people's intuitive impressions of how dramatic, frightening and surprising experiences seem to be 'printed' on the mind...what we are dealing with here is a stock of very vivid, disturbing and perhaps enlightening memories which are consciously turned over in the minds of initiates for years to come...when a Baktaman novice first realizes that he is (in some sense) being made into a virile, aggressive pig—a warrior and a father—he is not only struck by the absurdity of his previous assumptions about pigs, but he associates this revelation with the terrifying and agonizing experience of being beaten with stones, whipped with nettles and dehydrated almost to the point of death. It is this combination of cognitive and emotional crises that produces the distinctive mnemonic effect' (Whitehouse, 1996: 710). In examining the political implications of these rites Whitehouse points to ways in which their traumatic nature, combined with their secrecy, may 'generate intense solidarity among participants' which is linked to courage in war (Whitehouse, 1996: 711) and suggesting that, at least in some instances (Tuzin,1980: 73–4 & 78), 'although the authoritarian behaviour of initiators instantiates a striking imbalance of power, but once the metamorphosis of the novice is complete, the camaraderie engendered in their common experience of liminality is extended to their initiators. In a real sense initiators and novices undergo the experience together, and share its dramatic consequences' (Whitehouse, 1996: 712).

This language of liminality is interesting in that although Turner's work suggests important links between the bonds formed between initiates at the peak of the ritual process and expressions of *communitas* within religious and social movements (Turner, 1995: 108), he does not explore or explain the former phenomenon in great detail. This is partly because his emphasis is on *communitas* as a social modality in contrast to social structure (Turner, 1995: 131–2), rather than on a precise analysis of the small-scale social interactions that individuals might experience as examples of it. Related to this point is the humility demanded of both initiates and members of the groups that he uses as examples of permanent liminality such as the Franciscans (1995: 140–153).

The point he makes, that certain kinds of relationship and community are made possible by the renunciation of social structures that erect boundaries between people, is an important one, but in making it he eschews questions concerning the potential abuse of *communitas* by powerful groups and persons and avoids the possibility that resentment and anger, as well as fear, might be an emotion roused in initiates as an intended or unintended consequence of the ritual. However, given that the stated intention of many initiation rituals is the preparation of young men for warfare, it is not unreasonable to assume that this is a possibility in some cases. La Fontaine (1985), for example, discusses the *ilmugit* ritual of the Samburu, in which the *moran* (male initiates) are first exposed to intense heat and then splattered with a mixture of milk and water, an action which induces intense shaking, regarded by the Samburu 'as a sign of manliness and anger. . .the words of the elders indeed seem to provoke a manifestation of just that lack of control or respect, of which the elders accuse them' (La Fontaine, 1985: 157).

Secondly, there are difficulties in exploring the relationship between the ritual context and broader life experiences. For scholars exploring this point, the formality of ritual itself is a double-edged sword. It provides a discrete object of study that can be observed, but the focus on the mechanics of the ritual process can obscure more profound observations regarding transformations in consciousness that are connected to, but not bounded within the ritual itself. To give one possible example, understandings of a ritual that is intended to be a preparation for warfare could be enhanced by an exploration of informants' understandings of the relationship between their experience of the ritual and their experiences of war itself, as the ritual may be simply preparing the ground or providing a context which can be recollected and 'recognized' in the heat of battle. According to this paradigm, 'flashbulb memory,' is not a simple case of brainwashing, but rather a reference point for crisis and its transcendence. Similarly there may be instances where the formal ritual occurs to recognize and signify transformations in consciousness that have already occurred, and I would suggest that this proposition does much to elucidate descriptions of ritual in the context of tantric Buddhism.

For example, the hagiography of Machig Labdron relates a story of her initiation by Lama Sonam who her previous teacher (Lama Trapa) suggests has a connection with her through aspirations made in previous lives (Edou, 1996: 133). During the last in a series of initiations Machig's, 'body rose about one cubit metre above the ground. She displayed the twenty-four dance postures of the peaceful deities and sang in Sanskrit. . .and meanwhile her mind experienced the vajra-like meditative stabilization. . .absorbed in the limitless essence of reality. Next, without being in any way hindered by the clay walls of the temple, she floated straight through them, rose in the air and disappeared. . .around midnight, the five deities of the Mahamaya mandala with their consorts appeared to her in a vision and conferred on her the four initiations, complete in every detail' (Edou, 1996: 134). When the other disciples find her the next morning they 'pointed out that the evening before she had failed to obtain the main part of the empowerment, but the lama intervened: "What the rest of you have received is merely the initiation of the ritual substances, but Machig has obtained the empowerment into the ultimate nature of reality!" (Edou, 1996: 135).

Connected to this is the paucity of information about relationships between initiates, which may stem in part from a tendency to focus on initiates in relation to initiators and society more broadly and also from the seclusion of many initiates. While even 'secret' rites might be observed by anthropologists, the conversations that take place between participants, in which they might express reserve or even resentment of the rites or of those in authority, are less likely to be heard. I have therefore chosen to move from the more formal ritual arena into the realm of Western contemporary serial drama, and in particular the series *Skins* which focuses on the lives of a set of young people in a further education college in Bristol, England (usually attended by 16- to 18-year-olds). While the programme, given its postmodern Western setting, does not portray rituals, it does explore a time in young people's lives that can be considered a period of initiation, and it could be argued that watching such programmes has in itself some resemblance to ritual, especially as they contain a number of features, such as 'the indulgence of strong emotionalism; moral polarization and schematization; extreme states of being, situations, [and] actions; overt villainy, persecution of the good, and final reward of virtue; inflated and extravagant expression; dark plotting, suspense [and] breathtaking peripety' (Brooks,1976: 11–12) that also have much in common with melodrama. While melodrama has often been dismissed as 'low culture,' Brooks suggests that, 'at its most ambitious, the melodramatic mode of conception and representation may appear to be the very process of reaching a fundamental drama of the moral life and finding the terms to express it. . .we may legitimately claim that melodrama becomes the principal mode for uncovering, demonstrating, and making operative the essential moral universe in a post-sacred era' (Brooks, 1976: 15). Moreover, although Brooks hesitates to argue that it is the sacred itself which is being explored (because of melodrama's associations with modernity) he does suggest ways in which the genre's ethical concerns are related to it (Brooks, 1976: 11–21), and *Skins* presents a particularly good example of this idea, not least because of its focus on the bonds formed between the young people concerned and the ways in which adults often merely provide a sense of background authority or self-absorption in comparison to the all-consuming concerns of the teenage community.

Episodes 7 and 8 of the fourth series provide particularly useful material for developing the themes I have hitherto been outlining, in that they delve in some depth into ways in which this community can come into conflict with postmodern social structural authorities, represented by the college director, Professor Blood, and a counsellor in a psychiatric institution, Dr. John Foster. The three principal characters of these episodes are James Cook, a self-styled 'Jack the Lad' (he has this phrase tattooed on his forearm), Freddie McClair, his more responsible best friend, and Elizabeth 'Effy' Stonem who had a casual affair with Cook in the third series, but who has chosen a more stable relationship with Freddie in the fourth series, an act which provokes Cook to assault an innocent bystander, leading to a prison sentence. In episode five, Effy suffers a psychological breakdown and is placed in an institution following a suicide attempt. Episode 7 opens with her talking to John Foster about her brother, who was in a serious traffic accident in Series One that Effy witnessed. She relates this incident to John in a later session and is instructed by him to imagine that it had never happened and is then told that she can go home. It should be noted that this technique can be regarded as highly unorthodox from the point of view of conventional psychology, which is orientated to the uncovering rather than the erasing of memory, however, the commentary suggests that the writer was inspired by personal questions about the methodology of cognitive behavioural therapy. The theme of the erasing of memory continues, both symbolically (Effy's room has been repainted by her mother and all of her possessions placed in a cupboard) and in discussion with Freddie, who is concerned about her treatment, asking at one point, "did John steal your soul as well as your past?" It is also played out in the college, where Effy goes to arrange re-taking the exams she missed and is told by Blood:

"It's been a good year. . .every student received A to C grades (well we had a lot of people doing media studies). Nevertheless, our targets were met, except by you. You failed everything, which brings down the college average and affects the funding scenario. Do you see my dilemma?" Whereupon he shreds her old results and presents her with three A grades instead, suggesting that we are all living lies and that reality is all relative. Effy, confused by this, attends a celebration at the local pub where her friends read out their results and declares that she is leaving her friends because, "you have to make sacrifices to get what you want." Leaving the pub she bumps into Cook (who has escaped from prison), telling him that she does not belong at the party:

Cook: "Neither do I. . .we've got a lot in common me and you."
Effy: "Not anymore."
Cook: "Both stood in the rain. . .both miserable."
Effy: "You're no good for me Cook. You never were."

Cook: "If this was us, meeting for the first time, I'd do it all again. . .everything. I'd do it all again."
Effy: "What's that supposed to mean?"
Cook: "It means I still love you."

At this point in the episode, it is difficult to come to conclusions about Effy's behaviour, as she appears to be pulled between her friends and the possibility of a fresh start with better health and opportunities. While there are some sinister overtones to the scenes with John Foster, it is possible that they may simply be portraying her conflicted perspective regarding figures in authority. However, after one session with the counsellor, Effy seeming particularly confused, is sitting on a park bench when Cook approaches her, stating that, "I got a call from your man. He's all in a tizzy, so I thought I'd come down and hear your side of the story like." Denying all knowledge of Effy, she introduces herself as Elizabeth and goes out dancing with Cook, stating afterwards that she wants to do something bad, whereupon he leads her to the site of her brother's traffic accident (although it is unclear whether or not he is aware of what had happened there). As Effy begins to remember the incident her confusion and anxiety grow, and she continues to deny knowing Cook despite his protests, finally running into the road declaring that she wants to be scared and to remember. As Cook pulls her out of the path of collision with an oncoming car Effy kisses him, and asks him to take her to Freddie. Cook asks: "You remember me though? You know who I am?" and Effy replies, "How can I forget? You're my friend," before fainting in his arms. The theme of transcendent friendship is continued in a conversation between Freddie and Cook, when Cook realizes that Freddie was planning to leave.

Freddie: "She broke my heart."
Cook: "She broke my heart as well. You broke my heart. I bet you've broken hers at some point. So what are we going to do? Are we just three losers. . .or are we something better than that? Grow up cos I'm done here," an exchange that evokes the essence, if not the formal trappings, of an initiatory turning point in the story.

Waking up in the institution, Effy asks Freddie to remove John, which he does, but following a telephone call the next morning Freddie goes to John's house, where John admits that his motives are confused by his desire for Effy and murders Freddie with a baseball bat, ending the episode. This short scene transforms the focus of the drama from an exploration of conflicts between authority figures and friends into a carefully crafted comment on the abuses, and potentially very serious threats, of the contemporary world and its more unscrupulous inhabitants, that may, at times, be disguised beneath the cloak of conventional power systems. From the perspective of the story, this shocking event not only presents a stark contrast between two relations to Effy's sexuality; Cook's ability to sacrifice what he wants for an ethic of friendship and care compared to John's obsessive desire to possess which threatens both her identity and her life, but also throws up the difficult question of how Cook, who has no access to any responsible adult who will listen to him, might be able to alert anyone to the danger that Effy is clearly in. The last episode in the series, however, contains no scenes with adults at all, apart from a brief shot of the police as they try to catch Cook, and the adult role is instead taken by Freddie's younger sister who disbelieves a note (supposedly from Freddie) that states that he has simply run away, and demands that Cook try to find him. In the last few minutes of the episode, Cook spots John spying on a party in Freddie's shed and, unseen, breaks into John's home, finding Freddie's blood-stained tee-shirt and trainers. John enters the room with a baseball bat.

Cook: "What have you done?"

John: "Don't be stupid Cook. She told me all about you two. There was much to correct in that girl. I almost managed it. Perhaps I still can."

Cook: "You did something to my friend?"

John: "This is wasting time. Would you kneel down please?"

John hits Cook with the baseball bat, and Cook gets up smiling, saying, "You don't know what I am."

John: "I think I do. You're nothing. You don't deserve that girl and you know I do." Cook's response gives a strange twist to the notion of humility in *communitas* by saying, "I'm just a. . . waste of space. I'm just a stupid kid. I got no sense. I'm a criminal. I'm no. . .use mate. So please get it into your nonce that you killed my friend and I'm Cook!" The episode ends with Cook's war cry.

Conclusion

There is a certain irony in the fact that while psychological theories of the crowd and charisma are the most suspicious of collective emotions and charisma, a number of contemporary Western films and serial dramas (of which *Skins* is a good example) appear to suggest that the intimate relationship between psychologist and patient is potentially one of the most dangerous structures in modern society. Moreover, the series highlights ideas about forms of communitas between young people that are more difficult to access through more conventional modes of sociological investigation, precisely because they rely on unstructured friendship networks in which spontaneous sexuality and personal loyalties remain hidden from view. Nonetheless, I suggest that the evolution of Cook's character and personal transformations can be better understood within the framework of the anthropological literature explored in this chapter, not least because his emergence as an unlikely and apparently powerless hero conforms in many ways to the melodramatic genre of which the series is an example and thereby can be illuminated through discussions of the sacred and social solidarity central to the social theoretical models of Durkheim, Simmel and Turner. Moreover, Cook's chaotic conflicts with authority and undisciplined relationship with Effy prepare the ground for the challenges he faces at the end of the series, in that his shared memories with Effy help her to retrieve her identity, and his rage, rather then being checked or intimated by John's authority, is aroused by it, leading me to suggest that there are dimensions to Turner's humility in communitas that are hietherto underexplored in scholarly accounts of initiation and mystical communites.

Bibliography

Bolle, K.W. (ed.) (1987) *Secrecy in Religions*. Leiden, The Netherlands & New York: Brill.
Bowie, F. (2000) *The Anthropology of Religion: An Introduction*. Oxford: Blackwell.
Brooks, P. (1976) *The Melodramatic Imagination: Balzac, Henry James, Melodrama, and the Mode of Excess*. New Haven, CT & London: Yale University Press.
Campbell, J. (1996) *Traveller in Space: In Search of Female Identity in Tibetan Buddhism*. London: Athlone.
Child, L. (2010) 'Spirit possession, seduction, and altered states of consciousness' in Schmidt, B. & Huskinson, L. (eds.) *Spirit Possession and Trance: New Iinterdisciplinary Perspectives*. London: Continuum. pp. 53–70.
Child, L. (2008) 'Possession in contemporary cinema: Religious and psychological themes' in *Diskus* (the online journal of the British Association for the Study of Religion), vol. 9. http://www.basr.ac.uk/discus/diskus9/child.htm.
Child, L. (2007) *Tantric Buddhism and Altered States of Consciousness: Durkheim, Emotional Energy and Visions of the Consort*. Aldershot: Ashgate.
Dowman, K. (1985) *Masters of Mahamudra: Songs and Histories of the Eighty-Four Buddhist Siddhas*. New York: State University of New York Press.
Durkheim, E. (1995 [1912]) *The Elementary Forms of Religious Life* (translated by Karen E. Fields) New York: Free Press.
Edou, J. (1996) *Machig Labdron and the Foundations of Chod* . New York: Snow Lion.
Eliade, M. (1959) *Cosmos and History: The Myth of the Eternal Return*. New York.
Fontaine, J.S. (1985) *Initiation: Ritual Drama and Secret Knowledge Across the World*. Harmondsworth: Penguin.
Gross, R. (1987) 'Yeshe Tsogyel: Enlightened consort, great teacher, female role model' in Willis, J. D. (ed) *Feminine Ground: Essays on Women and Tibet*. New York: Snow Lion.
Gross, R. (1998) *Soaring and Setting: Buddhist Perspectives on Contemporary Social and Religious Issues*. New York: Continuum.
Guenther, H.V. (1995[1963]) *The Life and Teachings of Naropa*. Boston & London: Shambhala Publications.
Herdt, G. (1987) *Guardians of the Flutes: Idioms of Masculinity*. New York: Columbia University Press.
Herdt, G. (1990) 'Secret societies and secret collectives' *Oceania*. vol. 60, pp. 361–381.
Herdt, G. (2003) *Secrecy and Cultural Reality: Utopian Ideologies of the New Guinea Men's House*. Ann Arbor: University of Michigan Press.
Klein, A.C. (1999) 'Gurus and disciples in Tibet: Worlds visible and invisible' in Wolfson E.R. (ed.) *Rending the Veil: Concealment and Secrecy in the History of Religions*. New York & London: Seven Bridges Press.

Lindholm, C. (1993) *Charisma*. Oxford: Blackwell.
Norbu, N. (1986) *The Crystal and the Way of Light: Sutra, Tantra, and Dzogchen.* London: Penguin.
Otto, R. (1923 [1917]) *The Idea of the Holy*. Oxford: Oxford University Press.
Poole, F.J.P (1982) 'The ritual forging of identity: Aspects of person and self in Bimin-Kuskusmin male initiation,' in Herdt, G.H. (ed) *Rituals of Manhood: Male Initiation in Papua New Guinea*. Berkeley: University of California Press.
Ray, R.A. (2001) *Secret of the Vajra World: The Tantric Buddhism of Tibet*. Boston & London: Shambhala.
Shaw, M. (1994) *Passionate Enlightenment: Women in Tantric Buddhism*. Princeton, NJ: Princeton University Press.
Simmel, G. (1950 [1908]) *The Sociology of Georg Simmel* (trans. & ed. by Kurt H. Wolff). New York: Free Press.
Turner, V. (1995 [1969]) *The Ritual Process: Structure and Anti-Structure*. New York: Aldine De Gruyter.
Tuzin, D.F. (1980) *The Voice of the Tambaran: Truth and Illusion in Ilahita Arapesh Religion*. Berkeley: University of California Press.
Whitehouse, H. (1996) 'Rites of terror: Emotion, metaphor and memory in Melanesian initiation cults' *The Journal of the Royal Anthropological Institute,* vol.2, no. 4, pp. 703–715.
Wolfson, E.R. (1994) *Through a Speculum that Shines: Vision and Imagination in Medieval Jewish Mysticism*. Princeton, NJ: Princeton University Press.

SEVEN

Sacrament and Medicine
A Comparison of Roman Catholic and Native American Church Confession

Thomas J. Csordas

I want to compare two cultural variants of confession, which I will define as revelation or disclosure of personal or subjective information by an individual to another or to a group. The content revealed is sensitive in such a way as to create emotional or social vulnerability in the person making the confession. The individual or group to whom confession is made occupies, at least temporarily, a status socially recognized as qualified to receive and respond to the confession. This generic definition includes practices such as confession of a criminal to a police officer, confession of a sinner to a priest, confession of a friend to a confidant. Specifically religious variants have something to do with spiritual need for or value of forgiveness, absolution, healing, reparation, or self-transformation. This is the case for both variants with which I am concerned, namely confession within the Roman Catholic Church and within the Native American Church (NAC).

The purpose of this exercise is both to contribute to an understanding of confession as a general category of cultural practice and to elaborate an understanding of each variant through juxtaposing and contrasting it with the other. I assert that this is a legitimate undertaking despite the considerable difference between the two religious systems in which the practice of confession is embedded. Roman Catholicism is the largest and oldest among Christian denominations, always culturally inflected by the milieu of the global region, nation, or ethnic group in which it has taken root. The Native American Church is a religion barely more than a century old and limited to North American indigenous societies, though it too is culturally inflected by various tribal cultures and religions as well as varying degrees of influence from Christianity. The locus classicus for Catholic confession as a ritual practice is the encounter between penitent and confessor, the former understood as a sinner and the latter as one empowered to absolve the penitent from sin. The locus classicus for NAC confession is the encounter between patient and road man, the former understood as suffering from an affliction and the latter as one empowered to guide people as they follow the Peyote Road, the way of life prescribed for adherents of peyotism.

The first observation to be made in this comparison is that Catholic confession is defined in religious terms as a sacrament. Defined in theological terms as "outward signs of inward grace, instituted by Christ for our sanctification" (Catholic Encyclopedia 2009), our first question has to be whether the notion of sacrament is confined to the theological domain or whether, like the notion of charisma, may have some value when extrapolated as an analytic category for ritual analysis. Is the sacrament a culture-bound emic category of Christianity, or is there an empirically identifiable set of "outward signs of inward spiritual power" with a degree of etic validity, and specifically can it help us in our cross-cultural analysis of different forms of confession? The first step in addressing such a question is whether any help can be found in how the category of sacrament has previously appeared in the anthropological literature.

It is not surprising that the work on the ritual process by Victor Turner (1995), himself a Catholic anthropologist, has been taken up and applied to analysis of Christian sacraments by scholars in religious studies, ritual studies, and theology. In their work on pilgrimage, Victor and Edith Turner (1995) compare that ritual form to the sacraments which count as rites of passage such as Marriage and Holy Orders, and observe that in some respects Catholic pilgrimages are extended versions of the sacraments of Penance and the Eucharist. E.E. Evans-Pritchard, another Catholic anthropologist, observed that Robert Hertz intended to write a study of sin and pardon based on an interest in the "Sacrament of Auricular Confession" (Burton 1983). However, in order to find the notion of sacrament deployed as an analytic concept we must return to the work of Robert Ranulph Marett (1933), whose 1933 Gifford lectures were entitled "Sacraments of Simple Folk."

Notwithstanding that R.R. Marett was a scholar who unflinchingly used the now taboo word "savage" in his texts, and that his reputation is permanently marked by the most damning epithet of our profession, "armchair anthropologist," let us open our minds to the definition he presents at the very opening of the lectures:

Sacrament and Medicine 149

> For anthropological purposes a sacrament may be defined as any rite which by way of sanction or positive blessing invests a natural function with a supernatural authority of its own. By ritual the anthropologist understands an organized technique, approved by the society concerned, for dealing with the incalculable element in any critical situation of human life. Of all ritual forms, the sacrament is the most dynamic, coming to the aid of a given activity, at the point at which it finds itself baffled by nature in the shape of the contradictions of the sense-world, so as to turn it into a super-activity by bringing into play the latent energy of the moral personality (1933:1).

Marett feels obligated to justify use of the term, not insofar as we today would fear imposing a Western category on indigenous peoples, but insofar as it might be objected to as a misuse of a term hallowed by Christian usage within a claim that the savage is "capable of sacraments." His response is that Christianity borrowed the term *sacramentum* from Roman paganism by way of Roman law, and goes on to identify the issue of how to develop a repertoire of what we would call etic concepts for the comparative analysis of religion in face of the double risk of being misunderstood if one applies European terms to describe uncivilized thought and being even more totally misunderstood if one attempts to use the native idiom.

For Marett, ritual in general and sacraments in particular are purposive and not passive, not a matter of routine and repetition but of vigilance and a summons to exertion. For Marett, "The function of religion is not to lull the striving temper, but to compose it so as to intensify its force" (1933:7) as part of the human propensity to reshape the conditions of life. Sacraments are the most dynamic, creative, and life-enhancing forms of ritual precisely because they reinforce the effectiveness of "what are by their very nature active functions" (1933: 9). The sacrament consecrates a natural function and in so doing enhances its moral character by enlisting the creative imagination in service of the will to strengthen a sense of solemn obligation. Importing sacredness into an ordinary transaction, the sacrament "meets the world half-way" and "subordinates the material profit to the moral outcome," since the *mana* it bears, while an impersonal spiritual force, is also fundamentally moral in character. This mana brings both hope and fear to religious experience, and the element of fear makes sacredness both a peril to the unworthy and a positive means "to promote such repentance as results in renewed striving" (1933: 19), both features relevant to our concern with confession.

Interestingly from the standpoint of medical anthropology, Marett concludes his introductory discussion by referring to the sacraments he examines as "spiritual health-exercises" and "religious psychotherapy" aimed at "superior vitality," an "increase in vigour," and "spiritual well-being." From this standpoint, he says, "as civilized persons, who nevertheless retain a savage subconsciousness, we can take a practical as well as a scientific interest in the history of the sacrament, as being the method of trial and error whereby the association between religion and the good life has been chiefly promoted" (1933: 20–21). Each of his succeeding chapters is titled with what he calls a natural function subject to sacramental enhancement: eating, fighting, mating, educating, ruling, judging, covenanting, healing, and dying.

It is perhaps unsurprising that Marett, who was completely comfortable in using the terms *mana* and *grace* interchangeably, remains anthropology's foremost theorist of the sacrament as ritual form. Marett's definition allows us to suggest that the natural function consecrated by confession is speaking itself. Insofar as Rappaport (1999) argued that the advent of language brought forth the possibility of the lie, auricular confession as sacrament enshrines, enhances, and concretizes the ideal of truth in face to face utterance. Yet from the standpoint of contemporary anthropological thought this is not sufficient to justify adopting the concept in our comparison, if only because while Catholic confession is explicitly a sacrament in the emic view, NAC confession is not. At the least, if indeed the two forms of confession are commensurable, we ought to be able to identify an indigenous notion equivalent to that of sacrament. I suggest that the concept of "medicine" is such an equivalent, and furthermore that the ideas of sacrament and medicine can enrich one another by being placed in dialogue.

Introducing this dialogical pair of terms has immediate consequences for our comparison. The notion of medicine coincides with the aspect of a sacrament having to do with healing and the enhancement of well-being. However, the Native American concept of medicine goes beyond the sense in which it is used in the medical system and includes any vehicle of spiritual power. An object or substance that qualifies as medicine in this sense does not have its power by nature but is invested with its power by human agency through ritual action. This was brought home to me in discussing a statement by a Navajo healer that "the best medicine of all is water." This is true in part because water is a cosmologically fundamental substance; we are made in large part of water, and water is the basis of life. But there is a difference between water taken to quench thirst and water given to another as medicine. Water becomes medicine by being invested both with spiritual power and human care, which ultimately are virtually indistinguishable. Marett captures this well in saying that "Any projection of *mana* into an object such as food implies a moralization of that object, whether it be qualified naturally or not to assume such a character" (1933: 29). The medicine is not any water but ritually prepared water. But whereas in the Christian context blessing regular water so that it becomes "holy water" elevates it to the status of a sacramental but not a fully fledged sacrament, in the Native American view something of greater significance takes place in calling attention to the profundity of the mere existence of water in relation to life.

In our comparison of Catholicism and NAC, the juxtaposition of sacrament and medicine also immediately calls attention to the fact that the primary medicine in the NAC is peyote itself. Confession and ingestion of the peyote medicine are inseparable, and it is a short step to recognizing an analogy with the relation between Penance and the Eucharist in Catholicism, even though the latter are recognized as two distinct sacraments. In his discussion of healing sacraments, Marett has a useful insight here as well, observing that

> purity pivots round on itself from an abhorrence of evil to a rejoicing in spiritual cleanliness for its own sake. Purification and communion, the execration of our worse nature and the consecration of our better nature, are thus but two aspects of the same sacrament, differing only according as ritual happens to give prominence either to the imagery of rejection or to that of approach (1933: 188).

Recognizing that these two culturally divergent ritual forms partake of an ethnographically generalized pattern of confession and communion to some extent preempts the conclusion that the parallel is either a coincidence or too convenient. Yet we must acknowledge that the NAC in its various forms has been influenced to greater or lesser degrees by Christianity, not only in adopting the organizational form of a "church" in a bid for religious toleration, but in including the figures of Jesus and a Heavenly Father in some of its prayers, as well as revering a water spirit represented as a bird in a manner similar to how the Paraclete is represented as a dove. One distinguished Navajo road man acknowledged to me not only that as a child he attended a mission school, but that during this period he also assisted the priest as an altar boy at Mass.

Nevertheless, there are important differences. Most fundamentally, the Catholic penitent confesses in order to be absolved from sin and accepts a penance in order to atone for that sin, or in the post-Vatican II formulation to be reconciled to the deity. The NAC patient confesses in order to be healed from illness, specifically to accept responsibility for self-created obstacles to well-being and become re-oriented on the Peyote Road within the moral, social, cosmological, and spiritual order. This difference between sin and responsibility corresponds to a difference between worthiness and self-esteem as anticipated outcomes. The sinner who does not confess is precluded by unworthiness from participating in the Eucharist; the afflicted peyotist can partake of the medicine but is unlikely to experience its full benefit without becoming a confessing patient. The Catholic must return to confess again upon lapsing again into sin; the NAC adherent must again become a confessing patient by way of thanks to the peyote spirit or to renew the medicine's effect after it diminishes with time and the generation of additional self-created obstacles.

The relationship between the principal ritual participants is also of critical import. The anonymity of the Catholic penitent in a dark confessional separated by a screen from the confessor has given way since the reforms of the Second Vatican Council to a face to face encounter that, while it does not require identification by name, instantiates a greater degree of personalization and even intimacy concordant with a shift in emphasis from absolution to reconciliation as the desired goal of the sacrament. NAC confession is yet farther along on the continuum between anonymity and identity, such that a private consultation between patient and road man has always been face to face, and in a full-scale all-night peyote prayer meeting the patient is in the presence of other participants who include family members and acquaintances, even if some of the confession is made sotto voce to the road man. In this process, in relative terms it can be said that the road man has a more active role. While it is the case that not everything in Catholic confession depends on the penitent's examination of conscious, such that the priest can interrogate or question penitents for elaboration or clarification of their offenses, the road man's goal is not only to listen but to diagnose. This function includes identifying the type and source of a person's affliction, wrongs that they may have committed without awareness, and prescription for future comportment. It is based not only on disclosure by the patient but on revelation to the road man that can come through interrogation, inspiration, or even observation of the patient's action and demeanor.

A final point of comparison has to do with the relation between confession and communion in the two traditions, particularly in their most commensurable forms of private consultation between the two primary participants. In both situations, confession is a preparation for ingestion of the sacred substance, the consecrated Eucharistic host or the ritually prepared peyote. Contrary to what might be expected, rather than peyote being administered first so that its psychoactive properties amplify the spiritual power of confession and diagnosis, it is administered as the culmination of the consultation. Thus in both traditions confessions is preparatory. In effect, just as the message of Catholic absolution is "now you are worthy to commune with the divine in the sacramental presence," the "now your problems have been laid out before you and your spiritual affairs have been brought into order—with the medicine working within you, go away and think about it." Both forms of ritual ingestion confirm and consolidate the work already done.

Finally, however, this aspect of the confession-communion dyad differs in one deeply significant way, in that between the two traditions the valence of immanence and transcendence is reversed. To be precise, the transubstantiation accomplished in consecrating the Eucharist is the locus of divine transcendence, fundamentally changing its nature and rendering it otherworldly as a deity with a heavenly home. By contrast, the preparation of the peyote cactus as medicine is the locus of divine immanence highlighting that its already inherent psychoactive efficacy is of the earth and hence highlighting the spiritual profundity of the earthly order of being. In the Christian Eucharist, the process of ingestion is the locus of immanence in that the deity is incorporated physically into the communicant and the divine presence is a presence within. By contrast, with the peyote medicine ingestion is the locus of transcendence in that perception and imagination are enhanced and elements of everyday reality are thereby transfigured and elevated in spiritual significance.

Bibliography

Burton, John W. (1983). "Answers and Questions: Evans-Pritchard on Nuer Religion." *Journal of Religion in Africa 14*:3: 167–86.
Catholic Encyclopedia (2009). *Sacraments*. http://www.newadvent.org/cathen/13295a.htm
Marett, Robert Ranulph (1933). *Sacraments of Simple Folk*. Oxford: Clarendon Press.
Rappaport, Roy (1999). *Ritual and Religion in the Making of Humanity* (Cambridge Studies in Social and Cultural Anthropology). Cambridge: Cambridge University Press.
Turner, Victor (1995). *The Ritual Process: Structure and Anti-Structure* (Lewis Henry Morgan Lectures). Piscataway, NJ: Aldine Transaction.
Turner, Victor and Edith Turner (1995). *Image and Pilgrimage in Christian Culture*. New York: Columbia University Press.

EIGHT

Beyond Transcendence?
A Buddhist Perspective on the Axial Age

David R. Loy

Should your mind wander away, do not follow it, whereupon your wandering mind will stop wandering of its own accord. Should your mind desire to linger somewhere, do not follow it and do not dwell there, whereupon your mind's questing for a dwelling place will cease of its own accord. Thereby, you will come to possess a non-dwelling mind—a mind that remains in the state of non-dwelling....This full awareness in yourself of a mind dwelling upon nothing is known as having a clear perception of your own mind, or, in other words, as having a clear perception of your own nature. A mind which dwells upon nothing is the Buddha-mind, the mind of one already delivered, Bodhi-Mind, Un-created Mind... (Ch'an master Ta-chu Hui-hai, in *Hui Hai* 56)

A well-known line from the *Diamond Sutra*, one of the most important Mahayana Buddhist scriptures, is more succinct: "Let your mind come forth without fixing it anywhere." Whether or not this is the verse that precipitated the great awakening of the sixth Ch'an patriarch Hui-neng, his *Platform Sutra* makes and remakes the same point: "When our mind works freely without any hindrance, and is at liberty to 'come' or to 'go,' we attain liberation." Such a mind "is everywhere present, yet it 'sticks' nowhere." Hui-neng emphasized that he had no system of Dharma to transmit: "What I do to my disciples is to liberate them from their own bondage with such devices as the case may need" (Hui-neng 133).

The basic claim of such Buddhist texts is that the true nature of one's mind is formless, but it becomes "stuck" by identifying with particular phenomena, mental objects (e.g., one's self-image, ideologies) as well as physical ones. Such identifications occur because of ignorance of the basic "non-dwelling" nature of awareness, and awakening occurs when one's mind is liberated from grasping.

What does that imply about the relationship between *samsara*—this world of suffering, craving, and delusion—and *nirvana*, the goal of the Buddhist path?

> There is no specifiable difference whatever between *nirvana* and *samsara*; there is no specifiable difference whatever between *samsara* and *nirvana*. The limit [*koti* "sphere, bounds"] of *nirvana* is the limit of *samsara*. There is not even the subtlest difference between the two. (Nagarjuna, *Mulamadhyamikakarika* 25:19–20, in Candrakirti 259)

The implication is that *nirvana* is not the attainment of some other reality or transcendent dimension but realizing the true nature of this world, right here and now. This is consistent with one of the most celebrated verses in Buddhism, in which the Buddhist philosopher Nagarjuna—often acclaimed as "the second Buddha"—deconstructs the very concept of nirvana: "Ultimate serenity [*shiva*] is the coming to rest of all ways of taking things, the repose of named things; no truth has been taught by a Buddha for anyone, anywhere" (*Mulamadhyamikakarika* 25:24, in Candrakirti 262). We are not liberated by realizing any conceptual truth, for there is no such truth to identify with. This demotes all Buddhist teachings to *upaya* "skillful means," pointers that may be helpful but not if we take the finger for the moon.

Needless to say, there is much to say about such claims, but this chapter will not argue for or against this perspective. Instead, I will employ it provisionally as a heuristic tool to examine what happened during what Karl Jaspers (among others) named "the Axial Age." Various paradigmatic figures such as Deutero-Isaiah, Jeremiah, Ezekiel, Parmenides, Heracleitus, Socrates, Plato, Aristotle, Confucius, Mencius, Lao-tzu, Chuang-tzu, Mahavira, Shakyamuni Buddha, and the authors of the Hindu Upanishads all lived during this period, roughly 800—200 BCE, when profound and arguably similar transformations occurred in Israel, Greece, India, and China (sometimes Persia is also included, although Zoroaster was earlier). Although the precise nature of those transformations is controversial, one way to express it is that those civilizations developed a much stronger sense of transcendence, which created new possibilities along with new problems: the stronger dualism between this world and a "higher" one involved a greater felt demand for individual and social transformation, but the implicit critique of our "lower" world also had the effect of devaluing it.

This is of more than historical interest: in an important sense we still live in the Axial Age, motivated by the possibilities it opened up and struggling against its world-negating dualism. This chapter will use the Buddhist perspective adumbrating above to evaluate the role of *script* in the Axial transformation, as a new site of collective attachment that was both empowering and deluding. I will conclude by reflecting on whether we need to outgrow Axial dualism and replace its understanding of transcendence—e.g., God, Brahman, T'ien, the Tao and the Logos—with a more nondualistic appreciation of the evolutionary process.

The Axial Age

Jaspers was not the first to notice that something similar happened in Israel, Greece, India, and China in the middle of the first millennium BCE, but he gave it a name and popularized the idea of the Axial Age as a "turning point" in the development of human consciousness. During that period all four civilizations were independently experiencing similar stresses due in large part to new iron technologies, which enabled stronger, more efficient tools (hence more cropland and more crops, larger populations and population centers, more trade, wealth, and exposure to other cultures) but also stronger and more efficient weapons (hence more violent warfare, standing armies, imperial conquest and corresponding social crisis).

The late Israeli sociologist S. N. Eisenstadt provided a helpful summary of the consequences of the new Axial worldviews:

> The conception of a high level of tension between the transcendental and the mundane order, along with emphasis on this-worldly activities, tends to generate the highest level of free resources, the widest scope of markets, the greatest articulation of symbolic activities and of their institutional derivatives, and the largest variety of alternative conceptions of social and political order. (Eisenstadt 150)

In pre-Axial cultures people—as members, not individuals—are embedded in society and society embedded into its cosmic role, which meant that even rulers were not "free" but bound by the traditional functions of their position. There were no alternatives until stronger conceptions of transcendence developed, which provided "other-worldly" perspectives to evaluate given social and ideological structures. The political philosopher Eric Voegelin describes the Axial development as "the irruption of transcendental reality" in religious myth that amounted to "a major subjective orientation, a transition from consciousness that conceives of itself as fully immersed in the cosmos (the world of particular entities) to consciousness that is aware of its existence in tension between immanence in the cosmos and the pull of the transcendent pole beyond the cosmos" (Webb 115).

This included a radical restructuring not only of the way we understand the world but also of how we comport ourselves within it. Karen Armstrong's *The Great Transformation* emphasizes that the new religious programs "were designed to eradicate the egotism that is largely responsible for our violence, and promoted the empathic spirituality of the Golden Rule.... The Axial sages put the abandonment of selfishness and the spirituality of compassion at the top of their agenda (Armstrong 391, 392). As Armstrong also notices, this "social and psychological leap forward" involved the realization that each person is unique. "That is why so many of the Axial spiritualities were preoccupied by the discovery of the *self*" (Armstrong 397). The Axial Age was the origin of salvation religions, as well as the possibility of collective transformation. In contrast to pre-Axial cultures, where political and religious hierarchies were not differentiated—where rulers are sacred because those at the top of the social pyramid play a unique role in communicating with the deities that rule the universe—new conceptions of transcendence opened up the possibility of the divine's relationship with everyone, a challenge that created *the individual*. "For the very first time, individuals, not collectives, are told that there is only one universal God that reigns over the universe, but that this God seeks a relationship with every human being" (Rifkin, 213). This relationship meant that individuals could, at least in principle, dis-identify from the present social order by identifying with the alternative that the transcendental ideal provided.

The possibility of salvation or liberation implied a new understanding of time. Pre-Axial civilizations were conservative: time is cyclic, the golden age is in the past, so the task is to preserve or recover what is always (in an oral culture) in danger of being lost. "[I]n mythological cultures, people live in an endless now where personal histories don't exist and life is lived within a narrow circle of birth, death, and rebirth... Historical awareness introduces the idea that every event and every individual story is unique, finite, and unrepeatable" (Rifkin 211). Axial religions became future-oriented and often apocalyptic, looking forward to the day when the transcendent will irrupt into this world to resolve all its problems, and the gap between the two realities will be healed forever.

Axial transcendence also emphasized formalized law, which began to replace cultural tradition. "'Transcendence,' whether it takes the form of divine revelation or of theoretical cosmology, implies a search for authority outside the institutionalized offices and structures of the seeker's society. Even its most concrete form, the law code, implies a transfer of authority from the holders of office to the written rule. Transcendental impulses therefore constitute, by definition, an implicit challenge to traditional authority and indicate some dissatisfaction with it" (Humphreys 92).

The above quotation suggests the tension that limited the consequences of new Axial Age perspectives: emperors needed the universalistic and more portable Axial Age religions (emphasizing scriptures over particular places such as local shrines) to help unify the different peoples they conquered, but rulers also employed Axial Age perspectives for their own purposes. In place of local custom written law codes were instituted, which might have transcendental origins yet nonetheless implied reduced freedom for those subject to them and institutionalization of the power of those in charge of enforcing them. Jaspers refers to the collapse that occurred in all four Axial civilizations beginning about 200 BCE, when "great political and spiritual unifications and dogmatic configurations held the field" and great States "forcibly realized this unity." He describes this as "a loss of consciousness. Only a few suitable intellectual possibilities and spiritual figures from the bygone Axial Period were seized upon to impart spiritual community, lustre and concordance to the new State authorities" (Jaspers 194). Jaspers concludes that the Axial Age was "an interregnum between two ages of great empire, a pause for liberty, a deep breath bringing the most lucid consciousness" (Jaspers 51). Nevertheless, the fact that the new religions became script-based meant that Axial Age empires absorbed these profound developments into themselves as holy scriptures, cultural timebombs that would eventually explode into radical social transformations.

Let me give some content to these generalizations by looking briefly at the development of two Axial Age cultures: Abrahamic and Greek. This will emphasize the role of alphabetic script in their evolution, since that relationship is essential to the argument to be made afterwards.

Religions of the Book

> Every Axial culture became a text-based culture. Writing makes possible the great introspective religious traditions such as Buddhism, Judaism, Christianity, and Islam. All these have sacred texts. (Ong 102)

Israel became fully monotheistic only as the result of a long and painful process that included the destruction of the Jerusalem temple and Babylonian exile. J, the first biblical source, imagined Yahweh sitting and talking with Abraham, but by the time of Ezekiel God had become an overwhelming mystery (Armstrong 85). Elijah seems to have been the first prophet to insist on the exclusive worship of Yahweh, though he apparently did not doubt the existence of Baal. The first unequivocal assertion of complete monotheism is found in Deutero-Isaiah: "I am Yahweh, unrivalled. There is no other God besides me" [44:6].

This process was mirrored by a deepening subjectivity. "Man becomes aware of himself *as man* in the encounter with the God who addresses him. This also entails a fundamental rupture between man and cosmos. The cosmos ceases to be divine in its own right, as it was (probably cross-culturally) in the millennia of early human history" (Berger 146). In pre-Axial religions "the world of men and gods is hewn from the same matter" (Uffenheimer, in Eisenstadt 141), but henceforth for the Israelites there was a gap not only between humans and God but also between humanity and the rest of the world, as in the creation story in *Genesis*.

This individuation emphasized morality—how one acts in everyday life—over the ritual that predominated in pre-Axial religion. Prophets such as Amos, Isaiah and Jeremiah denounced the privileges of the priestly caste: all men are equal before God, and kings cannot do whatever they want, for they too are subject to a higher moral code. "The pagan gods depended upon the ceremonies to renew their depleted energies; their prestige depending in part upon the magnificence of their temples. Now Yahweh was actually saying that these things were utterly meaningless. . . . Isaiah felt that external observance was not enough. Israelites must discover the inner meaning of their religion. Yahweh wanted compassion rather than sacrifice: 'You may multiply your prayers, I shall not listen. Your hands are covered with blood, wash, make yourselves clean. Take your wrong-doing out of my sight. Cease to do evil. Learn to do good. Search for justice, help the oppressed, be just to the orphan, plead for the widow'" (Isaiah 1:15–17, in Armstrong 44).

"Classical prophecy" began about the middle of the eighth-century BCE, about the same time that the earliest biblical texts, forming the Pentateuch, were written down. In 587 BCE Jerusalem fell and the temple was destroyed; many of its residents were deported to Babylon. In exile religious focus shifted from temple worship to sacred texts—scripture—which were eventually collated and redacted into the *Tanakh* (Hebrew Bible). With the Roman destruction of Herod's temple in 70 CE and the eventual diaspora of the Jewish people, Judaism survived in large part by becoming a portable religion emphasizing textual study. As Torah study became a sacred act, the temple was in effect replaced by it.

It would be difficult to overemphasize the importance of script in Judaism. "The invention of the phonological alphabet in the South Sinai in the fifteenth century BCE almost certainly made the idea of an abstract monotheistic God thinkable for the first time" (Porush 553). With script language apparently achieves a life and meaning of its own. The Ark in the Temple that housed a record of the covenant between the Hebrews and their God was originally the focal point of worship because it served as the primary symbol of the presence of God. The story of Moses receiving the Decalogue on Mt. Sinai and destroying the golden calf can be understood as a shift in focus from graven images to a God who is now invisible but whose sacred words can be recorded and revered. Two contemporary by-products of this sanctification of script are the *mezuzah* metal cylinders attached to doorposts, which contain the first two paragraphs of the *Shema* liturgical prayer, and the *tephillin* phylacteries worn on left arm and forehead during prayer, which also contain sacred verses. Given such emphasis, the word "mysticism" of the Kabbalah becomes less peculiar, perhaps even inevitable.

Later Abrahamic developments emphasize scripture in different ways, but of course it is no less important for Christianity and Islam. Christianity focuses on Christ, the *Logos* incarnated as man, yet (especially since the Reformation) the Bible—God's word—became for most Christians the primary mode of access to the divine. For Islam the *Logos* is the uncreated Quran, the Heavenly Book dictated by the Archangel Gabriel to Muhammad. For all three religions God is formless and invisible, but we have access to the divine through God's *written* Word. Their adherents are encouraged to adhere to those words.

Classical *Greece,* where religious authority was weak and there was more competition among worldviews, offers a very different example of Axial Age transcendence: instead of the ethical monotheism of the Abrahamic traditions, the *Logos* was understood more philosophically and monistically by such pivotal thinkers as Parmenides and Plato. Greek Axiality involved the discovery or invention of what we now understand as *rationality*, which offered a different challenge to the *mythos* of pre-Axial cultures. Logic is a reflective activity that thinks about thinking, which emphasizes another function of Axial transcendence (from Latin *trans* + *scendere*, "to climb over, rise above"): abstracting (*ab[s]* + *trahere*, "to separate, draw out from") us from the given world by providing a theoretical perspective on it. As these etymologies suggest, theoretical thinking is a "second order" mental process that involves "rising above" the world as it is now, providing us with a conceptual (rather than an ethical) evaluation of it, and another possible way of changing that world.

The development of Greek Axiality was much influenced by the astonishing mathematical discoveries of Pythagoras. Mathematics for us is a science but "the father of numbers" was as much a mystic sage as a mathematician, and in fact our distinction between them would have made no sense in his time. Pythagoreans believed that numbers are the ultimate reality and that everything could be measured and predicted according to their laws and patterns. "The so-called Pythagoreans, who were the first to take up mathematics, not only advanced this subject, but saturated with it, they fancied that the principles of mathematics were the principles of all things" (Aristotle, *Metaphysics* 1–5). Pythagoreans also believed in the transmigration of souls and practiced Orphic-like purification rites and other rules of living to help their souls ascend to higher, presumably mathematical, realms.

Today we have lost the strangeness of the amazing realization that our world is a function of mathematical relationships whose truth is not dependent upon any particular physical arrangements. This suggests another, more abstract reality that is distinct from anything the senses can experience and not vulnerable to decay and mortality. That perspective was developed by Plato, the doorway to whose Academy announced: "Let no one ignorant of geometry enter herein." For Plato human imagination is mimetic and derivative, subject to the ravages of time; his philosophy seeks instead the *eidos* (ideas or forms) that manifest timeless Being, which are accessible only by reason. Everything in the physical world is an imperfect expression of such eternal and unchanging forms. In the parable of the cave (*Republic* book 7) one escapes the shadows of imagination for the changeless Being of the Sun (the One/the Good). Pure justice or beauty could not be experienced by our fallible senses but could be comprehended using the reasoning abilities that characterize our immaterial souls (*psyche*), which involved spiritual ascent to a higher reality. "Plato used the imagery and vocabulary of the Eleusinian and Dionysian mysteries to describe the process of illumination and recollection" (Armstrong 318). For Plato, as for Pythagoras and Parmenides, reasoning at its best is a mystical act.

Aristotle did not believe in Plato's forms and was not as influenced by mathematics, but he agreed that what distinguishes humans from all other beings is *theoria*, our ability to think rationally. "The life according to reason is best and pleasantest, since reason, more than anything else, is man" (*Nicomachean Ethics* 1178a). Our divine and immortal intelligence (*nous*) links us to the gods, for it gives us the ability to grasp the highest truth. In fact, *noesis noeseos*, "thinking about thinking," characterizes the nature of Being itself, which is an Unmoved Mover: the highest divinity is pure *nous*, self-absorbed and self-sufficient (Armstrong 327).

What role did writing play in this transformation? Plato (born in 428 BCE) was a member of the first cohort of Athenian boys taught how to read, and this crucial historical transition is reflected both in his relationship with Socrates (who wrote nothing and presumably could not read) and in his own later philosophy. Plato's early writings express the power of Socrates' dialogical style, while his later works record a more script-based way of thinking. According to Harold Innis the balance between orality and writing contributed much to the extraordinary cultural efflorescence of that transformative period (Innis 68–69).

In his controversial book, *Preface to Plato*, Eric Havelock pointed out that the etymology of our English word "idea" has visual connotations.

> Havelock argues that Platonic forms were conceived as analogies to visible forms, not just the perfect shapes of geometry, but the visible forms of the alphabet. Like letters, Platonic ideas were immobile, isolated, and devoid of warmth and secondary qualities; they seem to transcend the world at hand. As David Abram observes, the letters, and the written words they present, are not subject to the flux of growth and decay, to

the perturbations and cyclic changes common to other visible things; they seemed to hover, as it were, in another, strangely timeless dimension. (Davis 112)

As a response to our mutable world of suffering and death, the idealization of such a dimension is quite understandable, as well as the associated distinction between an idealized rationality and the more messy world of physical bodies and their emotions.

As with Abrahamic monotheism, the Greek case also suggests a significant relationship between the development of transcendence and a cultural shift from orality to literacy.[1] Let us look more closely at the connection between this transformation of human consciousness and stronger conceptions of transcendence. We will then consider further the problematical aspects of script, as a place where our collective awareness has become fixated, with dualistic consequences that call for a new paradigm today.

Script/ure

More than any other single invention, writing has transformed human consciousness. (Ong 78)

The consequences of script are difficult for us to comprehend, because we live on the other side of that great transition, which means that the way people in an oral culture experience their world is foreign to us.

The earliest writing systems—those of the Sumerians and the Egyptians—incorporated pictographs that kept them visually connected to the sensory world and thus "retained a large measure of the animist magic of archaic perception. Like many ancient peoples, the Egyptians believed that a name captured the essence of a thing, but they also held that such supernatural power lived in the inscriptions themselves—that spelling was, in fact, a spell" (Davis 25). Neither of these early writing systems developed the more radical and transformative transcendence of an Axial civilization. With the notable exception of China, the big jump occurred with alphabetic scripts, which use written symbols to re-present sounds: now the lines actually speak to you; you *hear* the words with your *eyes*! Vision becomes much more dominant, overshadowing the other senses and thus transforming the whole sensorium. In effect, this amounts to a type of animism that we have learned to take for granted. Inert objects now speak to us: "Stop here before proceeding"; "The name of this street is. . ."; "This shop is a place where you can buy bread." Today we live in a world filled with voices, not just birds and internal combustion engines, but voices that whisper or assault us, especially in urban areas.

We are all too familiar with the cultural advantages of script, and the problems for those who cannot read, but David Abram's celebrated book *The Spell of the Sensuous* gives us some sense of what has been lost:

> In indigenous, oral cultures, nature itself is articulate; it *speaks*. The human voice in an oral culture is always to some extent participant with the voices of wolves, wind, and waves—participant, that is, with the encompassing discourse of the animate earth. There is no element of the landscape that is definitely void of expressive resonance and power: any movement may be a gesture, any sound may be a voice, a meaningful utterance . . . To directly perceive any phenomenon is to enter into relation with it, to feel oneself in a living interaction with another being. (Abram 116–117)

As the focus shifts to printed letters "the stones fall silent. Only as our senses transfer their animating magic to the written word do the trees become mute, the other animals fall dumb" (Abram 131). One's relationship with the natural world, including our own bodies, is transformed, as our more visually based sense of self becomes alienated from them. "Transfixed by our technologies, we short-circuit the sensorial reciprocity between our breathing bodies and the bodily terrain. Human awareness folds in upon itself, and the senses—once the crucial site of our engagement with the wild and animate earth—become mere adjuncts of an isolate and abstract mind bent on overcoming an organic reality that now seems disturbingly aloof and arbitrary" (Abram 267).

In an unpublished essay on "The Axial Age and the Space of Writing," the Egyptologist Jan Assmann considers the consequences of alphabetic scripts for the new types of transcendence that developed in the Axial Age. "Without the invention of writing, without the use of writing for the codification of cultural memory, and without the processes of canonization, the 'Axial Age' would have never occurred. The Axial Age is nothing else but the formative phase of the textual continuity that is still prevailing in our western and eastern civilizations" (Assmann 13).

Oral cultures necessarily focus on preserving the old customs, since they must be transferred afresh to—that is, memorized by—each new generation. Such societies are naturally conservative, preoccupied with conserving what has been laboriously developed. By preserving tradition in a different way (externalizing memory in books), print frees awareness from that task, and thus encourages reflexivity, i.e., theoretical thinking, thinking about what one reads, which enabled the aspect of Axiality most emphasized in classical Greece.

Such reflexivity provides a strong incentive for originality. Assmann gives the example of Western music, which was transformed when notation developed in the late Middle Ages, allowing the creation and preservation of complex scores unthinkable in an oral culture. There is no possibility of a Beethoven symphony or a Wagner opera in an oral culture.

Writing enables the canonization of sacred scriptures that codify the teachings of religious founders. This happens in two stages, according to Assmann: in primary canonization, various versions of (previously oral) teachings are combined into one standardized text. Once collation is concluded, secondary canonization involves commentary and exegesis on the now-fixed canon.

> A non-literate society has an oral religion where several versions of the most important myths usually circulate, where the extent of the religion is limited by the reach of the spoken word, and where there is no fixed set of dogmas that the faithful must adhere to. A literate society, on the contrary, usually has a written religion (often in the shape of sacred texts), with a theoretically unlimited geographic reach, with a clearly delineated set of dogmas and principles, and with authorized, 'correct' versions of myths and narrative. (Eriksen 36)

One now has a new mode of access to the sacred: the recorded *Truth*, which not only needs to be explained but must be defended from error and heresy that might lead people astray.

As the main agent of "cultural memory," texts tend to replace more performative modes of religious practice: doctrine/dogma supersedes ritual, whereas in an oral tradition what you do is much more important than what you think. Thomas Eriksen points out that the judicial systems of non-literate cultures are based on custom and tradition, but literate cultures have law-making institutions such as legislatures. In place of a morality based on tangible interpersonal relations, the morality of literate societies becomes more impersonal and legalistic. "It should be clear by now that writing has been an essential tool in the transition from what we could call a *concrete society* based on intimate, personal relationships, memory, local religion and orally transmitted myths, to an *abstract society* based on formal legislation, archives, a book religion and written history" (Eriksen 38). And what is more abstract than transcendence: e.g., the monotheistic God of the Abrahamic religions, or the *logos* of Greek philosophy?

Assmann understands writing as "a special kind of symbols that bestow visibility to the invisible, stability to the volatile and wide dissemination to the locally limited," in contrast to orality which "uses sound symbols that are invisible, volatile and locally restricted" (Assmann 4). Script satisfies our desire to have something concrete to identify with, a fixed vehicle of salvation that can even be held in one's hands.

> The codification of revelation leads to an expatriation of the holy from the worldly immanence into transcendence and into scripture. The pagan or pre-axial cult-religions presuppose the immanence of the holy in images, trees, mountains, springs, rivers, heavenly bodies, animals, human beings and stones. All this is denounced as idolatry by the new scripture-based world-religions. Scripture requires a total reorientation of religious attention which was formerly directed towards the forms of divine imma-

> nence and is now directed towards scripture and its exegesis. Secondary canonisation means an exodus both of the holy and of religious attention from the cosmos into scripture. To the extra-mundane nature of God corresponds the textual character of his revelation. (Assmann 12)

Paradoxically, texts transcend this physical world: they attain a life of their own, liberated from the person who wrote them. Written words are in principle immortal, unchanging, with an origin now invisible and intangible. They have a meaning that transcends their material medium—but where does this meaning exist? Alphabetic script gives us a *transcendental* perspective because writing speaks to us of things and worlds unseen and unknown. We "see" them in the mind's eye, from the sounds heard and interpreted there, but where is that? This makes conceivable the possibility of a truth and reality that "transcends" any place and time—for example, a "higher law" that challenges us to change what we do, or the logical reasoning that reflexive theory employs.

"Writing creates an artificial memory, whereby humans can enlarge their experience beyond the limits of one generation or one way of life. At the same time it has allowed them to invent a world of abstract entities and mistake them for reality" (Abram 56). Concepts become more important than images: henceforth we can have doctrines about God but not depict him, which would be idolatry. In *Moses and Monotheism,* Freud understands the prohibition against making images of God as "the compulsion to worship an invisible God" that "signified subordinating sense perception to an abstract idea; it was a triumph of spirituality over the senses" (in Kearney 45). If Abrams is correct that by sanctifying script (fixating on those words, from a Buddhist perspective) the sacrality of our sensuous life in the world is lost, then it is difficult to avoid the awkward question: does our relationship to "sacred scriptures" amount to a new kind of idolatry? "An idol, in the theological sense, is a creation of man's hands, as the Bible says, in front of which we worship, and to which we attribute a power which transcends our own" (Ivan Illich, in Cayley 254). Are the Torah, the New Testament, the Qur'an examples of such creations?

According to a famous formula in the *Heart Sutra,* one of the primary texts of Mahayana Buddhism, "form (*rupa*) is emptiness (*shunyata*), and emptiness is not other than form." *Shunyata* is not "nothingness" but the formless potential that describes awareness prior to identification with any form. From that perspective, attributing ultimate value to any particular form is delusive, whether that is a golden calf or a religious dogma. Replacing a graven image with a written covenant has great consequences, but from a Buddhist perspective that shift is not liberative insofar as it replaces one type of clinging with another.

Erik Davis cites the great insight of both Plato and McLuhan that "technologies extend our creative powers by amputating our natural ones" (Davis 13). Writing is a case in point: as script began to speak to us, we became unable to hear what the rest of the world has to say. It is another version of the mythic scenario that McLuhan argued was the archetypal scene of all technology: Narcissus gazing into the pool, mesmerized by his own reflection (Davis 155). A classic example, of course, is a reader absorbed in his or her text.

The Problem with Transcendence

"Give me a place to stand and I shall move the earth," Archimedes is reputed to have said. Culturally, that leverage has been provided by (our belief in) transcendence, which offered the distance—the alternative perspective—necessary to evaluate both oneself and this world and to try to improve them. To paraphrase what Renan said about the supernatural, the transcendent is the way in which the ideal has made its appearance in human affairs. The world we live in today—including our concern for democracy, human rights, and social justice—would be literally unthinkable without the strong conception of an "other world" that the Axial Age developed.

> Axial Age thinkers . . . created alternative ideological systems to counteract and protest the empire and politics. They developed moral and legal systems outside the prevailing military and social structures of their day. These systems criticized the status quo and offered an ethical and often religious option rooted in humane values, such as personal responsibility to others, benevolence, virtue, compassion, justice, wisdom, and righteousness (dharma). This relativizing of the state and its cults brought human subjectivity and personal morality back into the center of religion—the covenant of the heart in Jeremiah, the Confucian virtuous gentleman, the Platonic wise sage, and the Buddhist enlightened monk—effectively undercut rigid class stratifications and the power of temple cults. (Armstrong 92)

Nevertheless, that stronger conception of an other and better world has also been problematic. The dualism between the transcendent and this world is also a split within us, between the "higher" part of ourselves (the soul, rationality) that yearns for escape from this vale of sorrow and the "lower" part that is of the earth (our physical bodies and emotions). The Axial legacy included Manichaeism and Gnosticism, which are only two of the more extreme examples of a more pervasive orientation that later included Cartesian mind/body dualism and, most recently, "transhumanists" who fantasize about escaping death by transferring their consciousness into silicon chips.

The example of transhumanism suggests the problem that encourages us to seek a "higher" reality: as the Buddha emphasized, this world is a place of suffering and death. Much of the attraction of the Axial religions is that they seemed to offer an escape from mortality, our dread of which also explains our fear and degradation of nature, animals, sex, and women (who bleed and remind us that we are conceived and born like other animals). It is no coincidence that the Axial Age was also an age of patriarchy: the dualism between higher and lower worlds became reproduced in the dualism between men and women.

> The male body becomes an instrument of dominance and control, while at the same time, women are held responsible for male sexual behavior. The female body becomes a symbol on which men project and act out a series of ideas about sexuality, birth, physical existence, and intimacy. The male body, in turn, symbolizes potency and power, capacities related to domination and conquest as religious values. For example, the biblical book of Hosea, which recounts what took place in the ninth century BCE, uses images of rape, prostitution, and domestic violence to describe God's relationship to Israel in a way that makes the voice of the rapist and batterer virtually indistinguishable from the divine voice. (Brock and Thistlewaite 82–83)

Although Axial religions emphasized the equality of all men (if not all humans) in relation to God, the hierarchical relationship between the transcendent and the human world also provided a model for inequitable social structures.

> Ironically, the "higher" religions create suspicion toward and a sharp critique of the military empires of their day by developing an alternative system that structurally resembles those very empires. The Axial Age thinkers were men in male-dominated societies, and they draw their structures and images from what they know, which is male dominance. Hence, their religions were partially co-opted into social systems of power and privilege, even as they sought to save people from them. Rather than consistently depicting male dominance, hierarchy, or militarism as the essential problem, they were often metaphorically and mythically appropriated to structure power within their own systems. Hierarchical images of totalitarian power were transmuted into benevolent images. (Brock and Thistlewaite 90)

Today we find ourselves increasingly challenged by another hierarchy of domination and privilege, that between *Homo sapiens sapiens* and the (rest of the) natural world. The Axial dualism between higher and lower worlds is replicated in the alienation between the collective "wego" of humanity and the rest of the biosphere, which is suffering the consequences of our institutionalized greed and exploitation. Rapid climate change—not just a future possibility but something that has already begun—makes it obvious that we must achieve a new relationship which acknowledges our nonduality with the earth and responsibility to the earth—our mother as well as our home.

To these three axiological critiques must be added that of the physical sciences, whose explanatory success constitutes the greatest challenge to any religious belief in a transcendent alternative to this world. It is difficult to avoid the conclusion that, although Axial-type transcendence has been historically important, it is no longer sufficient for what we know today. Such conceptions provided the symbolic leverage that freed us from the embeddedness of pre-Axial societies, but today we need to be liberated from its dualisms, which have outlived their role. Is there another paradigm that might offer the transformative leverage we still need, without devaluing this world? I conclude with some Buddhist-inspired reflections on what that paradigm might involve.

The Spirituality of Evolution

Axial religions have generally denied or ignored biological evolution, for their creation stories are more concerned with the relationship between this world and the "higher world" from which it originates. What might happen if we instead embrace evolution and make it central to our worldview?

That means asking whether evolution is really random and meaningless. According to the cosmologist Brian Swimme, the most mysterious phenomenon in the universe is that if you leave hydrogen alone for 14 billion years, it eventually transforms into rosebushes and giraffes and *us* (Swimme interview, 2). Fourteen billion years might seem like a long time but one could plausibly argue that it is actually quite a short period of time to evolve from Big Bang plasma (which after hundreds of thousands of years stabilized enough to became hydrogen) to a Shakyamuni Buddha or a Gandhi—unless, of course, physical matter is something quite different from the reductionistic way it is usually understood.

Many biologists balk at any notion of progress, but it is difficult to understand the development of consciousness in any other way. According to E. O. Wilson: "Progress . . . is a property of the evolution of life as a whole by almost any conceivable intuitive standard, including the acquisition of goals and intentions in the behavior of animals. It makes little sense to judge it irrelevant. . . . An undeniable trend of progressive evolution has been the growth of biodiversity by increasing command of earth's environment" (Wilson 187). The evolutionary biologist Theodore Dobzhansky agrees: "The evidence of progress and directionality in biological evolution is clear enough if the living world is considered as a whole" (Dobzhansky 119).

What we usually think of as evolution—the genetic variability that leads to more complex life-forms—is only one of three interdependent and progressive developments that together constitute a story as amazing as any religious myth. The first step was the creation of the heavier elements in the periodic table, which were formed when hydrogen fused in the super-heated cores of stars and supernovas, which later exploded, scattering those elements to coalesce into new solar systems. Elements such as carbon, oxygen, and calcium could now provide the material basis for the eventual appearance of self-replicating species about 4 billion years ago, including the appearance of human beings approximately 200,000 years ago. Last but not least are the cultural developments that have been necessary to produce highly evolved human beings such as the Buddha and (in our day) Gandhi and Einstein.

To me, at least, it seems implausible that all this is accidental, which does not necessarily mean that there must be some transcendental being outside the process that is responsible for directing it. Theists tend to see a Being outside these processes who is directing them. Many scientists see these developments as haphazard, including the evolution of life due to random DNA mutations. Is there a third alternative? According to Dobzhansky, evolution is neither random nor determined but *creative*. Can we understand this groping self-organization as the universe struggling to become more self-aware? In *The Universe Story*, Brian Swimme and Thomas Berry offer such a nondualistic interpretation: "the eye that searches the Milky Way galaxy is itself an eye shaped by the Milky Way. The mind that searches for contact with the Milky Way is the very mind of the Milky Way galaxy in search of its own depths." What is really happening when Walt Whitman is admiring a beautiful sunset? "Walt Whitman is a space the Milky Way fashioned to feel its own grandeur" (Swimme and Berry 45, 40).

Is this the answer to the old question, "If there is no self, as Buddhism says, then who becomes enlightened?" Perhaps my desire to awaken ("the Buddha" means "the awakened one") is nothing other than the urge of the cosmos to become aware of itself, in and as me. Is this the way the Buddha's enlightenment should be understood today? "Waking up" is realizing that "I" am not inside my body, looking out at a world that is separate from me. Rather, "I" am what the whole universe is doing right here and now: one of the ways that the totality of its various causes and conditions comes together.

After his own awakening, when "body and mind fell away," the twelfth-century Japanese Zen master Dogen Kigen described what he had experienced: "I came to realize clearly that mind is no other than mountains and rivers and the great wide earth, the sun and the moon and the stars" (in Kapleau 229). According to the Mahayana tradition, the historical Buddha (fl 6th-5th C. BCE) became enlightened when he looked up from his meditations and saw the morning star (Venus), whereupon he declared: "I am awakened together with the whole of the great earth and all its beings." Did he suddenly realize his nonduality with that star?

Every species is an experiment of the biosphere, and biologists tell us that less than one percent of all species that have ever appeared on earth still survive today. The super-sized cortex of *Homo sapiens* makes us co-experimenters and co-creators. (Is this what "created in the image of God" means?) With us new types of "species" have become possible: knives and symphonies, poetry and nuclear bombs. . . But it is also becoming more obvious that something has gone wrong with our hyper-rationality. Nietzsche's Zarathustra says that "Man is a rope stretched between the animal and the Overman—a rope over an abyss. . . . What is great in man is that he is a bridge and not a goal"

(Nietzsche 43–44). Are we a transitional species? Must we evolve further in order to survive at all? In Buddhist terms, our delusions of a self separate from others, and our collective delusions of a collective self separate from the rest of the biosphere, motivate us as species to do too many things that are self-defeating and sometimes self-destructive. According to Thomas Berry "the historical mission of our times is to reinvent the human—at the species level, with critical reflection, within the community of life-systems, in time development context, by means of story and shared dream experience" (Berry 159).

In short, we need a new, more therapeutic paradigm, which emphasizes not only realizing our nonduality with the earth but also the healing necessary to embody that healing, because we are sick, our societies are sick and our biosphere is sick. In the context of this essay, an important question is whether digital and interactive technologies such as the internet, which are transforming if not supplanting older media such as print, will contribute to such a development, but that issue is beyond the scope of this essay.

Figures like the Buddha might be harbingers of how our species needs to develop, in which case the cultural evolutionary step most important today involves spiritual practices that address the fiction of a separate self whose well-being is delusively distinguished from that of "others." Perhaps our basic problem is not self-love but a profound misunderstanding of what one's self really is. Without the compassion that arises when we realize our nonduality—empathy not only with other humans but with the whole biosphere—it is becoming likely that civilization as we know it will not survive the next few centuries. Nor would it deserve to. Perhaps we are challenged to grow up, or get out of the way. If so, it remains to be seen whether the *Homo sapiens* experiment will be a successful vehicle for the cosmic evolutionary process.

Note

1   Space does not allow a similar discussion of China or India, but I want to point out another significant parallel in the difference between early Pali Buddhism, which was an oral tradition, and the great rupture within Buddhism that occurred with the development of Mahayana (which eventually became the dominant tradition in Central and East Asia), a split that can be associated with the shift from oral teachings to written texts. Although script was not unknown in India at the time of the Buddha, he was the product of an oral culture and his teachings were transmitted by mouth for at least three centuries before being written down. When those original teachings were eventually recorded, new ways of understanding the Buddhadharma appeared in new types of sacred texts. In place of earlier focus on *stupa* cults and relic worship, devotion to the scriptures became emphasized, and there was a transformation in the way that the Buddha was understood in many of those sutras: no longer simply an awakened human, he became elevated into a transcendent being whose body, for example, could suddenly become radiant and illuminate all the world systems in the cosmos.

Bibliography

Abram, David. 1997. *The Spell of the Sensuous: Perception and Language in a More-Than-Human World*. New York: Vintage.
Armstrong, Karen. 2007. *The Great Transformation: The Beginning of Our Religious Traditions*. New York: Anchor.
Assmann, Jan. "The Axial Age and the Space of Writing." Unpublished conference paper. Cited with permission.
Berger, Peter L. 1979. *The Heretical Imperative: Contemporary Possibilities of Religious Affirmation*. New York: Anchor.
Berry, Thomas. 1999. *The Great Work: Our Way into the Future*. Harmony/Bell Tower.
Besancon, Alain. 2000. *The Forbidden Image: An Intellectual History of Iconoclasm*. Trans. Jane Marie Todd. Chicago: University of Chicago Press.
Brock, Rita Nakashima and Susan Brooks Thistlewaite. 1996. *Casting Stones: Prostitution and Liberation in Asia and the United States*. Minneapolis: Fortress Press.
Candrakirti. *Lucid Exposition of the Middle Way*. 1979. Trans. Mervyn Sprung. Boulder, Colorado: Prajna Press.
Cayley, David, ed. 1992. *Ivan Illich in Conversation*. Concord, Ontario: Anansi.
Davis, Erik. 1998. *TechGnosis: Myth, magic + mysticism in the age of information*. London: Serpent's Tail.
Dobzhansky, Theodore. 1967. *The Biology of Ultimate Concern*. New York: American Library.
Eisenstadt, S. N., ed. 1986. *The Origins and Diversity of Axial Age Civilizations*. Albany, New York: State University of New York Press.
Eriksen, Thomas Hylland. 2001. *Tyranny of the Moment: Fast and Slow Time in the Information Age*. London: Pluto Press.
Havelock, Eric. *Preface to Plato*. 1982. Cambridge, Massachusetts: Harvard University Press.
Hui Hai. 2006. *Zen Teaching of Instantaneous Awakening*. Trans. John Blofeld. Totnes, UK: Buddhist Publishing Group.
Hui-neng. 1978. *The Platform Sutra of the Sixth Patriarch*. Ed. and trans. by Philip Yampolsky. New York: Columbia University Press.
Humphreys, S. C. "'Transcendence' and Intellectual Roles: The Ancient Greek Case." In *Daedalus* (Spring 1975), special issue on *Wisdom, Revelation, and Doubt: Perspectives on the First Millennium B.C.*
Innis, Harold. 1950. *Empire and Communications*. Oxford: Oxford University Press.
Jaspers, Karl. 1955. *The Origin and Goal of History*. Trans. Michael Bullock. New Haven, Connecticut: Yale University Press.
Kapleau, Philip, ed. 1989. *The Three Pillars of Zen: Teaching, Practice, and Enlightenment*. New York: Anchor.
Kearney, Richard. 1998. *In the Wake of Imagination: Toward a Postmodern Culture*. New York: Routledge.
Nietzsche, Friedrich. 2003. *Thus Spoke Zarathustra: A Book for Everyone and No One*. Trans. R.J. Hollingdale. Harmondsworth, UK: Penguin.
Ong, Walter. 1982. *Orality and Literacy: The Technologizing of the Word*. London: Routledge.
Porush, David. "Hacking the Brainstem: Postmodern Metaphysics and Stephenson's *Snow Crash*." In *Configurations* 2.3 (1994), 537–571.
Rifkin, Jeremy. 2009. *The Empathic Civilization: The Race to Global Consciousness in a World in Crisis*. New York: Tarcher/Penguin.
Swimme, Brian. "An Interview with Brian Swimme: Awakening to the Universe Story." Online at: http://www.enlightennext.org/magazine/j34/swimme1.asp?page=2 Accessed 8 June 2010.
Swimme, Brian, and Thomas Berry. 1992. *The Universe Story: From the Primordial Flaring forth to the Ecozoic-a Celebration of the Unfolding of the Cosmos*. San Francisco: Harper.
Webb, Eugene. 1988. *Philosophers of Consciousness: Polanyi, Lonergan, Voegelin, Ricoeur, Girard, Kierkegaard*. Seattle: University of Washington Press.
Wilson, Edward O. 1999. *The Diversity of Life*. New York: Norton.

NINE

Freud's Last Theory of Mysticism
The Return of the (Phylogenetic) Repressed

William B. Parsons

When speaking of Freud's last theory of mysticism the implication is that there exist earlier versions as well, as if he had been struggling with the problem for a considerable length of time. The latter has not been sufficiently acknowledged, in part because what little that does exist of such ruminations have been obscured by Freud's much more famous and debated interpretation of what he called the "common-man's religion." The latter took as normative an understanding of religion which was Western, assumed institutionalized patriarchal forms of socio-cultural power, and valorized the monotheistic "mighty personality" of an exalted Father-God. Indeed, in entering into the long-standing debate over how to define the term "religion," Freud, in his *The Future of an Illusion*, defiantly chastised those "philosophers" who tried to "stretch the meaning of words" to the point that words like "God" and "religious" ceased to bear any resemblance to the Being worshipped by the common-man.[1] When one finally does turn to his views on mysticism one finds that it is usually located with respect to a single text written during the last decade of his life, namely, his cursory analysis of the famous "oceanic feeling" in the opening chapter of *Civilization and Its Discontents*. As is typically formulated, the "received view," so to speak, frames oceanic feelings as examples of Jamesian transient mystical experiences of unity, now psychoanalytically rendered as regressions to that initial developmental phase Freud called "primary narcissism." Oceanic feelings, while themselves potentially neutral are, when co-opted by religious institutions, framed as defensive, even pathological. Additionally oceanic feelings, based on the Mother, cannot displace the true origin of religion, the latter based on the culturally superior role of the Father and the wish for guidance and protection. So at least, has stood the psychoanalytic theory of mysticism for greater part of the last century.

The received view is misleading in a number of ways. In point of fact, Freud struggled with the interpretation and meaning of mysticism from early in his career until the very end. This essay proceeds to document such assertions, first by way of summarizing and re-framing some of my earlier work on the topic and then, relying on details of that narrative, going beyond it to offer a new thesis which, while hardly discontinuous with some of his earlier views, suggests that at the end of his life Freud was entertaining a new model for what constituted the content and nature of mysticism.[2]

1904–1927: The Psychoanalysis of Mystical Intuition

Even a cursory review of many recent and important essays on the topic of mysticism reveals that one would do well to begin by acknowledging, even if in a perfunctory way, the numerous debates that have accrued over its definition, use, and links to various interpretative strategies in the modern, academic study of mysticism. Indeed, one can go so far as speak of an imperative to qualify given that, among other things, the term *mysticism* is Western in origin, that it did not assume its status as a substantive until the 16th century, that many mystical authors never used the term at all, that philosophers have debated the epistemological status of assumed understandings of "experience," that it is often used loosely as a general, inclusive term signifying diverse altered states different in degree and perhaps in kind, that there is significant overlap and occasional blurring with similar terms (e.g., shamanism, spirituality, Gnosticism, esotericism), that there exists significant differences between how religious traditions are willing to define and utilize the term, and that many have rightly articulated how the term carries with it colonialist, orientalist, and modernist assumptions.[3] Yet despite this, most scholars are willing to use mysticism as "term of art." Certainly one can agree with the latter while also acknowledging the need for constant monitoring and qualification with respect to its use.

Of course Freud never entered into, much less knew anything about, modern debates over the term. Most psychoanalysts simply assume that Freud understood mysticism as consisting of the typically Jamesian episodic mystical experience proper. While he did use the term in such a sense, at least approximately so, it is further apparent, particularly with respect to the oceanic feeling, that he extended the term "mysticism" to incorporate other, related phenomena. In translating this discussion to the practical aims of this essay, then, and as a cautionary note to those particularly in the psychoanalytic world who remain blissfully unaware of the nuances of the term, we must be attentive to text and context, discerning what kind of religious phenomena Freud meant the term to designate as well as the interpretive models he offered concerning its origin and value.

In beginning, then, during the period 1904–1927, Freud's views were confined to what we would call "mystical experience." There are two texts which indicate that Freud held to a consistency of interpretation, espousing a psychoanalytic universalism which neglected differences between religious traditions and assumed a generic understanding of mystical experience, positing that the latter provided access to the workings of the unconscious. His initial interpretative foray is from a text that has been dubbed the "Goetz Letters," so named for the poet Bruno Goetz, author of a series of letters detailing verbatim conversations he had with Freud during the academic year 1904–05 while a student at the University of Vienna.[4] Goetz had been studying with the Indologist and Sanskrit scholar Leopold von Schroeder, known for his critical editions of Hindu scriptures as well as more historical and comparative work. Goetz had become especially interested in the *Bhagavad Gita*, relating to Freud how taken he was with its insight and profundity. While a detailed analysis of the letters have been undertaken elsewhere,[5] what is of importance for our discussion are two related points. First, Freud seems aware of the substantial debates over the meaning of nirvana which had occupied the emerging cadre of comparativists in the later 19th and early 20th centuries. Thus it is that Freud says "to take care, young man take care," for while it was right to be enthusiastic about such matters one should "keep that cool head" lest one go mad:

> If. . .one without the aid of a clear intellect you become immersed in the world of the Bhagavad Gita, where nothing seems constant and everything melts into everything else, then you are suddenly confronted by nothingness. . .Do you know what that means? And yet this nothingness is simply a European misconception. . .Or, if misunderstood, it is madness. . .What do these European would-be mystics know about the profundity of the East? They rave on, but they know nothing. And then they are surprised when they lose their heads and are not infrequently driven out of their minds.[6]

Second, and importantly, Freud indicates what he thinks is the correct way of characterizing the Hindu nirvana:

> The Bhagavad Gita is a great and powerful poem with awful depths. 'And still it lay beneath me hidden deep in purple darkness there,' says Schiller's diver, who never returns from his second brave attempt. . .The Hindu Nirvana is not nothingness, it is that which transcends all contradictions. . .the ultimate in superhuman understanding, an ice-cold, all-comprehending yet scarcely comprehensible insight.[7]

The interpretative key to the above lies in Freud's juxtaposition between madness and "superhuman understanding," the condensation of oceanic with Oedipal imagery, and his use of Schiller's poem "The Diver" to characterize the "awful depths" of the Hindu nirvana. The poem itself is quite short, depicting a young man who, on two successive attempts, undertakes the brave task of grappling with a whirlpool, described as an "ocean womb," that boils, hisses, and leads to the depths of hell, so that he might retrieve a King's goblet, the reward being his blessing, crown and daughter in return. The page emerges after his first attempt into the "purple darkness" below, exclaiming "Let him rejoice who breathes up here in the roseate light!" The page descends into the fateful whirlpool a second time at the behest of the King, only never to return.

The poem can be read as a metaphor for the psychoanalytic task: one "dives" into the "whirlpool" of the unconscious. The theme of "The Diver" is clearly Oedipal: wining the favor of the King, obtaining both his crown and his daughter. Importantly, while the poem has a tragic ending, Freud's characterization of the "Hindu divers" indicates that the mystic, unlike the page, succeeds in avoiding madness while gaining the "ice-cold, all-comprehending yet scarcely comprehensible insight." In sum, what we have here is a young Freud who is in the process of reading his own emerging view of the psyche and its dynamics back into the wisdom contained in an honored classic text. The Hindu philosophers dimly saw and existentially grappled with what Freud was clearly able to articulate as the hazards of the unconscious, the conflicts of Oedipus and the insights of psychoanalytic therapy. Freud was not endorsing the ontological views of Eastern religions but rather reinterpreting their seminal insights along the line of his emerging theory: nirvana was simply a culturally variant way of formulating the truths discovered and articulated by psychoanalysis.

The second text occurs in the midst of a discussion, in chapter five of *The Future of an Illusion*, where Freud rebukes what he calls the "desperate efforts" of philosophers to defend the legitimacy of institutional religion. In the passage below, Freud adduces the thought of Tertullian:

> The '*Credo quia absurdum*' of the early Father of the Church. . . . maintains that religious doctrines are outside the jurisdiction of reason—are above reason. Their truth must be felt inwardly, and they need not be comprehended. But this Credo is only of interest as a self-confession. . .If the truth of religious doctrines is dependent on an inner experience which bears witness to that truth, what is one to do about the many people who do not have this rare experience? One may require every man to use the gift of reason which he possesses, but one cannot erect, on the basis of a motive that exists only for a very few, an obligation that shall apply to everyone. If one man has gained an unshakable conviction of the true reality of religious doctrines from a sate of ecstasy which has deeply moved him, of what significance is that to others?[8]

Freud indicates that moments of religious ecstasy are far too subjective, rare and inaccessible to empirical, scientific verification to serve as the basis for the defense of institutional religion. On the other hand, the passage is littered with rhetorical questions and defensive rationalizations, which give one the impression that Freud is not denying that such altered states have some adaptive value for the "very few." Freud specifies the kind of knowledge that one might gain in such deep and rare states in the next chapter of *The Future of an Illusion* when, in returning to the epistemological status of mystical intuition, concludes that it "can give us nothing but particulars about our own mental life, which are hard to interpret."[9] While this comment is less detailed and positive than that offered in the Goetz letters, one could say there is a consistency of thought here. Both texts deal with Freud's interpretation of what James called the *noetic* dimension of mystical experience. In both texts one finds Freud distinguishing between mysticism and the "common-man's" religion. In both texts the knowledge gained through mystical intuition is akin to psychoanalysis in its inner trajectory and unearthing of unconscious content.

1927–1933: Roman Rolland and Oceanic Feelings

In 1927 Freud sent Romain Rolland a small gift: a copy of his newly published *The Future of an Illusion*. The correspondence between the two had started four years earlier. Freud had "revered" Rolland "as an artist and apostle of love for mankind" for many years, due chiefly to Rolland's literary productions (for which he won a Nobel Prize) and efforts to mediate between the French and Germans during the Great War (for which he was dubbed the "conscience of Europe"). For his part Rolland referred to Freud as the "Christopher Columbus of a new continent of the spirit" who had inspired his life and thought.[10] Freud knew that Rolland had attacked the mendacity of institutional religion, centering his critiques on Catholicism and the papacy, and so it is hardly surprising that he thought Rolland would like his own small work on the subject. In point of fact Rolland did, writing to Freud that his analysis was "just," and that it pulled off "the blindfolding bandage of the eternal adolescents, which we all are, whose amphibian spirit floats between the illusion of yesterday and. . .the illusion of tomorrow."[11] At the same time, he asked Freud to make a deeper analysis of another more primordial religious datum:

> What I mean is: totally independent of all dogma, all credo, all Church organization, all Sacred Books, all hope in a personal survival, etc., the simple and direct fact of *the feeling of the 'eternal'* (which can very well not be eternal, but simply without perceptible limits, and like oceanic, as it were).[12]

Rolland went on to say that it was the oceanic feeling, in its various nuanced forms, which was the "subterranean source" of all religions and, becoming autobiographical, that he was familiar with it, stating that he felt it as a "constant state (like a sheet of water which I feel flushing under the bark)."[13] Importantly, Freud understood it as such as well, for in summarizing the contents of Rolland's letter in the first chapter of *Civilization and Its Discontents* he describes Rolland's oceanic feeling as "a peculiar feeling, which he himself is never without."[14] This mystical phenomenon was not, then, an instance of the typical Jamesian transient mystical experience, for it was an enduring state. Indeed, if one turns to Rolland's substantial oeuvre, one finds that he distinguished between mystical experience proper and the later, more advanced, enduring, statelike oceanic feeling (which, without drawing an exact equivalence, is closer to the similarly more advanced and enduring mystical state Sri Ramana Maharshi refers to as *shahaj samadhi*).[15] Subsequent commentators, in establishing the "received view" of Freud's theory of mysticism, have interpreted Rolland's oceanic feeling as an instance of the Jamesian episodic mystical experience and Freud's interpretation of it as emphasizing the momentary regression to the "unity" of primary narcissism. But Freud interpreted the enduring state of the oceanic feeling as the preservation of (and not regression to) the limitless ego feeling of the infant which, in some cases, is never extinguished but remains alongside the more narrowly demarcated adult ego. Unfortunately, the ascendancy of the received view established the signature psychoanalytic entry into the comparative study of mysticism, which is as follows: insofar as the developmental phase of primary narcissism is universal one can posit the oceanic feeling as a core of mysticism everywhere, the latter differing only by virtue of differences in the cultural symbolic surround.

Along these lines it is significant to note that Freud, in his correspondence with Rolland, did address the interpretation of mystical experience proper. In so doing, he did not resort to the typical post-Freudian "received view" but regurgitated the line of thought apparent in the "pre-Rolland" texts of 1904 and 1927. This becomes immediately apparent when Freud, in the last paragraph of the first chapter of *Civilization and Its Discontents* and again replying to Rolland, turned away from the statelike oceanic feeling to address the relation between mystical practices and episodic mystical experience. He refers to "another friend of mine" who had assured him that through the "practices of Yoga" and by "fixing the attention on bodily functions and by peculiar methods of breathing" that one could evoke "sensations and coenaesthesias... which he regards as regressions to primordial states of mind." Freud goes on to state: "It would not be hard to find connections here with a number of obscure modifications of mental life, such as traces and ecstasies." Significantly, instead of offering a full analysis of such phenomena, Freud simply exclaims: "But I am moved to exclaim in the words of Schiller's diver: 'Let him rejoice who breathes up here in the roseate light!'"[16]

Tellingly, Freud once again adduces the same Schiller poem to speak to the wisdom of mystical experience. This line of inquiry is buttressed by subsequent exchanges by Freud and Rolland. In a letter to Rolland dated January 19, 1930, Freud, in returning to the issue of mystical noesis, affirmed that mystical practices could reveal "instinctual impulses and attitudes" which were "highly valuable for an embryology of the soul."[17] In 1933, in a passage directed to Rolland in his *New Introductory Lectures on Psychoanalysis*, one finds Freud employing a similar interpretative move. This becomes apparent when, at the end of Lecture 31, one looks at the imagery and linguistic construction of the "psychoanalytic motto" (namely, *Wo Es war, soll Ich werden*, or "where Id was, there Ego shall be"). In describing what it is that psychoanalytic therapy does, Freud clothes his remarks in typically poetic terms, speaking of rivers and oceans, of reclaiming land from the sea, and of Faust, Exodus and Genesis.[18] Then, drawing an analogy between psychoanalysis and mystical intuition, Freud remarks that "certain mystical practices" could pierce the usual barriers between the Id and Ego, so that one could gain insight into "the depths of the ego and in the id which were otherwise inaccessible." Casting doubt that "ultimate truths" and "salvation" could be had by such a route, he nevertheless went on to say: "it may be admitted that the therapeutic efforts of psychoanalysis have chosen a similar line of approach."[19]

1934–1939: Freud's Last Theory of Mysticism

Freud's correspondence with Rolland ebbed away during this last phase, and there are only a few references to mysticism. Most prominent and recognized among the latter is Freud's retort to Rolland's biographies of Ramakrishna and Vivekananda in his 1936 essay, entitled "A Disturbance of Memory on the Acropolis," which cautioned how mystical experiences could be tied to states of derealization and depersonalization, thus being ripe for those religious doctrines (notably *maya*) that emphasized the illusory nature of the world.[20] What remains to be investigated is one last reference to mysticism which lies, technically speaking, outside Freud's correspondence with Rolland. This "post-Rolland" reference occurs in the 23rd volume of James Strachey's mammoth *Standard Edition* of Freud's works where one finds a lone speculative entry, but a sentence long, among a series of entries of similar nature and length, in a section entitled "Findings, Ideas, Problems" (Freud's own title). The entry is dated August 22, 1938, and reads simply as follows: "Mysticism is the obscure self-perception of the realm outside the ego, of the id."[21] One could, of course, dismiss this as an echo of his earlier views and be done with it. Indeed, one would do well to heed the voice of caution, lest the romantic lure of the academic turned detective lead one to engage in seemingly excessive and unwarranted speculation. On the other hand, in this particular case there are a number of observations which can be made which, once contextualized within a working narrative continuous with the previous two sections, lead one to believe that in fact Freud was in the midst of developing a new and important extension of his interpretative model of mysticism.

Aside from his essay concerning his "experience" on the Acropolis, the only other project of note concerning Freud's application of his psychoanalytic method to religious phenomena from 1934 onwards remains his contested work *Moses and Monotheism*. There is a tangential, but not entirely insignificant, relation between the latter and Rolland. Freud had been asked by Victor Wittkowski to write something to celebrate Rolland's 70th birthday—a gift which later eventuated in Freud's writing his paper on the Acropolis. However, before the birth of that essay Freud had responded to Wittkowski, in a letter dated January 6, 1936, that he was old, infirm, lacking in creative output, and thus unable to produce anything of worth for Rolland. Referring to his book on Moses, Freud went on to say: "As recently as a year ago I succeeded in writing something that would have been of special interest to R.R., but it suffered from one defect which prevented it from being published, and since then my ability to produce has dried up. It is probably too late for it to revive again."[22] Surely there are several reasons why Freud would have linked Rolland with his book on Moses, not the least of which is the Mosaic emphasis on renunciation, secondary process thought, truth and justice. But what is of special interest to us is how the thesis of his Moses holds the interpretative key to his last theory of mysticism.

The pivotal point boils down to the explicit manifestation of Freud's more expansive view of the unconscious. One sees an inkling of this in his "Findings, Ideas, Problems" where Freud, in an entry dated July 20, 1938, just barely over a month before his entry on mysticism of August 22, states the following: "The hypothesis of there being inherited vestiges in the id alters, so to say, our views about it."[23] Clearly, then, his subsequent reference to mysticism of August 22 would include this latter view of the id. The notion of "inherited vestiges" refers to Freud's more cursory and Lamarckian views, outlined in works from *Totem and Taboo* onwards, of the phylogenetic transmission of traumatic primal events. In his *Moses* Freud took this view much farther in speaking to the matter of the "development" of religion. In *Totem and Taboo* he had offered a dubious thesis concerning the origin of religion: that it was the repeated murder of the alpha ape father in the small, wandering primal hordes which resulted in Totemic society, understood as the first organized and structured social community. The worship of the totem, with its attendant moral prohibitions against incest and murder, was the first, if rudimentary, form of religion. This traumatic "primal deed," as Freud was to call his psychoanalytic version of original sin, occurred so often and over so many generations that it became part of the id. In other words, as early as *Totem and Taboo* Freud was positing that alongside the normal developmental traumas unique to each individual was a deeper layer of universal traumatic events which were inherited and common to the mass of humanity. As he later put it in his *Moses*: "the archaic heritage of human beings comprises not only dispositions but also subject-matter—memory-traces of the experience of earlier generations."[24]

Freud's embracement of phylogenesis and the theory of Lamarck led to increasing consternation among the most loyal of his followers. As Ernst Jones so politely put it: "It is not easy to account for the fixity with which Freud held this opinion and the determination with which he ignored all the biological evidence to the contrary."[25] Indeed, Freud's defensiveness seems irrational enough to suggest the influence of deep psychodynamic forces. Along these lines one might note two significant facts. First, Freud's postulation of an "archaic heritage" allowed him to retain, even if in a stunted and distorted form, his original and quickly discarded theory concerning the role of actual seduction in the life of neurotics.[26] This becomes clear in his discussion of "primal phantasies," the essence of which is to account for, by way of phylogenetic transmission, the seemingly excessive nature of some of the sexual and aggressive phantasies which he found to exist in the life of his present-day neurotics. While actual physical seduction may not have occurred in such a person it definitely did occur many times over in the life of our ancestors. It is this fact that enables Freud to say the following:

> Primal phantasies. . .are a phylogenetic endowment. In them the individual reaches beyond his own experience into primaeval experience at points where his own experience becomes too rudimentary. It seems to me quite possible that all the things that are told to us to-day in analysis as phantasy—the seduction of children, the inflaming of sexual excitement by observing parental intercourse, the threat of castration (or rather castration itself)—were once real occurrences in the primaeval times of the human family, and that children in their phantasies are simply filling in the gaps in individual truth with prehistoric truth.[27]

The key phrase here is "beyond his own experience." Given the crucial nature of the role of Freud's abandonment of the seduction theory for the development of psychoanalysis and the debate that has raged over the extent to which he willingly or unwillingly did so, formulations such as the above take on added import. Freud is saying that one needs the influence of the archaic "deep past" to supplement the usual psychoanalytic focus on the more usual "developmental past" to account for the clinical data of neuroses. Indeed, the thesis of *Totem and Taboo*, usually the nexus of debates between psychoanalysts on the one hand and sociologists, anthropologists and theologians on the other, should be also seen as a theoretical outhouse, conveniently located in the repressed archaic past, for the compost of unresolved tensions in Freud's thought.

This avenue of inquiry is buttressed by the fact that *Totem and Taboo* was published in 1912–13, a time when Freud's chosen heir turned competitor Carl Jung was developing his theory of the collective unconscious and archetypes. It may well be, as others have pointed put, that such ideas were "in the air" and that Freud's version of the theory was psychoanalytically specific and lacked the religious connotations linked to Jung's notion of a collective unconscious.[28] Yet it is hard to dismiss the thought that Freud felt the threat of Jung's formulations. In acknowledging the existence of a common, universal dimension of the unconscious beyond that of the personal unconscious, of the need of the individual to reach "beyond his own experience," Freud was saying to Jung that yes, there does exist an archetype, but only one: Oedipus.

Now that the context has been established, we can understand how it impacted Freud's new understanding of religious ecstasy. As we have seen, in *The Future of an Illusion* Freud had spoken of such ecstasy in conjunction with Tertullian's *Credo quia absurdum*, offering that such states could cough up the contents of one's personal unconscious. In the "Goetz Letters," his *New Introductory Lectures on Psychoanalysis* and letters to Rolland, he likened mystical practices and the intuitive knowledge they uncovered to the practice of psychoanalysis. In his *Moses* Freud, in recalling the argument of *Totem and Taboo*, became more specific about the nature and extent of that intuitive knowledge. He begins by once again affirming that one's psychical life includes "not only what he has experienced himself but also things that were innately present in him at his birth, elements with a phylogenetic origin—an *archaic heritage*"[29] and then further: "If we assume the survival of these memory-traces in the archaic heritage, we have bridged the gulf between individual and group psychology."[30] Freud is here unambiguously stating the existence of a common storehouse of archaic memories buried deep within the phylogenetic dimension of the unconscious. He states that such memories were not accessed through direct communication or education. Such a thesis, he goes on to note, was not overtly stated in his previous writings:

> When I spoke of the survival of a tradition among a people or of the formation of a people's character, I had mostly in mind an inherited tradition of this kind and not one transmitted by communication. Or at least I made no distinction between the two and was not clearly aware of my audacity in neglecting to do so.[31]

Then, in speaking to the vicissitudes of group psychology, about the development of religion from Totemism through matriarchy and then to monotheism, Freud insists on the determinative dynamic factor of our archaic heritage and especially the primal deed. The rise of Moses and the introduction of monotheism were successful precisely because both recalled the memory of the great primal father and the various impulses linked to him. In speaking to the latter, and again referencing Tertullian, Freud goes on to state that such archaic experiences exercise "an incomparably powerful influence on the people in the mass, and raises an irresistible claim to truth against which logical objections remain powerless: a kind of 'credo quia absurdum.'"[32] Here Freud is not referencing Tertullian and religious ecstasy, as he was in *The Future of an Illusion*, to speak of the particulars of one's personal unconscious, but rather of the dynamic force of our common archaic heritage. The 'core' of the historical truth which determined the charisma of Moses was the complicity we all have in the primal deed:

> The first effect of meeting the being who had so long been missed and longed for was overwhelming and was like the traditional description of the law-giving from Mount Sinai. Admiration, awe and thankfulness for having found grace in his eyes—the religion of Moses knew none but these positive feelings towards the father-god. The conviction of his irresistibility, the submission to his will, could not have been more unquestioning in the helpless and intimidated son of the father of the horde—indeed those feelings only become fully intelligible when they are transposed into the primitive and infantile setting.[33]

Importantly, Freud adds that such intense awe and admiration, being feelings beyond the normal range of the personal unconscious, require a correspondingly altered state: "only religious ecstasy can bring them back."[34] In other words, what both motivates and is uncovered in religious ecstasy is the contents of not the personal unconscious but that of the universal memory-traces which define the content of our phylogenetically transmitted archaic heritage.

Concluding Reflections

Reviewing, then, Freud's evolving models for the interpretation of mystical phenomena, we can isolate at least three: 1) an early model of mystical experience and ecstasy that grants that mystical practices proceed along the lines of psychoanalytic therapy, uncovering the contents of the personal unconscious; 2) a model for a continuous mystical state, Rolland's oceanic feeling, which stresses the preservation of the feeling of limitlessness and eternity felt by the infant during the developmental stage of primary narcissism; 3) a later model of mystical experience and ecstasy which posits that the altered state of religious ecstasy allows for the uncovering and dynamic emergence of the memory-traces buried in our common archaic heritage, now clarified as a deep dimension of the unconscious that is phylogenetically transmitted from generation to generation.

This brings us to the domain of comparative mysticism which, as we earlier noted, Freud seemed to have little interest in, or at least displayed little knowledge of in his voluminous writings. Nevertheless, it is instructive to follow the gradient along which his thought takes one when bringing it to bear on the now quite sophisticated series of debates and issues which animate the field. For example, in dealing with mystical texts as diverse as the Hindu nirvana, Rolland's unorthodox, unchurched and nature-based mystical experiences and Western monotheistic ecstatic states, Freud was clearly oblivious to any claims to ontological status and difference. He did not, as did his colleague and fellow psychologist William James, allow for the possibility, with respect to the ontos of "the More," of an "unfinished" pluralistic multiverse in which we are like cats and dogs in their owner's library, hearing but not grasping the full meaning and import of the messages of the greater beings who determine much of their existence.[35] Nor was he interested in the current "constructivist" pleas for context and the allowance of real differences.[36] On the contrary, Freud was a true reductionist, reading his own psychology and reflections on the universal structure of the human psyche into mystical texts West and East. Yet despite this, Freud's ruminations do seem to indicate that he ranked mystical phenomena. Like R.C. Zaehner, he placed theistic forms of mysticism in a position of primacy.[37] Unlike Zaehner, he did so with respect to purely historical and psychological reasons: only monotheistic ecstasy can bring back the deepest memory-traces of the contents of our phylogenetically-transmitted archaic heritage.

However, at the end of the day one can debate just how much Freud's interpretative models offer to the scholar of comparative mysticism. With respect to the more narrow focus of this essay, certainly the positing of a phylogenetically transmitted archaic heritage has proven to be too irrational for even Freud's most ardent supporters to take seriously. But in resorting to such a hypothesis, what should not be missed is that Freud clearly thought that some forms of mystical experience necessitated "reaching beyond," as he put it, the more ordinary psychoanalytic focus on the individual's unique personal experiences and developmental trauma. In other words, Freud understood there was a something "more" to mysticism, even if his attempt to account for it may at times be better framed as reflecting the unresolved tensions of his thought and relations with competitors than successfully addressing the complexity of the topic itself.

Notes

1. Freud, *SE* 21: 32–33.
2. I am referring here to my *The Enigma of the Oceanic Feeling* (1999).
3. For definitions of the term see Bouyer (1980) and DeCerteau (1992). The various debates over the use of the term can be found in detail in my edited book *Teaching Mysticism*.
4. See Parsons (1999), chapter 2.
5. Ibid.
6. Ibid., p. 48.
7. Ibid.
8. Freud, *SE* 21:28
9. Freud, *SE* 21: 31–32.
10. For the entirety of the Freud-Rolland correspondence, see the appendix of Parsons (1999).
11. Ibid., p. 173.
12. Ibid.
13. Ibid., p. 174.
14. Freud, *SE* 21: 64.
15. See Osborne (1973).
16. Freud, *SE* 21: 72.
17. Parsons (1999): 177.
18. For a detailed analysis of this passage, see chapter four of Parsons (1999).
19. Ibid.
20. Ibid.
21. See Freud, *SE* 23: 300.
22. See E. Freud (1960): 427.
23. See Freud, *SE* 23: 299.
24. See Freud, *SE* 23: 99.
25. See Jones (1957): 313.
26. See Masson (1984).
27. See Freud, *SE* 15: 461.
28. See Jones (1957), chapter 13.
29. See Freud, *SE* 23: 98.
30. See Freud, *SE* 23: 100.
31. See Freud, *SE* 23: 100–101.
32. See Freud, *SE* 23: 85.
33. See Freud, *SE* 23: 133.
34. Ibid.
35. See W. James (1977): 140; 145.
36. See Katz (1978).
37. See Zaehner (1980).

Bibliography

Bouyer, L. (1980). Mysticism: An Essay on the History of the Word. In: R. Woods, ed., *Understanding Mysticism.* Garden City, N.Y.: Image Books.

De Certeau, M. (1992). Mysticism. In: *Diacritics*, 22, pp. 11–25.

Freud, E. ed. (1960) *The Letters of Sigmund Freud.* Translated by Taria and James Stern. New York: Basic Books.

Freud, S. (1953–1974). *The Standard Edition of the Complete Psychological Works of Sigmund Freud* (S.E.). Volumes 1–24. trans. and ed. J. Strachey. London: Hogarth Press.
 (1912–13). *Totem and Taboo. SE* 13: 1–161.
 (1916–17). *Introductory Lectures on Psychoanalysis. SE* 15–16.

(1927). *The Future of an Illusion. SE* 21: 1–56.
(1930). *Civilization and Its Discontents. SE* 21: 57–146.
(1934–38). *Moses and Monotheism. SE* 23: 3–137.
(1938). *Findings, Ideas, Problems. SE* 23: 299–300.
James, W. (1929). *The Varieties of Religious Experience.* New York: The Modern Library.
James, W. (1977). *A Pluralistic Universe* Cambridge, MA: Harvard University Press.
Jones, E. (1953–1957). *The Life and Work of Sigmund Freud.* 3 vols. New York: Basic Books.
Katz, S. ed. (1978). *Mysticism and Philosophical Analysis.* New York: Oxford.
Masson, J. (1984). *The Assault on Truth: Freud's Suppression of the Seduction Theory.* New York: Farrar, Straus and Giroux.
Osborne, A. (1973). *Ramana Maharshi and the Path of Self-Knowledge.* New York: Samuel Weiser.
Parsons, W. (1999). *The Enigma of the Oceanic Feeling.* New York: Oxford.
Parsons, W. ed. (2011). *Teaching Mysticism.* New York: Oxford.
Teresa of Avila, St. (1979). *The Interior Castle.* Translated by K. Kavanaugh and O. Rodriguez. New York: Paulist Press.
Zaehner, R.C. (1980). *Mysticism Sacred and Profane* (New York: Oxford).

Contributors

Yoram Bilu is a professor emeritus of psychology and anthropology at the Hebrew University of Jerusalem. His main research interests have been culture and mental health, folk-religion in Israel (religious healing, saint worship, messianism), the sanctification of space, and Jewish Moroccan culture. His last book: *The Saints' Impresarios: Dreamers, Healers, and Holy Men in Israel's Urban Periphery*. Brighton, MA: Academic Studies Press.

Louise Child is a Lecturer in Religious Studies at Cardiff University, U.K. She is interested in social theoretical approaches to the study of dreaming, possession trance and the supernatural and has published articles on the reception of these themes in contemporary film and serial drama. Her published book, *Tantric Buddhism and Altered States of Consciousness* (2007) applies the ideas of Jung and Durkheim to an analysis of dreams and visions in tantric Buddhism.

Thomas J. Csordas received his Ph.D. in Anthropology from Duke University in 1980, and is currently Professor of Anthropology at the University of California San Diego. Among his publications are *The Sacred Self: A Cultural Phenomenology of Charismatic Healing* (Berkeley: University of California Press, 1994); *Embodiment and Experience: The Existential Ground of Culture and Self* (Cambridge: Cambridge University Press, 1994); *Language, Charisma, and Creativity: Ritual Life in the Catholic Charismatic Renewal* (Berkeley: University of California Press, 1997; paperback ed. Palgrave 2012); *Body/Meaning/Healing* (New York: Palgrave, 2002); and *Transnational Transcendence: Essays on Religion and Globalization* (Berkeley: University of California Press, 2009).

Jonathan Garb is professor of Jewish Thought at the Hebrew University. In 2011-2012 he was a research fellow at the Tikvah Center for Law and Jewish Civilization at New York University. His fields of work are modern Jewish and comparative mysticism. His published books are: *Manifestations of Power in Jewish Mysticism from Rabbinic Literature to Safedian Kabbalah* (Magnes Press, 2004, Hebrew); *"The Chosen will Become Herds": Studies in Twentieth Century Kabbalah* (Yale University Press, 2009); *Shamanic Trance in Modern Kabbalah* (The University of Chicago Press, 2011).

Moshe Idel, Professor emeritus of Jewish Thought, Hebrew University Jerusalem, and senior researcher at the Shalom Hartman Institute. His recent books are *Saturn's Jews: On the Witches's Sabbat and Sabbateanism* (Continuum, 2011), and *Kabbalah in Italy 1280–1510* (Yale University Press, 2010).

David R. Loy was Besl Family Chair Professor of ethics/religion and society at Xavier University in Cincinnati, Ohio. He is also a Zen teacher in the Sanbo Kyodan tradition of Japanese Zen, offering retreats and workshops nationally and internationally. His academic field is Buddhist and comparative philosophy, with special interest in the interaction of Buddhism and modernity. His books include *Nonduality: a study in comparative philosophy* (Yale), *Lack and Transcendence: the problem of death and life in psychotherapy, existentialism, and buddhism* (Humanities Press), *A Buddhist History of the West* (SUNY) and, most recently, *The World Is Made of Stories* (Wisdom Publications).

Zvi Mark is the Levi Yitzhak of Berditchev Professor of Hasidism in the department of Hebrew Literature in Bar-Ilan University. His published books are: *Mysticism and Madness; The Religious Thought of Rabbi Nachman of Bratslav* (Continuum, 2009); *The Scroll of Secrets – The Hidden Messianic Vision of Revelation and Rectification in the Revealed and Hidden Writings of R. Nahman of Bratzlav* (Magnes Press, 2011, Hebrew).

William B. Parsons is Associate Professor of Religious Studies at Rice University. His publications include *The Enigma of the Oceanic Feeling, Religion and Psychology: Mapping the Terrain, Mourning Religion, Disciplining Freud on Religion, Teaching Mysticism* and dozens of essays in multiple journals and edited books. He has served as Chair of the Department of Religious Studies at Rice University, Director of the Rice University Humanities Research Center, Editor of *Religious Studies Review*, and has been a Fellow the Institute for Advanced Studies (IAS) at Hebrew University.

Philip Wexler is Professor of Sociology of Education and Unterberg Chair at the Hebrew University. His fields of work are Social theory, Education, and Mysticism. His current writing is about the intersection of social theory and Jewish mysticism. He is the author of a number of books, most recently including: *Social Theory and Education* (Peter Lang); *Mystical Society* (Westview); *Mystical Interactions* (Cherub).

Index

abhisheka, 138
aboriginal Australian totemism, 134
Abram, David, 164, 166
Abrams, Daniel, 4
Abrams, M.H., 110, 119, 120, 123
abstract society, 165
Abulafia, R. Abraham, 22
Adahan, Miriam, 29
Adam, Rabbi, 91, 92
Admor, 66
Ahijah the Shilonite, 91
Altglas, Véronique, 9
anthropological ethnographies, 10
anthropology, 19
'Arabi, Ibn, 32
'Arb 'a Turim, 22
archaic heritage, 182
Aristotle, 161, 162
Armstrong, Karen, 157, 158, 160, 167
Arush, Shalom, 61
Ascetic Protestantism, 111
asceticism, 116
Ashkenazi, R. Isaac Luria, 80, 84–85, 85–87, 88, 89, 94, 96
Ashkenazi, R. Lapidot, 96
Ashlag, R. Yehuda L., 8, 19, 20, 21, 23, 24, 25, 28
Assmann, Jan, 164, 165

Association of Jewish Studies, 20
auto-suggestion, 81–82
Axelrod, R. Abraham, 96
Axial Age, 157–59, 159–63
 collapse of civilizations, 159
 Greek, 161–63
 religions, 158
 scripts and, 163–67
 spirituality of evolution, 169–71
 transcendence, 158, 167–69

Ba'alei Teshuva, 52
Baer, R. Dov, 83, 90, 92
Bar-Yosef, Hamutal, 25
Bashir, Shazad, 5
Battle Plans, 28
Beit Yosef, 22
Ben Yehuda, 'Eliezer, 25
Bensaude-Vincent, Bernadette, 124
Berg, Philip, 21
Berger, Peter L., 159
Berland, Eliezer, 58
Berland, Tehilah, 58
Berry, Thomas, 170, 171
Besht, The, 6, 21, 22, 23, 50
 amnesia and, 82–84
 auto-suggestion and, 81–82
 charisma and, 79–81

hand gestures, 83, 84–85, 91
hypnosis and, 93–95
as a Jewish mystic, 95
Moses and, 92, 94
telepathy, 86
utterances, 90–91
visions, 85, 87
betrayal, 134
Bhagavad Gita, 175
Bi-Levavi Mishkan Evne, 29
Bilu, Yoram, 2, 5, 6, 8, 19, 31
Bloch, R. Yehuda Leib, 26
Bonhoeffer, Dietrich, 33
Boyne, Gil, 29
Braslav Hasidim, 6, 19, 31, 47–48
  border crossing with, 54–66
  compared to Chabad, 52–54
  factionalism within, 65
  gender and, 58
  history of, 50–52
  inclusive orientation of, 56
  Jewish House, 57
  link to Chabad, 66–68
  messianic vision, 64, 67
  Mizrahi Jews and, 59
  personal responsibility, 65
  redemption and, 53–54
  technology and, 59–60
Breiter, Yitzhak, 64
Brit Menuha, 22
Brock, R.N., 168
Brooks, P., 141
Brown, Benjamin, 26
Buber, Martin, 24, 80
Buddha, 170, 171
Buddhism, 3, 7, 129–30, 156
  Axial Age, 155–57, 157–59
  engaged, 9
  Mahayana, 155, 166
  Tantric, 6, 7, 8, 9, 130, 135–38

Campbell, J., 137
Candrakirti, 156
Cartesian mind/body dualism, 167
Castells, Manuel, 113
Catholic Encyclopedia, 148
Cayley, David, 166
Celebration of Discipline, 32
Centering Prayer school, 8
Chabad Hasidim, 47–48
  compared to Breslav, 52–54
  factionalism within, 65
  gender and, 58

history of, 48–50
holy letters, 62
Houses, 48, 57
inclusive orientation of, 56
link to Breslav, 66–68
meshichistim, 60
messianic ideas, 49, 64, 67
Mizrahi Jews and, 59
mysticism, 49
personal responsibility, 65
redemption and, 53–54
technology and, 59–60
chain of memory, 23
charisma, 79–81, 109, 148
Child, Louise, 3, 6, 8
Chosen Will Become Herds, The, 20
Christian Socialism, 111
Christianity, 3,
  confession and, 148
  emergent, 8
  water and, 150
Civilization and Its Discontents, 173, 178
classical prophesy, 160
collective
  consciousness, 134
  effervescence, 134
Collins, Randall, 110
communitas, 139, 140
concrete society, 165
confession, 147–53
connectivity, 85, 86
contextualism, 9
contraction, 66
Corbin, Henri, 118
Cordovero, R. Moshe, 21, 22, 23
cosmic social interaction, 119
cosmology, 114, 117, 119
Couliano, Ioan P., 81
Credo quia absurdum, 182
Critical Theory, 10, 123
Csordas, Thomas, 3, 6
cult of the individual, 122
cultural memory, 165
cultural relativism, 131
culturalism, 123

Dahan, Alon, 66
Davis, Erik, 163, 166
DBS database, 27
De Chardin, Teilhard, 32
Deleuze, Gilles, 63
democracy, 133
Derrida, Jacques, 5

Dessler, R. Elijah, 27
Diamond Sutra, 155
dibburim, 90
Divine Feminine, 120
divinity, 109
Dobzhansky, Theodore, 170
Dogen Kigen, 170
Dov-Baer, R. Shalom, 49
Dream Interpreted Within a Dream, A, 5
dualism, 167–68
Durkheim, Emile, 107, 113, 115, 122, 132, 134, 135

Edou, J., 140, 141
Efrayyim, R. Moshe Hayyim, 91
Eisenstadt, S.N., 157, 160
Eliade, Mircea, 5, 129
Elijah, R., 21, 23
Elor, Tamar, 28
Elyashiv, R. Shlomo, 23
Emerson, Ralph Waldo, 115
Enneagram, 8
Ephrayim, Shlomo, 51
Eretz Acheret, 20
Eriksen, T.H., 165
Erlanger, R. Yitzhaq Moshe, 22
esotericism, 19, 23, 26
Etkes, Immanuel, 26
Evans-Pritchard, E.E., 148
exotericism, 9, 24, 25
expressivist humanism, 110
extraordinary knowledge, 91

flashbulb memory, 140
Flood, Gavin, 117, 120
Forkes, R. David, 82
Forman, Robert, 3, 109
Foster, Richard, 8, 32, 33
Foucault, Michel, 20, 34
Freud and Augustine in Dialogue, 5
Freud, S., 166, 173–74
   Goetz and, 175
   last theory of mysticism, 179–83
   mystical intuition of, 174–77, 184
   primary narcissism, 173
   religious ecstasy, 177, 182, 183
   Rolland and, 177–79
functionalism, 115
fundamentalism, 113
Future of the Illusion, The, 173, 176, 177, 183

Garb, Jonathan, 2, 4, 5, 6, 8, 57, 118, 119
Gerondi, R. Yonah, 22

Giller, Pinchas, 19
Ginsburgh, R. Yitzhaq, 20, 29, 66
Ginzei Meromim, 24
Gnosticism, 167
Goetz, Bruno, 175
Great Maggid of Miedziresz, 80, 88–91, 93
Great Transformation, The, 157
Greek Axiality, 161–63
green philosophy, 115
Greetham, David, 4
Greisman, Nechama, 58
Grodzinsky, R. Hayyim 'Ozer, 31
Gross, R., 137, 138
Guattari, Felix, 63
guru yoga, 136
Gush Emunim, 67

Habad, 6
Ha-Kohen, R. David, 24
Halakhah, 4, 23
Ha-Levi, R. Hayyim David, 31
Haredi kabbalah, 8, 21, 25–27
   discontinuities in, 27–30
   psychology, 29
   research on, 30–31
   women and, 28
Haredi-National groups, 25
Harvey, David, 113
Hasidism, 6
   boundary crossing in, 54–55
   modes of behavior, 94–95
Havelock, Eric, 162
Haver, R. Yitzhaq, 24
Hazon 'Ish be-'Inyanei, 27
Heart Sutra, 166
Heelas, Paul, 109, 110, 113, 122
Heikhalot literature, 88, 89
Heller, Tziporah, 28
Herdt, G., 130, 131
Hertz, Robert, 148
Hervieu-Léger, Danièle, 23
Hillel, R. Ya'aqov Moshe, 25, 28
Hindu Tantra, 120
Hinduism, 117
Hirschenson, R. Hayyim, 31
Hollenback, Jess Byron, 117
homosociality, 131, 132
Hui-neng, 151
Humphreys, S.C., 158
Huss, Boaz, 3, 19, 20, 117
hypnosis, 93

Idel, Moshe, 1, 3, 5, 6, 8, 118, 119, 120

ideology of textology, 1
Ikon group, 8
Illich, Ivan, 166
imitation Dei, 121
individualism, 123
Innis, Harold, 162
In Praise of the Baal Shem Tov, 91
Institute for Advanced Studies, 2, 3, 11, 20
intersubjective magic, 81
Israel, monotheism in, 159
Israel Science Foundation, 19
'Iyyun circle, 22

James, William, 114, 115, 121, 123, 184
Jaspers, Karl, 156, 157
Jewish/Judaism
  Rabbinic, 92
  renewal movement, 21
  scripts and, 160
Jewish mysticism, 3
  contemporary society, 7
  Israel and Western centers, 4
  Jewish culture and religion, 4
Jones, Ernst, 181
Joseph, Rabbi Jacob, 85, 93
Julius and Gwenn Knapp Foundation, 11
Jung, Carl, 182

Kabbalah, 6, 7
  classical, 19–20, 21
  contemporary, 19–20
  continuous, 25
  empowerment and, 118
  exoteric, 27
  Haredi, 25–27
  languages of, 25
  Lithuanian, 23, 24, 31
  Lurianic, 82
  modernity and, 21
  new age, 117
  periodization of, 23–25
  post-modernity and, 21
  publishing and, 27–28
  sexualization of, 120
Kabbalah Center, 26
Kabbalah: New Perspectives, 1, 20
Kabbalat Ha-Ge 'onim, 22
kabbalistic thought, 8
Kagan, R. Yisra'el Meir, 27
Karelitz, R. Abraham Yesh'ayahu, 27
Karo, R. Joseph, 22
Katz, Jacob, 47
kavvanot, 23

Kearney, Richard, 166
Keating, Thomas, 8
Kempis, Thomas à, 33
Kesef Mishne, 22
King, Martin Luther, 80
Kirchner, Suzanne, 110
Klein, A.C., 136
Kohen, R. David, 26, 118
Kol Haloshon, 27
Kook, R. Avraham Itzhaq Ha-Cohen, 8, 20, 23, 24, 25, 28, 118
Kripal, Jeffrey, 29

Labdron, Machig, 140
Lash, Scott, 116, 123
Leib, R. Aryeh, 51, 82, 83, 84, 89, 91, 93
Leiner, R. Mordekhai Yosef, 31
Lights of Repentence, The, 8
Likutei Halachot, 65
Lindholm, C., 130
literary theory, 4
Loewe, R., 5
logos, 165
Loy, David, 3, 7, 8, 111
Luhrmann, Tanya M., 29
Luria, R. Luria, 87, 95
Luria, R. Yitzhaq, 21, 22, 23
Luzzatto, R. Moshe Hayyim, 21, 22, 23

Ma'arekhet Elohut, 21
Magid, Shaul, 21
Maharshi, Sri Ramana, 178
Manichaeism, 167
Manifestations of Power in Jewish Mysticism, 2
Marcuse, Herbert, 115
Marett, R.R., 148, 149, 150, 151
Mark, Svi, 3, 5, 6, 8, 19, 20, 23, 24
Marx, K., 10
McLuhan, Marshall, 166, 167
meaning, 107
medical anthropology, 149
Meir, Jonathan, 19
Merton, Thomas, 8, 32, 33
Mesilat Yesharim, 22
Mesmer, Franz Anton, 95
mesmerian theory, 95
messianism, 53, 54, 55, 113
Metaphysics, 161
mezuzah, 160
Mishna Berura, 27
monotheism, 159, 163
Mopsik, Charles, 120, 123
Morgenstern, R. Yitzhak Meir, 8, 22, 28

Moses and Monotheism, 166, 180, 182
Mulamadhyamikakarika, 156
Munzer, Thomas, 113
Mussar, 4, 22, 23, 27
Myers, Jody, 21
mysticism
    asceticism and, 116
    canonical sociologies of, 6
    Chabad, 49
    Christian, 32
    comparative, 4, 184
    empowerment and, 117
    Freud and, 7, 174–77, 179–83
    Islamic, 7–8
    new, 112–16, 117
    noetic dimension of, 177
    place in religion, 107–8
    prevalence of, 109
    psychological-experiential readings, 88
    religiosity, 122
    self-deification and, 111
    as a social process, 123
    social structures and, 130
    society and, 107–9, 112–16
    spirituality and, 9, 11, 110, 122
    transcendental forms, 116
    types of, 3
    Western Christian, 7
    women and, 26
mystics
    continuous, 23

Nachman, Rabbi, 48, 50
    background of, 53
    borders and, 55
    communication with, 64
    death of, 51
    as exemplary model, 57
    gender and, 58
    as Messiah, 51
    pilgrimages to tomb of, 52
    portrait of, 63
    tomb of, 58
    writings of, 62
Nagarjuna, 156
Nahmanides, 21
nanotechnology, 124
Nathan, Rabbi, 61, 62
Native American Church, 147
    comparison with Catholicism, 151
    confession and, 152
    medicine and, 151
    water and, 150

Neshek, 56
Neuro-Linguistic Programming, 28, 29
New Age Romanticism, 113
New Age spirituality, 3, 9, 10, 11
New Age Tantra
New Introductory Lectures on Psychoanalysis, 179, 182
New Monasticism, 8, 9
New Mysticism, 116, 117
new vitalism, 123
ngondro, 138
Nicomachean Ethics, 162
Nietzsche, F., 23, 170, 171
nirvana, 152
nomian practice, 26

Occupy Wall Street, 9
Odesser, R. Israel, 52, 58, 63
Old Worlds, New Mirrors, 5
Open Secret, 5, 25
Ordinary Rascals, 32
Otto, R., 129
Otzar Hahochma database, 27

Papua New Guinea, 130–33
    initiation rites, 138
    rites of terror, 138–39
Paquda, R. Bahya Ibn, 22
Parsons, William, 3, 5, 7
Pedaya, Haviva, 94
Pelikan, Jaroslav, 33
Pentacostalism, 32
Pereq Shirah, 83
Petaya, R. Yehuda, 24, 26
Piyyut, 4
Platform Sutra, 155
Plato, 162, 166
Pliskin, Zelig, 29
political theory, 2
Poole, F.J.P., 138
Posen Foundation, 31
Preface to Plato, 162
primary narcissism, 173
psychological-experiential readings, 88
Pythagoras, 161

Quakerism, 113

Rabinovici, Eliezer, 11
rationalization, 109
Ray, R.A., 138
Raz, Amir, 93
Rebbe, 47–48, 49,

57, 60, 65
  background of, 53
  communication with, 64
  death of, 50
  as descendant of Rabbi Nachman, 66–67
  as designated Messiah, 49–50
  as exemplary model, 57
  gender and, 58
  messianic vision of, 67
  personality cult of, 61
Reiner, Elhanan, 87
religion of humanity, 113, 122
religious
  creativity, 116
  ecstasy, 177, 182
  knowledge, 91–93
  salvation, 116
Renovaré, 32
Republic, 162
Revelation and Rectification, 6
Rifkin, Jeremy, 158
righteous man, 81
Rigler, Sara Yoheved, 28
Rishonim, 22
ritual secrecy, 131–33, 136, 140
Rolland, Romain, 177–79, 180, 182
Rollins, Peter, 8
Roman Catholic Church, 147
  confession and, 147, 152
Romanticism, 110, 113
rupa, 166

Sabbatai, R., Israel ben, 87
Sabbatainism, 113
Sabbath meals, 7
sacramentum, 149
sacred forces, 135
Sambia, 130
Samburu, 140
samsara, 152
sanctification, 108
Schneerson, R. Menachem Mendel. *See* Rebbe
Scholem, Gershom, 1, 24, 80, 107, 108, 112, 113, 119, 122
Schwartz, R. Itamar, 29
Scroll of Secrets, The, 19
secrecy, 133–35
secularized socialization, 121
Sefer Ha-Bahir, 21
Sefer Ha-Temuna, 21
Sefer Raziel ha-Malakh, 83
self, 158
self-deification, 111

self-sanctification, 108, 109
self-spirituality, 10
sexuality, 123
Shach, Rabbi, 65
Shahaj Samadhi, 178
Shalif, Yishai, 29
Shamanism: Archaic Techniques of Ecstasy, 5
Shamantic Trance in Modern Kabbalah, 5
Shapiro, Theodore, 93
Shar'abi, R. Shalom, 19, 21, 23
Shaw, M., 136
Shick, R. Eliezer Shlomo, 52
Shiv'a 'Enayyim, 22
Shivehei ha-Besht, 81, 87
shluchim, 48
Shmeruk, Chone, 91
Shneurson, R. Menahem Mendel, 19, 25, 26
Shulem, Barukh, 29
shunyata, 166
Shuvu Banim, 58
Simmel, Georg, 116, 122, 132, 133, 134
Sinaitic revelation, 88, 90
Skins, 141–44
Smith, Joseph, 80
social
  movement theories, 10
  relationality, 115
  sciences, 2, 54
  theory, 2
Sociology, 2, 6, 19
  classical, 107
  functionalist, 115
  mysticism and, 107–9
  of religion, 2
Sorokin, Pitirim, 113
Sorotzkin, David, 5
Soteriology, 108
Spector, R. Yitzhaq 'Elhanan, 31
Spell of the Sensuous, The, 164
spiritual revolution, 2
spirituality, 9, 32, 111, 113, 114, 122
  evolution, 169–71
  movements, 10
  mysticism and, 9, 11, 110
Standard Edition (of Freud's works), 179
Steiner, George, 5
Sternhartz, R. Nathan, 51
Strachey, James, 179
Sufi Bodies, 5
Sufism, 5, 7, 31, 32
Sulkhan 'Arukh, 22
Sutcliffe, Steven J., 9
Svirsky, Efim, 29

Swimme, Brian, 169, 170
symbolic interactionism, 115

Tantric, 31
   Buddhism, 6, 7, 8, 9, 130, 135–38
   discourse on secrecy, 9
   new age, 117
Tantric Buddhism and Altered States of Consciousness, 8
Tau, R. Tzevi Yisra'el, 25
tephillin, 160
Tertullian, 176, 182, 183
Thistlewaite, S.B., 168
Tikkunim, 51
Tilly, Charles, 110
Tiqqunei Zohar, 83
Totem and Taboo, 180, 181, 182
Toulmin, Stephen, 111, 114, 115, 121
Tov, R. Israel Ba'al Shem. *See* The Besht
transcendence, 158, 167–69
transhumanism, 167
transitive magic, 81
Troeltsch, Ernst, 1, 107, 109, 111, 112, 113, 123
truthfulness, 133
tsaddiq, 61, 62, 63, 65, 66, 81
Tsogyel, Yeshe, 137
Turner, V., 139, 148
Tuzin, D.F., 138, 139
Tzevi, Sabbatai, 80, 88

Universal Story, The, 170
Unmoved Maker, 162
Urban, Hugh, 9

virtuality, 63
Voegelin, Eric, 157
von Schroeder, Leopold, 175

Walker, Daniel P., 81
Wallace, Anthony, 112
Webb, Eugene, 157
Weber, Max, 1, 6, 80, 107, 108, 111, 113, 116, 118, 121
Weiss, Yoseph, 55
Werczberger, Rachel, 3, 21
Wexler, Philip, 2, 6, 8, 9, 28, 31, 113
White, D.G., 110, 117, 120
white philosophy, 115
Whitehouse, H., 138, 139
Wilson, E.O., 169
Wink, Walter, 32
Wittkowski, Victor, 180
Wolfson, Elliot, 3, 5, 6, 19, 25, 66, 118, 119, 123, 129, 135
Wood, Mathew, 9, 10
World Congress of Jewish Studies, 20
Wrong, Dennis, 115, 121

Yad Ha-Hazaka, 22
Yam Ha-Hokhma, 22
yihudim, 23
Yitzhak, R. Yoseph, 49
Yosef, R. 'Ovadyah, 25

Zaehner, R.C., 184
Zalman, R. Shneur, 21, 48
Zionism, 21
Zohar, 83
Zoroastrianism, 156

Studies in Mystical Traditions

Philip Wexler and Jonathan Garb
General Editors

The role of mysticism is dramatically changing in Western society and culture as well as in the relationship between spiritual traditions throughout the world in the era of globalization. After Spirituality: Studies in Mystical Traditions seeks to develop a wide range of perspectives—anthropological, cultural, hermeneutical, historical, psychological, and sociological—on mystical and spiritual centers, figures, movements, textual and artistic products. The series will appeal to broad audiences, ranging from scholars to students to teachers.

For additional information about this series or for the submission of manuscripts, please contact:

Philip Wexler and Jonathan Garb
philipwexler@mscc.huji.ac.il | jgarb@mscc.huji.ac.il

To order other books in this series, please contact our Customer Service Department:

(800) 770-LANG (within the U.S.)
(212) 647-7706 (outside the U.S.)
(212) 647-7707 FAX

Or browse online by series:

www.peterlang.com

www.ingramcontent.com/pod-product-compliance
Ingram Content Group UK Ltd.
Pitfield, Milton Keynes, MK11 3LW, UK
UKHW022239230426
12048UKWH00018BA/1351